And Perhaps . . .

And Perhaps...

The Story of Ruth Dayan

By Ruth Dayan and Helga Dudman

Harcourt Brace Jovanovich, Inc. · New York

Contents

Illustrations

Between pages 112 and 113

And perhaps these things never happened at all . . .
Perhaps—it seems now—
I never rose at dawn to work in the fields
By the sweat of my brow,

And never, high on the sheaf-laden wagon
During the long
And scorching days of harvest, did my voice
Rise in song?

And I never bathed in your silent and blue
Innocent gleam,
O my Sea of Galilee—
Was it real? Or did I dream a dream?

—RACHEL (1890–1931)

Foreword

You can divorce a husband, but not a legend.

In this case there was not the slightest reason for saying good-bye to the legend. A long love affair with a force of history may be easier to maintain than a marriage, especially when one woman has long faced both across the breakfast table.

As for the divorce from the man himself, that is something else again. Ideals may remain unchanged over the years, but people rarely do. Perhaps in time even charisma evaporates from the breakfast table.

Two weeks after the Dayans' divorce, we were once again driving north, as we had so often during more than a year working on this book. It was our last trip together, one of many made back and forth across Israel and back and forth over Ruth's life, following the threads of her past. Criss-crossing the country's roads and its people, these threads are interwoven more tightly than in calmer lives, and circumstances have broadened the warp to crowd in more patterns than usual.

Ruth's memory is a special form of total recall that seems close to self-hypnosis. She does not just describe past details with fascinating immediacy; she is actually right back there in the past. It is as if a button somewhere clicks and she is once again reliving part of her life. So she does not view long-gone events with detachment.

"A psychologist friend told me this is a certain kind of mental failing," she said, "but I don't remember the term that was used." For abstractions, her memory is less impressive.

On the road through Galilee Ruth began typically, "I stayed overnight at an Arab hotel in Nazareth a while ago. I was with two women friends, one Arab and one Jewish. We were in the Golan Heights during the day and then went to Nahalal for the fiftieth anniversary celebration of the village. Moshe was the main speaker, and he talked about the differences and the similarities between the 1920's and the 1970's.

"In my hotel room that night I tried to go over the past, too. I often use the past in trying to deal with the present. I couldn't sleep. It was terribly hot and the room was full of mosquitoes, but the moonlight over Nazareth was beautiful. I sat by the window swatting mosquitoes and thought of another Arab room that was also very hot and also filled with moonlight and mosquitoes. It was the Hotel Philadelphia in Amman, and the year must have been 1929, because I couldn't have been more than twelve. My parents had taken me to Jerash, a wonderful archeological site, but instead of being pleased I was sulky and cranky and a terrible nuisance.

"That night in Nazareth I thought about another night some years after 1929. I was in Angkor Wat in the Cambodian jungle and there, too, I was surrounded by beauty and loneliness. And that took me back to the time on the island of Rhodes when Moshe was with the Mixed Armistice Commission and I was alone with the moonlight reflected on the ancient blue tiles of the Roman baths. That memory led to one of a strange night in a convent in Sardinia, where I was badly hurt in a car accident, and a nun prayed by my bedside till morning."

As our car wound through the hilly outskirts of Nazareth her voice and manner changed when she talked of the appointment ahead. She had plans to open a Maskit branch in Nazareth. Maskit is the arts-and-crafts firm she founded in 1954, which, under her direction, now does an international business.

She is a superb and most unfeminine driver, which is in contradiction to her emotional warmth and vulnerability. There are plenty of other paradoxes: she has always been shy, but is happiest among people. She has always loved the sea, but never learned to swim. "An introvert trying to behave like an extrovert" was one friend's description.

Her appointment list is always exhaustingly varied and crowded: with a bereaved mother who lost her son in the Six-Day War; with a rabbi on the problems of the Falasha Jews of Ethiopia; with a Norwegian gentile girl on the obstacles to her marriage to an Israeli paratrooper; a meeting of the Brit Bnei Shem, an organization devoted to the promotion of understanding between Arabs and Jews which she was asked to head after the Six-Day War; with a Yemenite grandmother who once wove baskets for Maskit; with an ambassador's wife; with three boys in wheelchairs, all polio victims, who have learned metalwork and are eager to make jewelry for Maskit; a première of her younger son's newest film. But what is uppermost in her mind at all times is the basic purpose of any project.

"Our younger daughter, Reumah, is the one who's considered efficient, cool, and well organized," Ruth's father has remarked. "But I think perhaps Ruth's way of working—all that rushing in what looks like disorder—really has the more ultimate organization."

By sheer chance the name of Moshe Dayan did not come up on any of the news broadcasts we heard on the car radio that day. On other occasions, statements by the Minister of Defense had suddenly filled the car. Ruth listened to the familiar voice with thoughtful concentration, not because it was her husband, but because it was Moshe Dayan.

The distinction was confusing but somehow complete, and it simmers down the Dayan generations. When the first granddaughter was three, she once asked, "Grandpa, are you Moshe Dayan?" At about the same age her brother announced one evening, "I want to watch television, and I want to watch Grandpa watching Moshe Dayan."

On our drives north we usually stopped at Nahalal, the village where Ruth and Moshe met, married, and lived as farmers. Ehud (called "Udi"), the older son, now runs the family farm. "I was in Nahalal last week, too, for Udi's birthday. We had a little party just for the family—Moshe, and Assi and his wife." (Ruth's daughter, Yael, was in Paris with her husband and two children.)

"Moshe arrived from Tel Aviv after I did, and when he came in he kissed me. Udi, who is quite a combination of fantastic joker and sensitive boy, watched this and said with a laugh, 'Well, that's the nicest birthday present I could have received.'

"And I said, 'But why shouldn't Moshe kiss me? We've known each other for thirty-seven years!'"

Nahalal and Zahala are the two contrasting homes in Ruth's married life, and for all of our trips except the last her starting point was Zahala, a Tel Aviv suburb built for army personnel, where the Dayans lived for eighteen years.

The name "Zahala" is an acronym constructed from the Hebrew letters that stand for "Israel Defense Forces" (Zva Haganah L'Israel), but in Hebrew the word also means "jubilation." The atmosphere of the place is suburban, but all the addresses are biblical. Ruth's, since 1953, was Number 11 Joab Street. (Joab was King David's complex commander in chief.)

The Zahala house is not easily forgotten by anyone visiting it only once. The guard on twenty-four-hour duty in the sentry box outside and the ten telephones inside are the least of it. The atmosphere is the opposite of something designed by interior decorators, and for Ruth, who planned its character and worried over every detail, housekeeping was a kind of legend-keeping.

Even the ashtrays were engraved with illustrious names, and the silver fruit bowl was inscribed "With the Compliments of General Ne Win, Chief of Staff, Burma" (now President of Burma). The small-scale cannon near the front door that fired gunpowder during the Turkish rule in Palestine five hundred years ago was given to Moshe Dayan after the Sinai Campaign by the monks of Saint Catherine's Monastery.

And so on, through a dazzling and almost endless list—the carved red dragon presented by an Armenian bishop, the ancient brass tray with Hebrew letters brought from Damascus by an Arab from Bethlehem, a gold cloisonné tea set from a Russian Orthodox priest, the silver Thermos from the Italian Foreign Minister, the antique gold statue of a dog given by a Panamanian general . . .

But of course, the most overwhelming objects are in the archeological collection that each year has required more and more shelves and cases throughout the house and that is Moshe Dayan's deepest personal concern. Sliding glass doors with bullet-proof Venetian blinds look out upon the garden, and above the doors are set two of the finest pieces in the collection —a rare, six-thousand-year-old mask from Hebron, and a regal stone head from the time of King David that looks, Moshe Dayan is sure, exactly as David did.

"On the day of the divorce," Ruth said, "when I walked out of our house for the last time, I took only a few things of my own, things Moshe would never miss. His collection is magnificent, but it is clear to me that he is in love with the past and fascinated by people long gone. I took things that are of value to me because I remember the faces and the stories of the men and women who made them and who are my friends.

"I took the Book of Ruth inscribed on an eggshell, because the man who made it memorized the Scriptures during his years in a Russian prison. I took my little arts-and-crafts collection, a few dolls from Africa, an alabaster box from the Taj Mahal, and a little carved wooden group from Peru. Instead of the usual Nativity scene, the artist made a miniature orchestra for me.

"I looked at the room with the teakwood Damascus cabinet and its collection of Roman glass, and the silver Sikh sabers, and the life-size portrait of Yael that the artist Chaliapin gave Moshe, and for one long last moment I saw all the treasures and tributes that had been part of our years together. Then I walked through the front door and out into the pouring rain.

"There were no tears this time, and I am a woman who cries easily. My secretary, Mickey, was waiting in the car outside the gate. I handed her the odds and ends I was carrying and kissed the guard good-bye. He was the one crying, as I left, and the rain fell on both of us."

The garden of Ruth's new house will be very different from the almost surrealistic mixture of classical grandeur and romantic tangle behind the Zahala house, for that gothic garden is rooted in the past. There Moshe planned a landscaped setting for an exalted and continuing intellectual treasure hunt for some elusive prize. Pillars of granite and basalt, floodlit all night, rise theatrically among cactuses and rosebushes carefully placed to give the illusion of depth. One of the floodlights rests in a stone wheel used to grind flour a few thousand years ago; others, behind Roman and Greek pedestals, light up the white bougainvillia from Ethiopia and the pomegranate trees from Galilee.

Towards the rear of the garden are two stone structures where part of the archeology collection is kept. One houses a row of twenty-one mummy cases painstakingly glued together by Moshe from jagged fragments dating back four thousand years; each stands taller than a man's head and has a lid in the form of a face. They are spectacular, especially by moonlight.

Ruth's new garden will need no massive stone wall like the one dominating the Zahala garden. For this wall, built after the Six-Day War for security reasons, Moshe designed niches between the stones to hold pottery and stone jars, bits of carved hieroglyphics, statuettes of birds and animals by artists who lived two thousand years ago and whose work puts the day's headlines in their place.

"When I clanged the iron gate shut that last day and heard the metal clash on metal one final time," said Ruth, "I thought to myself: I am free. As I looked back through the grillwork and saw the garden, I felt as though I were stepping out of an amazing fairy tale that I had never wanted. I was leaving behind an emotional isolation that had become oppressive and un-bearable—for Moshe as well as myself.

"I was glad it was all intact, as a comfortable home for Moshe to return to, and also, selfishly, to keep the memory of our family's place so that, in my thoughts, I too could return. Because I knew I would never—could never—go back there myself."

Just inside the front door, near the shelves from which Ruth took her little handicraft collection, a telephone rests on a small table. The stool next to it was carved in Africa, but the table itself was made by Moshe at Nahalal over thirty years ago. The top is a thick slab of oak rimmed with its own bark, and it rests on a base which was the trunk of a plum tree that fell in the garden long ago. The table has a purposely rustic look; but when Moshe made it, the advantage was that it cost nothing. It is the only piece in the house that remains from Nahalal, the village where all this started.

—Helga Dudman

And Perhaps . . .

1 · Nahalal Nights

I felt wonderfully happy, sitting up in the eucalyptus tree
waiting for Moshe, and absolutely free of doubts, which was
unusual. I was seventeen years old and a high-school dropout,
finished with city life and my parents' comfortable home in
Jerusalem. Moshe was nineteen, and a farmer. That was one
of the many things I liked about him in those first few weeks
we knew each other. He was so unlike all the schoolboys with
whom I had been in and out of love. Moshe was someone who
went before daybreak to plow a frozen field, who knew how to
handle a scythe and how to make things grow. Also, he was
exceptionally intelligent and handsome, and he loved Tolstoy
and Dostoevsky.

My eucalyptus tree, that autumn evening in 1934, seemed an
odd and therefore suitable place to wait till Moshe came
along for our regular walk. While waiting I carved our initials
on a branch: "RS" and "MD"—for Ruth Shwarz and Moshe
Dayan. I suppose they are still there, much higher up by now,
for the trees at the agricultural school in the village of Nahalal,
where I was a new student, have grown tall since then.

The trees are at the rim of the Nahalal Circle. This first
moshav, or co-operative village, was carefully planned by the
architect Richard Kaufmann in a series of concentric circles
—school, library, dairy, and other shared institutions in the
middle; then a ring of farm homes; then a ring of fields. Later

I came to think of it as very much of a closed circle. But just then I did not feel at all an outsider on the rim of things, as I often had before and would again.

Though I liked Moshe tremendously when I carved those initials, marriage was not in our minds. My school friends and I had grown up in a movement that considered marriage an old-fashioned, bourgeois custom, and Moshe saw it as a complication. Still, my enthusiasms had changed since my arrival at the school six weeks earlier, when I wrote to a friend:

I've come here with the feeling that I'm entering a nunnery. I'm going to stop wasting time with boys and getting all mixed up with them. From now on, that's over. I will devote myself to work and learning to become a good farmer. Involvements with boys only confuse me.

I suppose I have walked past that tree and around the Circle thousands of times since then, under circumstances changed by time and people. My memory weaves back and forth, back and forth, to events and their parallels; but this is not the way a weaver works with his loom, for I have woven on looms and I know that when you throw a real shuttle, you see any flaw in the pattern right away.

We were lucky, my Jerusalem friends and I, for we were brought up in a movement whose ideals were more real and exciting than our schoolwork. We had a huge challenge and little cynicism; we wanted to return to the land, and my best friends did join kibbutzim, which was the aim of all of us. That is why a whole generation of classmates did not go on to university. Some were brilliant students—which I certainly was not—but they saw their duty in rejecting the academic world of their parents. I left school a year before my friends. My mother and father, who both had university careers, understood. Father's attitude was, "Our eldest daughter is not the studious type. All her friends, all those activities, all that fiction she reads are at the expense of her studies. But she should do what she wants."

I saw no point in wasting another whole year on irrelevant books when my life was obviously going to be with chickens and cows. I had wanted to leave even earlier, but my first application to agricultural school was turned down because I was too young. Now, at last, I was starting at the Nahalal Agricultural School for Girls, in the green valley between Nazareth and Haifa.

Probably I would marry, I thought, sometime in the distant future; he would be a kibbutznik, and we would live forever in a world of farms. But that was far off. When Moshe and I walked in the fields around and around Nahalal Circle, we discussed our views of life and saw our futures taking separate paths, for we were very different in background, in personality, and in youthful ideology, which occupied all of us very much.

Moshe used to tell me not to go to a kibbutz, though that had been my aim for so long. "You'll just end up ruining your life," he wrote in one of his early letters when I was away briefly in Jerusalem. "You'll marry some fool, have six children, and then get divorced."

At villages such as Nahalal, I soon learned, divorce was rare, because everybody was far too busy keeping his farm going. At a kibbutz, after a regulated day's work, there might be time for the luxury of emotional troubles that divide couples. But at Nahalal the chores were endless. There were suicides, not divorces.

In the moshav where Moshe grew up, all members receive the same amount of land and facilities but live in their own homes with their families, and their income is set by their own work. Initiative is encouraged in a moshav and productivity is the main value; in a kibbutz the most important consideration is the social structure and a close, communal form of life.

As a moshav boy, Moshe has always been a complete individualist. The movement to which I belonged emphasized the importance of the group; and I have always loved being among people and part of a unit. Some of this is paradoxical, because I was shy and afraid of ridicule. I never believed I would be chosen for positions of leadership, yet I always was. If for some reason I was not picked I was terribly offended, while at the same time I continued to be surprised by each election. It was the same with boys. I thought most girls were prettier than I, yet boys flocked around me. I was a tomboy, insisted on wearing my hair cut short like a boy's and had no interest in clothes; yet I loved sewing and knitting and making decorations.

I was romantic and poetic about farming because I came to it out of choice. Those like Moshe, born to the hard realities of mud and smells and backbreaking work, did not share my lyricism about every chore. But even Moshe once expressed beautifully his feeling about fruit trees, a branch of agriculture he did love. In a letter written not long after we met, he described grafting new shoots in the orchard:

I remember every one, when it was done and when it will blossom, and I feel toward each like a father to a son. Most of all, more than with the apples or the pears, I have this feeling with the plum trees. I think perhaps because we have so few of them.

My own enchantment made practically no distinctions, and I enjoyed every moment of becoming a farmer. I loved learning to make cheese and I loved baking bread, thousands of loaves; I even liked the washboards in the laundry, in spite of blisters and backache, because this was a challenge and symbolized what

I wanted my life to be. I am still romantic about that past, but I am not sure I would like to be a farmer today. Everything now is infinitely cleaner and easier, and whenever I visit Udi, our son who runs the farm Moshe and I worked at Nahalal after we married, I know it is not the same place at all. It is more efficient, and all the old experiences are gone.

Milking at two in the morning, alone in the cowshed, had a special beauty for me always—at school, afterwards at the farm of Moshe's parents, and later still when we had our own farm. You are there in the stillness, with only the sound of the animals moving in their stalls and the swish-swish of the stream of milk into the pail, and only the light of a lantern. I used to milk with my head against the cow's flank, listening to her heartbeat. That steady pulse, and the rhythm of your fingers working, and the milk swishing down, and the warmth from the cow in the freezing shed all made for a unity between animal and milker that nobody who has not actually done this—and I mean by hand, not in the mechanized way of today—can even imagine. When you are finished, the cow turns her head and gives you a look of thanks, or so it seemed to me, and I loved this moment especially.

Technique was essential, bringing all the fingers into play. This we first practiced on a rubber udder, for you may not learn on real cows; they grow used to a certain pair of hands, and changes in touch will make them refuse to give milk, which is thoroughly exasperating. When I began helping Moshe's parents, one of the Dayan cows, Kochba, developed a loathing for me and would give no milk, no matter how dutifully I tried.

Moshe encouraged me to specialize in the dairy branch. He considered some of the subjects at the agriculture school a lot of nonsense. But he said that knowing how to handle cows would certainly be useful for whatever my future might be.

Before all these delights entered my life, and before I ever talked to Moshe, and before I unroped my eiderdown blanket and steamer trunk from the top of the bus that brought me to Nahalal from Jerusalem in September 1934, I had by sheerest chance already spent some time at Nahalal at the summer camp for members of the socialist youth movement. I even heard Moshe give a speech around a campfire, under the impression that he was somebody else.

Our camp was on a pretty hill; there was a spring near by and a field belonging to the village. I was an enthusiastic camp scout, and every summer we ran two-week camps for younger children from Jerusalem, Tel Aviv, and Haifa. That year I was a senior counselor in charge of about two hundred children. But, like any camp counselor anywhere in the world, the first thing I did when we all arrived in July was to see which of the boy counselors seemed worth falling in love with for two weeks. A Jerusalem boy gave me a pair of long overalls from America to help against mosquitoes (mosquitoes always look for me, perhaps because I respond so dramatically to bites). Bloomers were being worn that season—shorts did not arrive in Palestine until a few years later—and in those long American overalls I must have stood out from the other girls. The younger children, of thirteen and fourteen, were assigned to village homes where they did farm chores during the day, for summer camp in Palestine was a matter of real, not make-believe, work. On that first day, we counselors gossiped about camp the year before, when we had been on a hike in Galilee and lost our way, and were picked up by a Syrian army patrol. We spent the night in Damascus; it had been a wonderful adventure.

The first evening at Nahalal we had a bonfire and met with the boys and girls of the village. The moon was full, we ate roast corn and baskets of grapes from the fields, and we sang songs—the main activity in the evenings before radios came to places like Nahalal. There were speeches, too. One was given by a handsome Nahalal boy whose topic was "The Structure of the Moshav." He explained that the moshav was an agricultural settlement in which every farmer lives and works separately, though purchases and sales are co-operative and mutual help is a basic principle. This was all new to me, with my kibbutz ideas, but even so I did not keep my mind on much of what was said. Besides, my camp adviser was sitting next to me.

"Don't pay any attention to those moshavniks," he whispered. "They're all a terrible bunch." Kibbutz boys did not like moshav boys, and vice versa, and it is still that way today. "And especially," he went on, "see that you stay away from the boys of two families here—the Dayan family and the Uri family." These were influential names in the moshav movement and both families lived in Nahalal. For some reason I got the names mixed up. The attractive boy discussing the structure of the moshav, I thought was the son of the Uri family, and while my adviser warned me against contamination, I decided this Uri boy was worth getting to know.

But we were sitting at opposite ends of the bonfire and did not meet. We did not meet at the next campfire, either, when the village boys and girls invited us for an evening of more speeches, though this time I was the center of attention. One of the children in my group was bitten by a scorpion and I made a big fuss, because for city children this was an event; at Nahalal a scorpion was nothing unusual. And I was the only girl in long overalls. But I never met the handsome boy.

Two days later camp broke and my friends and I returned to Jerusalem—they to finish high school and go on to kibbutzim, I just to pack my things, say good-bye, and return to Nahalal.
· · · · ·

A few weeks later I knew very well that the boy I had watched at the campfire was Moshe Dayan. He knew that I spoke English, and that interested him. He was always eager to learn, and we decided that I would teach him English on our walks and give him lessons at his home twice a week. He claimed that he remembered the girl in the long overalls, but I had the feeling that, really, he did not.

I was also getting to know how things worked at school. Classes started at 6:30 A.M. Then came five hours of practical work, with more classes in the afternoon. Certain assignments, such as work in the cowshed, brought privileges of better food and more hours of freedom.

One important fact was that Hannah Maisel was away that year. She was the school's founder, a legendary woman who ran the place with an iron hand. But this year she was on another assignment and a man was in her place as director. With him there, we found we could do things, like climb back through the dormitory windows at three or four in the morning, that would have been unthinkable under Hannah Maisel.

I had four roommates, all from Europe. This was the time of Hitler's rise, and girls from Germany and Poland, sometimes older than the usual students, could come to Palestine on student visas. But they were allowed to stay as long as they were in school or they happened to marry local boys. Fictitious marriages were sometimes arranged so these girls would not be sent back to Europe.

I became busy "integrating" these newcomers, a habit from home. Some spoke a little English and I remembered a bit of German from my kindergarten in Heidelberg. But I was rather snobbish and my best friends were among the second-year students, mostly sabras who spoke Hebrew, knew our songs, and knew the ways of the school and the village. They knew that "going out" in Nahalal society meant stealing fruit from the school gardens or cakes from the kitchen, and that the water tower was the place where everybody met after school. That was where the village boys passed on their way from the cowsheds to the dairies, carrying across their shoulders the milk buckets attached to either end of a wooden yoke. Each boy had his own style of carrying the yoke. Moshe, for instance, as he stopped by at the water tower to chat with us, carried it across one shoulder.

The first week of school I was elected to the council of incoming students. As usual I was surprised, and as usual I would have been offended if I had not been elected. Two weeks later I was chosen to represent the school on a "committee of two," which was to organize joint sports events between the school and the village. The other member, picked from the village, was Moshe. No sports events ever came of this, but

Moshe did write a humorous poem about the effort. We began to talk. Moshe wanted to know about city life, and I found I was interested, after all, in the structure of the moshav. Anxious to do the right thing, I resigned from the other committee because I was soon much too busy with Moshe to give it much time. And I forgot all about my intention of entering a nunnery.

Moshe casually invited me to come to his home, and I think I fell in love with the atmosphere of the place on that first visit. My own home was so different, equipped with every kind of convenience available in Palestine. I saw this farmhouse in the way a city visitor today would see and be charmed by rural simplicity.

It must have been a Friday, because everything in the Dayans' two-room house was spotless. The wooden planks of the floors and the walls glowed from being scrubbed. There was not a picture or a rug anywhere. The chairs were the old-fashioned folding kind, wooden seats with iron backs, that might have been taken from some ancient theater. An old teakettle boiled on a kerosene stove next to Shmuel's chair, and in my mind it became a samovar; I soon learned that Moshe's father could easily drink nine cups of tea in a sitting.

There was not a frill anywhere. The bedcovers were white sheets; in the kitchen, the icebox for a family of six was an old insulated chest used by the German army as a medicine kit in World War I. The house had no bathroom; the toilet was a long way off towards the cowshed, and in the winter, as I learned later, you would sink to your knees in the incredible mud of Nahalal.

Moshe's own little room, built on to the house by him and Shmuel, had cracks between the planks; the main house at least had double walls. In Moshe's room there was nothing but a bed and table. His brother and sister slept in one of the other rooms —Zohar, the light-haired nine-year-old boy who was called "Zorik," and Aviva, nearly thirteen, a radiantly beautiful girl with long black hair. From that day until she died in 1968, Aviva was one of the people I felt closest to. The parents, Shmuel and Devora, slept in the second room, and there, too, was the cot of Devora's completely paralyzed mother. She needed constant care, and Devora and Aviva gave it without a murmur.

Devora, with her jet-black hair worn in a coronet and covered by a kerchief, impressed me from the first. She looked as though she had stepped out of a Russian novel; I was in a very Russian period just then, and Devora was steeped in Russian culture and literature. It was considered a waste of time at Nahalal then, but Devora always had flowers in her house. She especially loved violets because they reminded her of the Russia she had left twenty-five years earlier. There was a little bed of them under the walnut trees at the front of the house, and jasmine climbed the wall. The heavy perfume of jasmine in the Dayans' garden, combined with the barnyard and cowshed odors and the smell of farmers coming home from work, is something I shall never forget. For me, Moshe had a special, infinitely fresh and clean aroma, like that of fresh milk and new-mown hay. Devora was always immaculately clean, which most of the Nahalal people of those days, including myself, were not.

Today every house in Nahalal has a flower garden, but years ago Devora's idea of investing precious work hours in something that you could neither eat nor sell was considered odd. Even with all the rough farm work there was whimsey too: one of the family's horses was called "Isadora Duncan."

So I fell in love with this Russian family that, at least outwardly, looked so happy. This, I thought, was what I had been dreaming of; this was exactly the way I wanted my own life to be. The way they all sat down together for meals at a rough wooden table lit by a kerosene lantern, with Shmuel presiding like a patriarch, was a joy to me; in my own family we ate at peculiar hours and hardly ever together. After supper Shmuel, the patriarch, often washed the dishes, which my emancipated mother would never have thought of letting my father do. And then Shmuel would roll on the floor playing with the younger children.

Though I admired Devora tremendously, I did not understand until afterwards how much she had given up to come to Nahalal, and how much she continued to give up. With her mind and education she could have been one of the country's leaders. Instead she remained at the farm, holding the family together, driving herself physically with the hardest chores, which a simple laborer could have done. All this I did not realize until later; that, and the problem Devora must have had with me, because it is not easy to be a mother-in-law and there was much tension between us.

I loved the literary discussions and the wonderful food: there was no money, but the wooden table was spread with fresh salads, home-baked bread, rich farm cream and butter; and I was always hungry.

The Friday evening bath was a fascinating ritual for me, coming from a home that had a conventional bathroom with hot water. There was none at the Dayans', only a cold-water tap for doing dishes. Friday afternoon we filled a big Arabian copper washbasin with water and set it over a wood fire outside; then we each took a turn in the kitchen for a hot bath in the laundry tub. After that we changed into clean, but wrinkled, clothes; there was an iron that you heated with a hot coal, but it was only used for special clothing. Sheets were hung to dry on the line, but carefully by the corners; folding them over the line made a crease. Devora was a perfectionist about all such domestic duties and would go over the spots here and there that I missed, which made me feel dreadful.

To get the weekly portion of meat for Saturday dinner meant a two-hour wait in the butcher's queue. Devora would prepare cutlets late Friday night and then go to bed; Moshe and I would come back much later, very hungry. We did not think about the next day's dinner, and sometimes we sat down to the cutlets and ate them. I should have known better, but I was thoughtless and it did not occur to me that we were being terrible.

Devora soon asked me to come to the house for the day, from time to time, to take her place running things. She went to Tel Aviv to the Working Women's Council, and received a few pennies for expenses; these she would pay me if I took over the chores. I was happy to, and loved the darning and cooking and scrubbing and everything, even though it made a heavy load with schoolwork. Moshe did not like the whole idea. He didn't like his mother being away, and he didn't like his mother deciding who would take her place. Shmuel liked it even less. He had made inquiries about my parents, whom he had met at Merhavya when I was a baby, and decided they were wealthy, bourgeois, and unsuitable for his own pioneering family.

One evening, sitting under the walnut tree in front of the house wrapped in the scent of jasmine, I overheard Shmuel and Moshe talking. Moshe mentioned that he was going to Jerusalem with me.

"I don't like the idea of your being with that Shwarz girl," Shmuel said. "She has bourgeois values."

Suddenly I felt involved in some terrible mistake, because the family did not want me. My impulse was to go into the house and say, "I've heard what you said, and I won't ever come back," and walk off into the village night, just as in a Thomas Hardy novel, trailing the scent of jasmine.

But I didn't. Moshe said later that this was all nonsense, to pay no attention, that his father was just old-fashioned. And I said, "But he doesn't understand me at all! He doesn't know I'm against bourgeois values! After all, I'm going to a kibbutz!"

In the end the family accepted me, and I was soon staying all night at the Dayan farmhouse instead of crawling back through the dormitory window. It all would never have happened if Hannah Maisel had been there.

The nights of Nahalal seemed to me then, as they do still, incredibly romantic. The moon was huge; we had hayrides in the horse-drawn cart and bonfires and endless Russian songs to balalaika accompaniment. Here Moshe had a real distinction, for he has always been incapable of carrying a tune. The

other young men had beautiful voices and some were musicians.
Moshe was tone-deaf, something all our children inherited.
But this did not bother me. I found everything Moshe said
important; he did not have to sing it.

One of the exciting things we did was "taking the bull for
a walk." This meant hitching to a cart a bull who had not
been near a cow for a long time and driving him out for
exercise. It was on one moonlit night when such a bull was
drawing the wagon that Moshe paid me his single compliment.
He was driving, a tricky business, and I was sitting next to him.
In the back of the cart, in the hay, were some village boys and
girls from the school; they were all singing, and a boy called
Shlomo was playing the harmonica.

Suddenly Moshe said to me, "Has any sculptor ever wanted
to make a bust of you? With a profile like yours . . ." I was
stunned and ecstatic. It was such an extraordinary approach for
Moshe, who never talked like that. The bull must have been
surprised by something too, for at that moment he gave a lurch
and the wagon jerked towards a row of eucalyptus trees. A
twig snapped across my forehead, cutting it just enough to draw
a little blood. There was much excitement and Shlomo stopped
playing the harmonica. Moshe was considerate and attentive.
I remember every detail exactly.

But with all the romance, work was the center of our lives.
My first assignment at school was the bakery: four hours,
starting at 2:00 A.M., baking the day's bread for a hundred girls.
"And a real loaf, looking just like a loaf should, comes out
every time!" I told my mother excitedly when I went home
for the weekend. I was pessimistic about my abilities and thought
it a miracle that I was actually creating beautiful, normal loaves.
And I loved the baking. You were up to your elbows in dough,
kneading and shaping it, dipping your hands in water to keep
them from sticking, waiting for that magic moment when the
dough no longer stuck but made a special squelching sound,
the sign that it was ready to be shaped and left to rise; then
the marvelous smell of baking bread, and finally, baked bread!

My mother, of course, would take it for granted that if you
followed the recipe the result could hardly be otherwise.
Moshe's mother, on the other hand, had made herself go through
the same work just twenty-one years earlier and wrote her own
description of the price of this accomplishment—the stiff fingers,
the aching back, the whole "superhuman effort."

Moshe began turning up in the bakery at two in the morning
to help chop wood for the bakery oven and learn an English
word or two. By four he would be back at his parents' farm for
the milking.

From the bakery I was transferred to the dairy to learn cheese-making. I loved this too, especially finding out how to make real Swiss cheese, holes and all. We made all kinds, from simple, white cottage cheese hung to drip in a cloth to interesting, smelly French varieties. These we proudly took to the dining room, but the girls could not bear the smell and sent them back.

From the cheeses, I asked to be transferred to the cowshed, considered the "hardest subject" in the curriculum. The dairy-science teacher was famous for her strict discipline. She instructed us, "You will start scrubbing down the cows, and of course everything else in the shed, at two-thirty in the morning to prepare for the milking. You will carry in the alfalfa from the barn. As you will notice, alfalfa is eight times heavier than hay."

She went over the cowshed lanterns with a white handkerchief to see if we had removed all the soot, and I was in awe at this Dickensian touch. But the cowshed had its advantages. There was more free time in the evenings and more opportunity for Moshe to come and help. From the time he was a child, he could handle any problem with cows.

I was assigned to the quarantine shed and twelve sick cows. But how do you go about milking twelve sick cows who do not want to be milked? Alone in the barn at three in the morning with only the light of a lantern and twelve animals who kicked wildly when approached, I did what I always do at such times. I sat down and cried.

Moshe arrived out of the night and took over masterfully. "You tie their back legs, like this, and fasten the rope to the beams, so they can't kick," he explained. One cow, part Dutch and part Arab, had been queen of the dairy, the champion milker; now she was sick with a disease that makes cows abort. I could not bear to see the wild look in her big eyes; on the other hand I was filled with admiration for the way Moshe handled everything. It was strictly against the rules for him to be in the quarantine shed at all, because of the danger of infection; only the student assigned to this shed was allowed near the animals, and each time I left I had to wash thoroughly with disinfectant. Still, Moshe came, and continued to come, every night before going to milk his family's cows.

In the dormitory, things were as they always are when girls live together. From gossip I learned that Moshe had been friendly the term before with another student, who was late in returning for the second year. I decided to make the sacrifice and, just before she came back, announced dramatically to Moshe, "I will give you up!" Nonsense, said Moshe, and told me it had not been at all important.

Packages of food came from home with delicacies unknown at Nahalal, for in the mid-thirties, under British rule, Jerusalem had imported food. This was my chance to introduce Moshe to some good things from the outside world. A tin of pineapple from one of these packages was probably his first taste of something that was not grown on the farm.

But I was not always successful in impressing him. I thought I was quite a good horsewoman and one day Moshe and I took two of the Dayans' horses and rode several hours to visit the kibbutz where my sister, Reumah, was staying. I did my best to gallop expertly. Moshe only laughed and said, "Maybe in twenty years you'll be able to sit a horse properly." I was terribly offended; but a few days later I saw Aviva riding bareback over a hill, her black hair streaming behind her. It was one of the most beautiful things I have ever seen, a picture of grace and freedom, and I realized that in this a girl from the city could never compete with a child born on a farm.

In our long talks, I tried to convince Moshe of the beauties of kibbutz living. But it was hopeless, for Moshe despised that way of life. I still saw my life as a farmer on a kibbutz, and he saw his as a farmer on a moshav. Perhaps he might live in one of the new border settlements planned as security outposts; this he considered more of a challenge, and more important to building the country than staying in a safe, established place like Nahalal.

I told Moshe about my childhood in London and we discussed books. He knew Russian literature in Hebrew translation, but only a few English classics had been translated into Hebrew, and he was eager to learn them. We talked about the Haganah, the illegal underground defense organization, and about the future of the country. There was barely a word about marriage. I, especially, looked down on the institution. If you happened to be expecting a baby, so all of us brought up in the kibbutz movement believed, that was when you got married. Even at the moshav, a marriage ceremony in those days was nothing to get excited about.

The first time I took Moshe to Jerusalem to visit my family, Mother was struck by how involved I was. She was used to my turning up every few months with another boy and being very excited about each one; this time I was committed in a different way. After lunch Moshe stayed with Father—he was silent and shy most of the time, Father told me—and I followed Mother upstairs, asking, "Mother, don't you think he's unusually intelligent? Mother, don't you think he's the most handsome boy you've ever seen? Isn't he wonderful?"

When the rains came to Nahalal that winter I became ill with an infection picked up in the cowshed and was sent home for two weeks. Moshe sent me letters every day, long, analytical and sometimes poetic, which I think, reflect the Russian moodiness that affected us both.

"Everything is muddy, dark, and gloomy, and so it seems inside myself, too," one of these letters begins. "And there is no mud anywhere in the world like the mud of Nahalal." He interrupts his writing for a trip to the cowshed, to carry the milk buckets on the wooden yoke, and describes all the things that can go wrong on such a farm chore.

"But now I am back home. The rain is leaking through the roof, but it's not too terrible—a fire, a kettle, a letter to Ruthie, and Dostoevsky for the twentieth time. How he purifies one with his concept of suffering . . ."

He gives paragraphs of advice on the conduct of life, as though he were twenty years older than me instead of only two. I must finish my studies, that is essential, "for we must often do things that seem unpleasant." One must have a specific, carefully thought-out program for the future; one cannot just stumble ahead. "One must follow a definite plan—until, of course, the plan changes."

Moshe wrote about the comforts of city life, and about my parents. "We two are so different—in inclination, in background, in potential, in sex, too! In everything!" He brooded on the differences: "If only I had your possibilities, your rights with respect to your family instead of merely obligations, then I in your place would unquestionably finish my studies. For my own sake, first of all. If only it were possible, I'd say we should sit down together, and study together."

A wife, he explains, is not in his future; nothing but much backbreaking work. He is a son of Nahalal, and its destiny is his. Unless, perhaps, he goes to the new settlement being planned for the swamps of Hula up north, "some real paradise with malaria and tuberculosis and shortage of working hands and all the rest," and he doubts whether this difficult future would suit me.

He is taken with the idea of dynastic continuity. We had just read a wonderful new novel, *The Forsyte Saga,* and in the letter Moshe says that "it is a good thing to carry on the tradition of your family. Every family has its saga—the Dayan saga, the Schwarz saga . . ." And then this rather lofty phrase from a boy of nineteen: "After all, Ruth, you are still very young and your whole life is ahead."

There is more description of the wind and the rain; and then, "Get well quickly . . . And Ruthie, if I don't get a whole packet of letters from you, then——! And not that I don't remember how you look, but do go have a photograph taken and send it to me. A real one, of your face."

Before returning to school I went to a party in Jerusalem that was in direct contrast to our Nahalal nights. Held at the home of a Jerusalem judge, it was for the twenty-first birthday of my friend Zelda, and among the guests I met for the first time were Captain Orde Wingate and his exquisite bride, Lorna. This visionary British officer, whom Moshe was soon to come to admire in action against Arab bands in the hills around Nahalal, was something like Moshe in his lack of interest in social gatherings. He arrived late for the party, in a beige smoking jacket with a bright red lining that impressed us all. Lorna, who became a good friend after her husband's death in Burma, seemed unattainably beautiful.

I must have looked peculiar, because I had borrowed a mauve evening dress from Mother, which could not have suited my short, boyish hair. I liked the idea of dressing up theatrically for some festive and rare event, but for normal life I preferred the Nahalal ways.

Back in the dormitory we had a new topic: Wilhelmina. Wilhelmina was not a student, but a young Jewish woman from Germany who lived in Haifa and was a friend of my German roommates. Her temporary permit to remain in Palestine was about to expire and now, in the late fall of 1934, she was going to be sent back to Germany.

One way to help such cases, I knew, was by arranging a marriage with a Palestinian. Our boys even traveled to Europe for the purpose of marrying a girl—any Jewish girl—and returning home with her. Usually these marriages were just for the record, but sometimes they turned out happily—more happily than some with romantic beginnings. A cousin of Moshe's from Nahalal married a girl from Poland to bring her to Palestine; the anniversary of their "fictitious" wedding was happily celebrated thirty years and several grandchildren later.

So the solution to Wilhelmina struck me as obvious: Moshe was available and patriotic. I said to him, "Moshe, you must marry Wilhelmina." He was not enthusiastic. Moshe was not interested in marrying anybody. He had never seen Wilhelmina, who, I was told, was not very attractive, spoke no word of anything but German, and was nearly ten years older than Moshe. But I thought this was all irrelevant and told Moshe it was his duty to marry her, for this was another way of building the country.

He finally agreed, and I rushed about making arrangements. I sent word to Wilhelmina in Haifa that her worries were over, she would not be sent back to Germany; she was going to marry Moshe Dayan and become a British subject and receive a Palestinian passport. I gave the rabbi of Nahalal the details and we set a date. On the happy morning, I took a day off from school, met Wilhelmina as she got off the bus from Haifa, and introduced her to Moshe. They hardly talked, and what conversation there was, I translated from Hebrew to German and back. I had found a second witness from the village but had forgotten to buy a ring. This was no problem, though, for under Jewish law a bride may be married with an ordinary coin, or anything round.

After the ceremony the bride and groom said good-bye, which I translated, the first Mrs. Moshe Dayan took the bus back to Haifa, and Moshe went back to the cowshed. I was pleased that things had turned out so well. But Father, being a lawyer, was irritated when I told him of my achievement, and said, "What a foolish thing to do!"

For the prospect of marriage between Moshe and me was beginning to take shape. Not that there were any romantic vows; that was foreign to both of us. But Moshe was eager to study, and for this we thought of going to London together. For practical reasons, we decided, it might be simpler to be married. Devora, the freethinking intellectual, was beginning to wonder how the neighbors felt about a young girl spending the nights under the family roof. My own parents, equally freethinking intellectuals, had themselves married at an even earlier age for, as they said, "practical" reasons.

I was sound asleep one afternoon on my bed in the dormitory, for I had been up for fourteen hours since the early milking, when I was awakened by excited whispers around me: "How are we going to tell her?" "What should we do?"

"What's it all about?" I asked.

"Moshe's been hurt."

I didn't wait for details, though as I rushed out I heard something about an Arab boy who had crept up behind Moshe in the fields and struck him over the head. Quarrels over land rights were a source of friction between the villagers and the neighboring Bedouin Arabs.

At his home, I found Moshe very still on his cot, his head bleeding. I did not leave the house for three days. This was the first of many times at Moshe's bedside. In the future, there were to be hospital wards and nurses; this time, my introduction to the feeling of helplessness and tension that follows wounds and accidents was in a simple farm home, which now held two patients, for Moshe's paralyzed grandmother lay motionless in the adjoining room. But Moshe has always been exceptionally strong. He recovered more quickly than anyone expected and was soon back at the plow.

And, it seemed, we really would be getting married. But of course, a problem cropped up: the first Mrs. Moshe Dayan. We had all forgotten about Wilhelmina, and she had to be found and divorced. Where was she? Nobody knew; and as the owner of that precious Palestinian passport, she might, for all we were aware of, have gone off to America or Australia. But I tracked her down and she had no objection to the divorce. The papers were signed, and Moshe faced his next wedding free from the shadow of bigamy.

July 12, 1935 was set as our wedding date; the same, according to the Hebrew calendar—Yud Aleph be Tammuz—on which my parents had been married twenty years earlier and on which our three children would be married in the future. Invitations went out to my family's Jerusalem friends, who included most of the city's noted citizens; on Moshe's side, besides the whole village of Nahalal and leaders of the moshav movement, there were the Bedouin encamped in the nearby hills.

I took Zorik and Aviva for their first trip to Jerusalem, on a shopping tour; and I bought myself a very inexpensive wedding band. Perhaps the most excited and sentimental of all was Devora. She went to a great deal of trouble to find a length of white crepe for a bridal gown, which I promptly refused. Instead, I wore a peasant-embroidered Rumanian blouse that Mother gave me, and a blue *sarafan* (peasant dress) made by a friend. For a veil, my grandmother, Pnina, produced a gray chiffon scarf embroidered with pink flowers. For the ceremony, I was barefoot. Moshe wore khaki trousers, a short-sleeved open-necked white shirt, a khaki cap, and sandals.

Not one of my friends from the youth movement came for the wedding. This was nothing personal against Moshe, but, rather, a reproach to me for abandoning all my antibourgeois convictions. "I strongly disapprove of your going through with this ceremony," one boy wrote me, and listed all his ideological objections.

On the other hand, the Bedouin guests, who had never heard of socialist idealism, enjoyed a noisy "sulha." This Arab tradition is a festivity to celebrate a reconciliation after a quarrel, with many blood-curdling shrieks. The sulha at our wedding marked a temporary end of bad feelings between Nahalal and the Arabs, for the latest eruption had been just two months before, when the Bedouin boy split open Moshe's head.

The first guest was Dr. Arthur Ruppin, one of the most famous men in the history of agricultural settlements. He arrived when I was still in my working shorts and told me, "I came an hour early so that you will be able to tell your grandchildren that Arthur Ruppin was the first guest at your wedding."

The Jerusalem guests came in a bus and stayed overnight at Nahalal, because travel at night was hazardous; rooms were found at the school and with friends in the village. My parents brought smoked meat, sausages, and other delicacies; the rest of the refreshments were all home-grown—corn boiled in enormous washing tubs, mounds of grapes and plums, homemade grape wine, and a potent Nahalal specialty, wine made of grapefruit. After the ceremony in the garden, conducted by the same rabbi who had not long before joined Moshe and Wilhelmina, there was dancing on the grass and Russian songs; Devora's fragile carpet of violets under the walnut tree was badly trampled that day.

Soon after the ceremony I changed from my wedding dress to my work clothes and went off to the cowshed, for the cows still needed to be milked. "Maybe Ruth didn't really have to go off to milk, but undoubtedly she liked the idea of it," my mother observed later. But that was not at all how I felt: I heard the cows lowing and knew nobody was going to worry about them except me.

My father's law partner, Dov Joseph (Governor of Jerusalem during the War of Independence and later Minister of Justice), went looking for me among the guests and finally found me in the cowshed, where he extended his felicitations.

Moshe was shy and reserved. My parents and friends remember me as lighthearted, and enjoying every dance. But then the sky grew dark and the huge summer moon of Nahalal rose above us. I think that neither Moshe nor my parents missed me when I again slipped out from the gaiety, to be alone.

I went to the grove of plum trees, not far from the house, the ones Moshe had written about so paternally the winter before. Now they were laden with fruit. It was near midnight of a decisive day in my life. I stayed there for what seemed a long time, and I knew those moments would never come again. The moon shone on the plum trees. Like every bride, I felt a sense of finality. But I was unsure of what would come now.

2 · London with Moshe

Moshe objected strenuously to one aspect of the wedding, the gifts. These were mostly checks given by friends of my parents to help finance our studies in London. Being showered with money was against Moshe's philosophy of life, but he was eager for the chance to learn and accepted it for the trip to England.

Our travel arrangements were fourth class, four pounds sterling (about thirty dollars). When Father learned about our ideas of thrift he said, "No, that's impossible. I'll pay the difference and you'll go at least third class."

Moshe was firm about not letting porters carry our luggage aboard. No hired laborer was going to be paid to carry the belongings of a moshav son; so, true to the pioneering socialist ideology of those days, Moshe took every piece of luggage aboard himself. Ours had a Middle Eastern flavor, since the overflow was bundled into a Bedouin rug of red camel hair.

As we stood on the deck of the *Mariette Pasha* watching the shoreline of Palestine disappear, I realized there were tears in Moshe's eyes. He was leaving home for the first time in his life. This was the only time I have seen him moved to the point of visible tears.

It was ideology all over again when the *Mariette Pasha* arrived in Marseille. Moshe heaved the eiderdown and the red Bedouin rug down the gangplank and I followed with assorted bundles. We made a rather lunatic pair. Both of us insisted on wearing sandals, not the usual thing for European autumn. Moshe refused to wear a necktie. I refused to wear the dignified dresses Mother had bought in Jerusalem's best shop, and spent the next five months in pleated skirt and blue blouse, the uniform of the youth movement, with bandages on my bare legs marking old mosquito bites.

The night we spent in Paris, Moshe, again for ideological reasons, refused to leave his shoes outside our hotel room to be polished. This might be the custom in capitalistic countries, he knew, but no man born free should cause another to stoop to polish his shoes. His solution, to me, was "Go out and buy some shoe polish."

"But I don't know the French for 'shoe polish,' " I said, starting to cry.

This was the beginning, in tone and content, of the arguments ahead of us that winter, which was far from a romantic European honeymoon. When we looked for a place to stay, not a single suspicious London landlady believed that such a curious pair were actually married. We would produce our marriage license, much of it in mysterious Hebrew letters. "And where is this here Palestine supposed to be?" we were often asked as we stood forlornly at the front door in our sandals.

Moshe was supposed to study agriculture at Cambridge. Chaim Weizmann had, at Shmuel's request, arranged for an exemption and Moshe was admitted with a high-school matriculation certificate. But he needed to know more English first. He settled down to English grammar, for Moshe is thorough and disciplined in anything he believes important, but his only real pleasure that winter was standing on two wooden crates in our landlady's garden and watching a litter of bulldog puppies next door.

Our first London purchase was two secondhand bicycles at ten shillings each from the Caledonian Market, to save money on transportation. I had an hour's trip from Finsbury Park, where we finally found a bed-sitting-room, to a class in pottery-making. Moshe had an equally long ride to a drawing class he enrolled in to cheer himself up. We used to arrive on our bicycles for rendezvous with various wealthy friends of my parents. My parents always looked respectable, while we must have seemed very peculiar as we tied our bicycles to the railing of the underground station at Piccadilly for a dinner invitation to some elegant establishment like the Princess Restaurant.

We argued constantly about directions as we cycled through the London fog. "We're going the wrong way," Moshe would growl in Hebrew, dubious and depressed and feeling out of place.

"No, I know this is right," I would insist, and of course I always was. My superior knowledge must have been infuriating to Moshe, who has always been the leader in command of any situation. It was no wonder he was in a dreadful mood; he hated the weather, hated his ignorance of English, hated being dependent on me for simple conversations and directions. Every letter from home telling of the growing troubles between Arabs and Jews added to his feeling that he was in the wrong place at the wrong time. He thought constantly of returning, though he well knew the importance of staying and studying. Each time he was at his lowest a cable would arrive from my parents: STAY IN ENGLAND FIFTEEN POUNDS FOLLOW.

For me, London was just the opposite—a city I knew well, the place where I had spent my childhood. I had lived there from the time I was two, when my parents left Palestine to study in England, until I was nine. When we left I was a proper English schoolgirl. But although I felt self-confident about the London streets with Moshe, I had been a fearful little girl in those early years, in tears most of the time. My first bicycle rides were with my mother and I hated them. Mother traveled around London on a bicycle and used to put me on the seat behind her, telling me to hang on, which I did with tears streaming down my face. Mother kept hoping I would learn to enjoy this fun but I never did, and my constant crying exasperated her. "At least decide on some good reason for crying, if you insist on doing it," she would say.

That was how London was when I was a child. During my stay there with Moshe, I had no trouble finding work teaching Hebrew, at a religious school, and I tried to get Moshe a job there.

"No," said the headmaster, "that will not be possible. Your husband does not wear a skullcap and this is an Orthodox establishment." Besides, Moshe's English was not yet good enough. Still, I had the job and raced home on the bicycle to tell the good news and describe the effort I had made for him, too.

Moshe greeted me with different news. "I've bought tickets. We're going home." He had received a letter from his cousin in Nahalal telling of a new settlement being formed, to be called Shimron. Moshe was needed, and he could no longer endure being in a place where this was not the case. In February 1935, we left London and returned to Palestine.

To explain how I, having been born in Haifa, and taken my first steps in the co-operative village of Merhavya, south of Nazareth, nevertheless became an English schoolgirl; and why, although I have a remarkably fearless mother, I turned into a crybaby, I must first describe my parents. English became my mother tongue as much as Hebrew because of a secret society that my parents organized when they were in high school in Tel Aviv. That youthful conspiracy caused them to go to England when I was a baby.

Mother and Father had an unusually close marriage. They met when Mother was twelve and Father fourteen, and married six years later. Mother was brought to Palestine from Russia by her parents when she was eight. Her father, Boris Klimker, a Sorbonne-educated chemical engineer, was one of the first "capitalists" in Palestine and founded an oil factory. His wife, Pnina, was an unusual woman. A nurse and midwife, she learned fluent Arabic and worked among Arab patients in Safed and Nablus, where, fifty years ago, Jewish professional women were practically unknown. The Emir Abdullah of Jordan personally invited my grandmother Pnina to come to Amman and attend the royal harem, where a palace would be at her disposal, an offer she reluctantly declined.

But my grandparents had a difficult home life and were married and divorced twice from each other. Both were freethinkers and political liberals—a viewpoint shared by my mother's grandfather—and this thinking I inherited, as a matter of course, from my parents.

When he was fourteen, Father was sent alone to Palestine by his Russian parents because they were worried he might become a Russian revolutionary; they preferred him to grow up a Zionist. But the Herzliya Gymnasium in Tel Aviv, Palestine's first Hebrew high school, where my parents met as students, had the reputation of being "a hotbed of free thought." It was also a training ground for the country's future leaders, and Zvi Shwarz and Rahel Klimker became socialist activists. With a few slightly older students—Moshe Sharett, Dov Has, Eliahu Golomb, Itshak Olshan, all destined for national fame—they organized a secret society, putting their names to a compact that required each signer "to devote his life to the country's service." The student conspirators set up a hierarchy so that each member would "receive orders" from someone above him in the ranks. Father's commander was Dov Has, who became a founder of the Haganah and was instrumental in creating the beginnings of Israel's air force.

Social justice, equal rights for women, a natural and antimaterialistic way of life, and love based on freedom rather than conventional rules were among the principles of my parents and their friends in high school during the fading years of the Turkish Empire. But Mother approached everything with a practical attitude. Free love, for instance, was all very fine but not always practical. "We knew we would be together, so we decided we might as well get married" was the phrase she used more than half a century after the event. They were the second two graduates of the high school to marry; the first were the parents of Yehudi Menuhin, although the violinist was born in New York.

As for women's rights, Mother has said that she hardly thought them worth all the agitation, particularly since some practical aspects were overlooked. She saw that the Arab women of Palestine occupied a low rank and she wanted that changed. But when a Mr. Sulzberger divorced his wife in the Old City forty-five years ago, an Arab woman asked my mother, "Is this such a good idea? Now she has no place to go. Wouldn't it be better if he just took a second wife? Why must he divorce the first?" Mother thought there might be a certain logic to that.

It turned out to be handy for my socialist father to have a capitalist for a father-in-law. Grandfather's factory in Haifa supplied war materials for the Turkish army, and his employees were therefore exempt from Turkish military service. When father's call-up orders for the Turkish army came in 1917, the high-school society sent him his first instructions: "Stay out by taking a job in the factory." During World War I many Palestinians had no strong feelings for either side. Father and his friends considered the German presence in Palestine "culturally progressive" and there were few reasons, then, to hate Germany. Mother was a pacifist and did not consider World War I a valid instrument for furthering social justice. That both her children grew up to marry soldiers—my sister, Reumah, is the wife of Ezer Weizmann, former commander of Israel's air force—is described by Mother as "an ironic trick of fate."

I was born in Haifa on March 6, 1917—just eight months ahead of the Balfour Declaration—in a stone house near the seashore built by the German Templars, a sect that settled on the Palestine coast a hundred years ago.

No doctor was present at my birth, not because of any pioneering rigors but because of Mother's principles. She was nineteen and believed that childbirth was a healthy, natural process. She also believed that jobs must be given to new immigrants, and among the unemployed new immigrants in Haifa was an inexperienced young midwife from Germany. The birth turned out to be difficult and dangerous, and a doctor should have been present; but we all survived and I became, I am told, a good-natured, easygoing baby who seldom cried. That started a few years later.

As a little girl, I was afraid of practically everything, while Mother is afraid of nothing. I have never seen my mother cry; I doubt whether anyone has. She believes this total absence of fear must be described as "some kind of emotional atrophy."

I have always had enormous admiration for my mother. Her fearlessness is something she shares with Moshe, and the two of them got along from the start. Yael has the same character, and she has always felt close to her grandmother. Mother's companionable ways with Moshe were certainly unlike those of the usual mother-in-law. During the early forties, for example, the two of them were driving along a road forbidden to motorists because it was exposed to snipers. Mother, one of the first women in Palestine to hold a driver's license, was at the wheel.

"We're not supposed to be driving along here, right?" Moshe asked Mother, coming out of one of his silences. He paused, added with satisfaction, "And we're driving along here, you and I, right?" and sank back again into his own thoughts.

A few years later, during an Arab riot, when Mother was driving her car with two Haganah officers and a quantity of illegal ammunition in it, the car was practically overturned by a mob of Arabs. The two Haganah officers turned pale. Mother felt nothing, absolutely nothing.

Shortly after Yael was born, Mother became the talk of Jerusalem with her crazy drive across the Sinai Desert. A grandmother at the age of forty-one, Mother helped us with Yael the first week and then left to join Father in Cairo, where they were both to fly to South Africa. Mother was to catch the plane that flew from Lydda Airport to Egypt. But a sandstorm had grounded all planes. So Mother took her Morris Minor and persuaded an Arab friend who knew the terrain to go along as relief driver. There were no roads in Sinai, only camel tracks. Army lorries passed once every two weeks, and there were only two police stations between Gaza and Cairo, over three hundred miles. The sandstorm covered the track. Mother's guide was terrified by the roaming Bedouin and the hyenas; she cheered him up with Arab parables. Somewhere between the two police stations, the car sank deep into the sand. Mother sensibly let the air out of the tires and drove to Cairo on the rims, making it, nonstop, in sixteen hours. Even she admitted that this was an idiotic escapade, but they made it, though nobody could understand why.

It must have been hard for so cool and practical a mother to have a timid daughter, fearful of ridicule, who daydreamed of proving her worth.

Early in 1918 the Turkish forces were defeated in northern Palestine and the British took over my grandfather's factory. On orders from the secret society, my parents went with me to Merhavya, to be teachers at this co-operative farm village. Today it is a veteran moshav; a kibbutz, the spiritual center of one of Israel's socialist parties, also bears the same name. Among the occasional visitors was a farmer called Shmuel Dayan, from the co-operative settlement of Degania, on the shores of Lake Galilee, where Moshe was born.

My parents received further orders: go to London to study.

When the time came, the nation would need leaders with higher education.

Because neither of my parents spoke much English, although Father knew Turkish and Arabic, they spelled their name to the immigration authorities—who accused them of being bolsheviks —in a way that seemed logical and that spelling has remained.

I felt a lonely stranger in my London school. We spoke Hebrew at home, but my romantic imagination was nourished by the English classics. My parents and their friends discussed socialist theories, but my great ambition was to be part of a "poor but happy family," and I saw the homes of the neighborhood's poor children in a rosy literary light. There was Dad and Mum, and all six children, one of whom seemed always to be in a wheelchair and another who was always called Lily. I did not realize then that Dad was unemployed and Mum drank; what charmed me was the family together at teatime, and hot cross buns. My parents were always too busy for this. Years later, the Dayan family eating supper by lamplight in a rough farmhouse attracted me in the same way.

Mother studied chemistry at London University, and after a day in the laboratory she used to play the piano at home. My ballet lessons absorbed me. That is, I loved the magic of dancing but, like so many other little girls, I was not at all fond of the drudgery of practice, and was terrified of the walk home from ballet class in the dark. But when Mother played Chopin waltzes, I loved improvising to her music. I was never musical, but those moments helped me reach my mother.

Father was more understanding. He has been known to cry at the movies and has even felt nervous in tense situations, just like everybody else. Mother considers his behavior more admirable than her own because, as she says, "When you are born with a blind spot for fear, you deserve no credit for being unafraid." As for my miserable moods, Father remembers that "they usually passed quickly."

Father is warm, charming, and scholarly. In London he studied for two degrees. His dissertation in political science at London University was on "The Social and Political Ideas of Maimonides." At the same time, though completely nonreligious, he studied rabbinical subjects at Jews' College. Both my parents gave Hebrew lessons, met influential English families, and earned a comfortable living. Father could even afford to go to Germany for visits when Mother studied for a year at Heidelberg University, and my first schooling was in German, at a Heidelberg kindergarten.

My own ideology at the time turned me into a thief. My idea was "to give things to poor children," and I stole pennies from the newsstands on the way to school to buy presents for children I considered less fortunate than myself. These gifts were usually things like celluloid fish, but I gave one little girl my small emerald ring. I told Mother it had slipped down a drain. Somehow my fibs and thefts were never discovered.

I enjoyed morning prayer at school, especially the poetic sound of "Our Father Which art in Heaven." One evening, Mother happened to overhear me reciting the phrases. Without any fuss she explained to me that I was Jewish and arranged to have me excused from school prayers. And that was that. I was not bothered by it; there were too many other things to worry about, such as the mysterious streak of moving light on my bedroom wall, made by a crack in the window blinds, or the unknown terrors in the gaslit London streets, especially the dark side streets beyond the lamplighter's area. I was upset by the brass headboards of our old-fashioned beds, for they gave off electric shocks whenever I touched them. Mother did not feel those shocks, for her fingers were callused from chemistry experiments. She thought my overactive imagination was at work again.

Many things confused me. Moshe Shertok (Moshe Sharett, later Israel's second Prime Minister) visited my parents often, and I thought he was Charlie Chaplin, because he had the same small mustache. When this was cleared up, I thought he was my uncle, for the mustache was also like my father's.

In class, when I knew the correct answers, I was too embarrassed to stand up and recite them, so I whispered the answers to my friends. One of my teachers commented, "Ruth must learn not to sulk when reproved."

I liked to embroider on plain facts. For a paper on botany I produced something complete with birds, butterflies and curlicues. It was too ornate, though underneath all the adornments the material was correct. Fairy tales were more interesting than schoolbooks, and I especially loved *The Little Mermaid.* I knew practically by heart the story of the princess who sacrifices herself to be near her prince: *"I know what you want all right,"* said the sea-witch. *"And it's very silly of you! Nevertheless you shall have your way, for it will bring you misery, my lovely princess. . . ."* Forty years later, on a visit to Copenhagen, I bought another copy of the book and went to see the famous statue of the little mermaid. That day, pranksters stole its bronze head. On February 10, 1972, my second visit to Copenhagen, the front page of the newspaper ran a picture of her covered with white paint. I felt that someone was trying to destroy my mermaid.

I enjoyed making decorations for my room and sewing clothes for my dolls. But my parents were brilliant and academic, and I knew my interest in dolls showed a lack of character. In 1925 a baby sister, Reumah, was born. I was delighted to have a real live doll at home, and also a real English nanny to take care of us. Our nanny loved the baby but found me tiresome. She could not understand my fondness for spiders. I used to watch them spinning their webs by the hour. I loved the way they touched and retouched at certain points—the wall, a twig—making a lovely, delicate, satisfying pattern. English spiders, I have noticed, make much more formal patterns than do our Israeli spiders.

In my last year at school in London, assigned a composition on "the greatest moment of my life," I chose for my topic, "Being at Trafalgar Square on Memorial Day," and described how impressive it was to see all the traffic coming to a stop to participate in that vast stillness. I had never been there during this celebration, but my description must have been convincing, for I received the highest mark in the class.

That year Mother reluctantly changed her course of studies from chemistry to education; even for her the hours of laboratory work were too much in addition to caring for two children and giving Hebrew lessons. In October 1926, seven years after we arrived in London, our family returned to Palestine, the homeland of which I had no recollection.

3 · Sirius

I hated Palestine from the moment we returned. After polite and respectful London, Jerusalem seemed to me rude and noisy. At school nobody wore blazers, and nobody stood up deferentially to recite in class. It was chaotic, and I stayed away as much as possible. In a way, I had always felt something of a stranger in England; now I felt very much a stranger in my own land.

Later, when I found my way among the children of Jerusalem, and especially after I met Zvi, life became fascinating. In the early thirties, boys of twelve and thirteen were in the Haganah, the Jewish underground defense organization, and most Palestinian children were obsessed with the concept of courage; the main occupation was proving your bravery, which was a long way from my London fear of shadows on the wall. Zvi was even more involved than most with the idea of courage and heroism, and, like me, he was an outsider. When we first met, he thought of me as an unattainable little rich girl and I thought of him as a boy out of a Dickens story.

But all that was still ahead, and until I joined the scouts I was lonely and miserable. My parents, on the other hand, were delighted to be back. At first we lived in a house in Musrara, a district inhabited largely by Arabs and facing the walls of the Old City of Jerusalem. Both Mother and Father speak Arabic well; Father even knows literary Arabic, and Mother had spoken it as a child in Jaffa.

Father received a position as a lecturer, and Mother naturally was not intimidated by the economic crisis of 1927 in Palestine.

"You won't be able to get a job," a friend warned Mother, "because if the husband is working, the wife is not allowed to. There aren't enough jobs to go around."

"Just watch and see," said Mother, and a week later she had a job teaching in a kindergarten, for which she had trained in England. A few months later she accepted a new post, organizing an after-school playground for both Arab and Jewish children. Coexistence of Arabs and Jews as a principle for a playground attracted her. In that neighborhood the Arab children came from rich homes and the Jewish children from poor ones; yet there they celebrated one another's holidays and learned one another's customs. Mother also knew the importance of taking children off the streets—the slums of Jerusalem then were difficult and depressing—and giving them some aim and constructive interest in life. I know people today whose lives were changed because they came to know my mother when they were children.

As for me, I sulked in my interesting, comfortably furnished home. For a time I carried on my furtive habit of illegal social work and stole to give to the poor just as I had in England. Like a great many other children, I even decided to run away from home. We planned it carefully, another girl and I, selling our schoolbooks to finance our escape, and started to walk along the railroad tracks that lead from Jerusalem to Tel Aviv. The stationmaster noticed us, of course, and we were taken home.

My sister, Reumah, was too young to be a friend, but I made dresses for her dolls and invented toys and games for her. And our house filled up with animals. My parents liked them and considered animals educational, so I was luckier than many of those children whose parents came from Eastern Europe, where a fear of animals, especially dogs, was common among Jews. I have loved animals all my life, but as a child I was often afraid of them and felt I had to overcome this fear.

I felt very unsure about the bats we had in the living room. Mother brought them home from a cave near Jerusalem, because she was sure they would be educational, and they lived behind a glass shelf on a diet of insects. I was terrified they would get into my hair, but since Mother thought they were interesting there was nothing I could do.

The Arab-Jewish riots of 1929 were the background to my dreams of glory. In August there were murders in Jerusalem, in Galilee, and in Tel Aviv; one hundred and thirty-three Jews and one hundred and sixteen Arabs were killed. Tension was high between the two communities and the British authorities. Mother's playground closed for exactly one week; then it reopened and remained so until the riots of 1936, with Mother walking home alone, often at night, through the narrow alleys of the Old City.

Mother was both fearless and a pacifist. I wanted to be both, too, but I was torn in different directions when our house became a Haganah defense position. We had moved to the Rehavia Quarter of Jerusalem and an Arab attack seemed imminent. Haganah men were stationed on our roof, and the adults in our four-story house stocked stones with which we were going to defend ourselves. I had fantasies of being a heroine, of somehow displaying fearless initiative and singlehandedly saving everybody from a screaming mob. What frightened me most was the thought that I would be cheated of this triumph, for the women and children were to be evacuated to the nearby Ratisbonne Convent, as indeed we were for two days; but fortunately the attack never materialized.

I continued to dislike school and had no feeling of belonging until my parents sensibly transferred me to another, more congenial school, and encouraged me to join a scouting movement. This changed everything in my life. There were two scout movements in Palestine—a very minor historical fact today but one we considered profoundly important at the time. The one I joined was geared to the pioneering socialism of our country and trained members to join kibbutzim after finishing school. The one Zvi joined when he was asked to leave ours because of "undisciplined behavior" had the usual scouting aims of Sir Robert Baden-Powell's organization in other countries.

Our group's activities and ideology attracted me more and more, with evening meetings in our hut, hikes in the countryside, and summer camp. Most of my friends were boys and I turned into a tomboy; my hair was cut short, like a boy's, I wore a boy's shirt, and went barefoot whenever possible.

The first time Zvi and I spoke is as clear to me today as it was on that summer afternoon in 1930. Parts of our attachment were typical of any youthful romance—jealousies, quarrels, reconciliations. But these ordinary emotions were played against a backdrop of Jerusalem in a period and mood that is gone forever, and Zvi's story gives an unusual picture of a complicated, gifted boy who chose to be what the times demanded.

In May 1941, when he was twenty-six years old, Zvi was killed off the coast of Lebanon on a secret commando mission in behalf of the British army. He was in command of a boat called *Sea Lion* and its crew of twenty-two Haganah volunteers. Major Sir Anthony Palmer, a member of an aristocratic British family and an artillery officer assigned to the British army's special operations branch, went with the men of the *Sea Lion*. In our military history, they are known as the "Twenty-three."

All vanished without a trace. They were assigned to sabotage the oil refineries at Tripoli, in Lebanon, which were providing fuel for German and Vichy French planes. Something went wrong, and the mystery of their disappearance was never solved.

Three weeks before, Moshe had lost an eye in another mission in Lebanon, planned within the same framework as the *Sea Lion* operation. Zvi was by then far higher than Moshe in the Haganah command, and I have no doubt that if he had lived he would have headed our army—or become a writer. His son, who lost his father when he was eight months old, is well on the way to realizing Zvi's boyhood dreams.

When he was fifteen and I was thirteen, we began a love affair that dominated both our lives for two years. I say "love affair" although it was quite pure. Our youth movements saw to that. Generally, we were passionately involved in romance, as distinct from sex—just the opposite of the climate today.

The first time we spoke was at the close of scout camp, in Rehovoth. At camp that summer I was still a little snob, not interested in mixing too much with other children. Zvi was the same, but for different reasons. I had noticed him before at scout meetings, and saw that he paid no attention to girls, yet always seemed to be showing off. He dressed differently from the other boys, and always wore his scout hat. Although Zvi also lived in Rehavia among Jerusalem's "intellectual snobs," he was not "one of us" and his family was considered odd. In fact, he lived with a very strict aunt and his background was tragic. When he was eleven, he had seen his mother burn to death while his father tried to smother the flames with a blanket. After that he refused to speak to his father and went to live with his aunt. He used his dead mother's family name of Toledano, a well-known name among Sephardic Jews; but the annals of early military history use his real family name, Spector.

Zvi had an inferiority complex and his behavior was strange, but he was outstanding. Whenever we put on a school play it was Zvi who wrote it and made the scenery as well. He liked being at the center of things, but felt very much apart.

On the drive back to Jerusalem from the camp, Zvi was sitting next to me on a jerrycan on which I was drumming with a stick. To be cute, I drummed on his head too. A day later he sent me a note. In his diary, he discussed the problem of how to sign it—such matters used to be taken very seriously. He recorded that another boy suggested, "Well, you could sign it, 'A friend—and more.' "

I answered it immediately, which surprised Zvi, but I had only been waiting for such a signal. From then on, most of my time in class was spent writing notes to Zvi. I had been a fairly good student, but I began to neglect my homework because Zvi was so much more interesting. He was two years older, a year ahead

in school and a good student; so he began helping me, especially
with algebra.

One midnight in 1931 Zvi wrote in his diary, "Ruthie, if you
ever read this, don't laugh at me . . ." Now, forty years later, I
am holding his diary—on the cover he wrote in block letters,
"The Diary of a Bloated Fool: Z. Toledano"—and on nearly
every page he found room for the words, "I love Ruthie." His
diary is mine now because a few years ago his older brother decided it should go to me, since most of Zvi's thoughts at the
time were taken up with me, as were mine with him.

Some of Zvi's darkest moods, and he had many, were expressed
only to this diary: "I was born bad. . . . Diary, go to Ruth and
to my aunt and tell them I'm bad for everybody . . . perhaps I
should commit suicide, that's the easiest thing. But Shlome says
that's egotism. And I don't want people to say, after I'm dead,
that I was an egotist."

He often sounded like any confused schoolboy: "Only now
the question has come to me, Am I really in love? And what is
love, anyway? How much longer will I be with Ruth? And I
still don't know what love is!" This is followed by: "Just returned terribly tired from a Haganah meeting. And tomorrow
there's an exam in algebra. . . ."

School seemed pale to us, for everything around us outside
was exciting and adventurous. The Arabs and the conflict with
the British and the underground Haganah were the realities
that provided the challenges we sought. I doubt whether children today can have as much fun as we did. Zvi and I invented
a whole world of our own. We had a cave in the Valley of the
Cross where we stored stray bullets that we found as an arms
cache against the Arabs and the British, and a hideaway against
the world. We had a special whistle—and a secret sign at the
window of my house that meant my parents had gone out. I
often had to stay home with my sister, and when my parents had
left the house, I would close the shutter at one window so Zvi,
standing under the olive tree across the street, would know the
coast was clear and he could come up. And we had our own
star, Sirius, the brightest in the heavens. We agreed that whenever in the future either of us saw Sirius, we would know that
we were somehow again together, even if one of us were dead.

Zvi's love for me was the most unselfish I have ever known.
He was the one who was always prepared to give without taking;
he was the one human being ready to stand outside my window,
under the olive tree, in the freezing rain of a Jerusalem night,
waiting for two hours to see whether I might give the signal. I
never see the star Sirius without thinking of Zvi. It appears at
different times in different years but somehow, when I need it,
it is there—as it was when I drove to Jerusalem after learning

that Reumah's nineteen-year-old son was wounded at the Suez Canal. Sirius shone above me all the way, as I drove in tears through the dark; and the boy recovered. And Sirius was the only star in the sky when I flew across Europe to America after telling Moshe that I wanted a divorce. I am sentimental enough to find comfort in this big, bright, often solitary star, and in its strength and brightness I still see Zvi's square face and blue eyes.

At the beginning of our relationship my parents were quite fascinated by Zvi; but they disapproved of him later and thought I was too young to carry on such an intense friendship.

Zvi had a wonderful sense of humor, though, like any boy, he took himself seriously. Some of his diary entries described ordinary events, such as party invitations: "Another party next week, and I'm not going to be asked. And they'll be bored, because a party without Zvi isn't a party. They'll ask me why I didn't come, and I'll say I didn't have time. The important thing is to preserve my self-respect. Which nobody else in the class does."

At times he composed richly detailed fantasies, like this one, which he called "From My Imagination" (since my parents did not care for Zvi, they always appeared in his daydreams as tremendously impressed by his valor):

The scouts' hut is completely filled with members and many parents. Her parents are there too. Suddenly there is an attack and shots are fired. And I'm there, in this vision, as a young officer commanding a unit. We're all on horses, well armed. I choose a pistol and give the order to fall to the ground and approach the back door, one by one. Then I give a stream of further commands. Then I take the pistol and draw my sword from the scabbard and everybody sees it. She and her parents, too.

And so we vanquish all the attackers, who were 240 in number, all armed, who wanted to pillage and murder. Then two high officers come and give me an honorary rank and a gold medal. All this is seen by her and her parents. Then I reorganize my unit, which admires me very much because of my modest behavior.

Now someone is needed who will take some of the wounded to the city and buy supplies. I ask for volunteers but nobody comes forth. Finally she alone advances and volunteers, but I do not accept her as I don't want to send her out. Finally I myself go. Then I speak a few words to the group, but since these words change every five minutes I'm not reporting them to you, my diary. . . .

One of our favorite tests for courage was to enter the Arab cemetery at night, a frightening business. Zvi was already training himself to lead men into danger and carried his Haganah pistol, yet at the same time he saw our actions with an ironic, detached writer's eye. One moonlit night the two of us sat among the tombstones; afterwards he wrote in his diary: "Sitting with Ruth in the cemetery, and the moonlight gleamed on my pistol. I'm sure it made an impression on Ruth. A beautiful scene for my future book."

Zvi always behaved like a gentleman. He knew that he had to restrain himself:

I'm like a piece of fire that is going to explode. . . . I want to embrace Ruth. . . . When I saw her I could hardly keep from hugging her. So I ran away. . . . I'm eating my fingernails. . . .

I shouted at Zvi for looking at other girls and flirted with other boys, including his brother, to annoy him—a talent that left me completely five years later. I was honestly astonished by the things that used to happen to me, because I was convinced most other girls were prettier. But things did happen. One mad boy actually brought a knife to school and said he was going to stab Zvi. Another boy told me that he must talk to me or else something tragic would happen: "I have some poison," he told me, "and I'm not joking. If you don't talk to me, I'll poison myself." So I talked to him. But I told him I loved Zvi.

We expected to marry and have six children. We discussed the idea of going to Australia, for in those days, before the state of Israel was established, young people who later were to give their lives for their country were quite capable of considering life elsewhere. "I dream of Australia, and of life with her there. Sometimes a path back to her after a previous marriage," Zvi wrote when he was sixteen, revealing his troubled attitude towards family life. He wrote stories and nearly a whole novel about our life in Australia, where we lived in a house he built in a tree.

"I wore my brother's work clothes," Zvi wrote in his diary about one of our school's work days at a kibbutz. "Ruth likes me in work clothes, I think because they make me look stronger." It is true that I was attracted by what seemed to me the idealism of simple labor; and that is just what drew me to Moshe a few years later, when he, too, really lived the life of a simple, dedicated worker.

Zvi got into trouble because of a letter I wrote to another boy —one called Moshe, an early admirer of mine. In this letter I explained to Moshe that I was afraid I could no longer see him because of my love for Zvi. My letter fell into adult hands, and my parents, horrified that a girl of fourteen had such thoughts, forbade me to see him. Father took me up to the roof of our house and lectured me calmly. He gave me some good advice: "Don't ever put things like this down in writing," a wise policy I have not always followed.

"Ruth isn't to blame, I am," Zvi told his diary after this episode. "And I don't hate her parents; but I wish her father would lecture me, instead of her." Except for Zvi, nobody has ever so wished to protect me.

But my parents' order did not stop us; it only made everything more exciting. For two years we saw each other every day, and not only at school. I was terrified of disobeying my parents, yet I did so month after month after month. Mother and Father thought they were leaving a demure little daughter at home when they left on their weekend walking trips—but in their absence I would invite our whole scout group to my house for parties, terribly nervous that something would be broken and I would be found out. But I never was.

We both seemed to have an early conviction that married life is not easy. Our youth movement did not place much importance on domestic cosiness. Zvi wrote:

> Ruth doesn't want to study and is having a hard time organizing her life, just as I once did. And my relationship to her has changed. I have no wish to share my life. She said today that it seems as though we're already married, and she doesn't want that. Because the relation between a man and his wife is always terrible, and that she wants to avoid.

Naturally, we had our little fights. After one of them I sent Zvi a paper heart, and a week later he wrote: "I was afraid we would come together again, and we have. What fine material for a romantic drama! I saw her wandering around my house . . . but pretended not to see her. We walked along, then she asked if I wanted to talk to her. I didn't, because I knew I would be lost again. . . . I told her to go home, and she was disgusted because she hadn't gotten out of me the words she wanted to hear. . . . We passed an Arab house and then, in the fields, I kissed her. We can't separate even if we wanted to. . . ."

On one of our solitary hikes, we walked to a spring in the Judaean wilderness, desolate yet beautiful country that Zvi knew like the back of his hand. That day I took along sausages and a little saucepan. At the end of the three-hour walk we came to the spring, and I cooked our lunch with the feeling that this was really a family meal; I, too, tended to change my mind about the desirability of family life.

We ate under a ledge of rock by the waterfall, where its echo sounded through the caves above. There was not a soul around, and except for that echo and the water and our voices, it was silent. I suspect we broke the desert stillness by shouting at each other about kibbutz ideals. I was steeped in them, but Zvi came to oppose socialism when he joined the Baden-Powell scout movement. When Zvi told a classmate he thought I "did not have the character to go to a kibbutz," I was terribly hurt.

For our picnic that day I had also brought along a tin of fruit, a delicacy in those days, and introduced Zvi to that side of gracious living—a bit like the gesture of the tinned pineapple with Moshe four years later. So that while I was the one who had my heart set on kibbutz simplicity, I also liked to show off to boys who were actually leading that simpler life.

"Maybe together we can solve the problems of life," Zvi wrote. "A farm on the banks of the Jordan, perhaps, alone among the Bedouin. First, we'll be there unmarried; occasionally one of us will go to the city to bring regards to our friends . . . I have Ruth, she is mine. But time alone knows what the years will bring."

In the battlefield of his mind, Zvi saw what he called a "vision of our conflict with the Arabs. He described it in great detail. My role is amusing, considering the trouble he had with my parents. As to the war "on all four borders that would probably take six days," it shows an uncanny imagination for a boy in the year 1931.

Zvi's Vision

This will be strange for you, Diary. A new kind of writing. The time is a time of preparedness by the Jews of the land to free their country by force, since every other method has failed. I am at this time the head of the Jewish Defense. Before this, my vision has showed me the period of acquiring arms and other arrangements necessary to break out successfully, once and for all.

Then comes the day of the uprising. At this time Ruth, who is already grown up, is with her parents in Haifa. I travel north to make all final arrangements. I go on my motorcycle and meet Ruth and her parents just outside Haifa. They greet me and invite me to eat with them; I ask them to save a room for me and say I will soon return. Then I go to a meeting with a number of loyal Haganah comrades.

I am given final plans. We organize details of attack and defense— on the coastal front against England, which is still trying to hang on by her fingernails and to help the Arabs. I inspect all lookout points and check ammunition. I am given various letters from abroad concerning immigration policy, and also available ships and arms supplies from Germany and so on.

Finally I stand up, look at my watch, and say in a clear voice, "In another eight hours, that is at 3:00 A.M., the war will start." I describe Attack Plan A, the coastal defense, and Plan B, on the southern and eastern fronts against attacks from Arabs. There are good chances of finishing with England in such a way that she will let us deal with the Arabs ourselves and just stand aside and watch. And after the war we will settle accounts, either by reparations or some other method. We will see. After this the war will be just with the Arabs, who apparently will attack us on all fronts, though not from overseas. When England will no longer be an octopus on the seas we will be able to bring immigrants from abroad much more easily. And ammunition too. And then its 100 per cent sure victory will be ours.

I sit with my seven council members to make final plans. There are more phone calls and telegrams. Suddenly Ruth enters the room with her mother, and they show me a document signed by the supreme commander of the army. They point to the name at the bottom. They ask if I am he. I smile haughtily and answer yes. I pretend not to pay any further attention to them and continue with my work.

I get into my car and say good-bye to Ruth and her family. They ask me where I am going and I say I must get to the front. That I

had to deal with all four borders, and that it would probably take
six days.

On the way to Jerusalem we were stopped twice by British patrols
but overcame them. At 2:30 A.M. I was in Jerusalem and in the last
half hour I prepared the army. At 3:00 A.M. exactly six of our airplanes appeared and bombed the area. The Old City was taken immediately, without casualties on either side.

The British army, six battalions, was captured by us and moved to
Nablus as prisoners, and guarded for days and nights by the Israeli
army. It was wonderful to see our soldiers . . . just like a real army of
any country. The country was in the hands of the Jews.

I have no time to go on now; I must arrange these thoughts for a
book, as they seem to me very close to the target.

The next entry in Zvi's diary is in a depressed mood, full of
black thoughts and the unhappy situation at home. Somewhat
later, as we were beginning to drift apart, he wrote:

The days rush by like arrows, and cannot be returned. Nothing in the
world can bring back the past. So much has happened in the last
month, and I have changed completely. I've become harder, more
realistic. The sensitive Zvi is gone. I'm growing up. I wrote a poem
the other day that is completely different from the poems I once
wrote. This change, this new manliness is also apparent with respect
to Ruth. I think of her now as a child who needs my protection, and
I must take care of her without any help from her. The main thing
is that she should love me, and I her.

After two years, Zvi and I drifted apart. There was no particular reason, except perhaps ideology, for Zvi began to criticize
my kibbutz aims, much as Moshe was to criticize my social outlook a few years later. I began to remember that there were
other boys in the world.

The year I left Jerusalem for Nahalal, Zvi went to England to
study at a university. But there was not enough money, and he
returned after just two years, and became a full-time officer
in the Haganah.

Stories of his bravery are related in the book *The Secret
Defence*, which tells of the Haganah's underground operations
during World War II. An example of his character is recalled
from the period of Arab attacks against Jewish settlements. Zvi
was with a group defending Kibbutz Kiryat Anavim against a
number of Arabs shooting from under cover of rocks. Zvi suddenly jumped up, ran towards the attackers, and in full view
began shouting at them in juicy Arabic: "You cowards and sons
of cowards! You don't dare come near us, you hide behind rocks
without showing your heads, you haven't the courage to attack,
you're just making a lot of noise!"

When he returned to his men, they asked why he had en-
dangered himself needlessly. "What do you mean, needlessly?"
Zvi replied. "They've stopped shooting, haven't they?"

He brought illegal immigrants from European camps to the shores of Palestine under the noses of British patrols. The immigrant ship in his charge had reached the coast and most of the refugees were already swimming ashore. Suddenly a British police boat came into view and began scanning the area with searchlights. The ship's captain, frightened, announced that he was going to surrender the ship.

Zvi had a large key in his pocket. In the dark he pushed its cold metal into the stomach of the captain and ordered him to his cabin. The captain, convinced the key was a pistol, obeyed. Zvi locked him in his cabin and returned to the sailors. "I've arrested your captain. I'm in charge here now, and order you to continue with this operation." When all the refugees were safe on land, Zvi himself swam ashore.

The Secret Defence describes Zvi as a man whose qualities of leadership were apparent in every situation in which he found himself, though he was quiet and slightly built, with "the face of a boy, one of those boys who are described as looking a bit like an angel." He loved adventure "but he did not pursue it; there was no need to, for adventure pursued Zvi." Yet he was an outstanding student and able to adjust to academic life, something that not all Haganah boys of those days could do.

When Zvi returned from England I was already married, and he married not long after. Soon we both became parents. We saw each other from time to time; he visited us when Moshe and I were at Shimron, and when Moshe was in prison he sometimes took me and Yael for an outing. I continued to think of Zvi whenever I saw our star, Sirius. But I was incapable of thinking seriously about any man besides Moshe.

Zvi volunteered for the command of the *Sea Lion* just a few days before its mission began. He was still limping from a motorcycle accident, and wore a wooden brace on his leg. For months after his ship was lost, I had nightmares of that wooden brace floating in the sea. Tense relations between the British and the French prevented a thorough investigation of what really happened off the coast of Tripoli, which was guarded by French government troops.

The final official document on this little-known action of the early days of World War II is a letter from the Supreme Command for the Middle East, dated Cairo, 19 October 1942 and marked "Top Secret." It conveys "high esteem for the strength of spirit and bravery with which these men took upon themselves this dangerous mission for the British Army," and expresses profound regret for the loss of the Twenty-three.

Zvi's younger brother Yeshaiahu was killed in November 1949 in the Negev, during our War of Independence, at the age of nineteen. From time to time I see his two surviving brothers— one is a member of a kibbutz, the other a photographer for our

Ministry of Defense. Zvi's widow, Shosh, often visits me, and is now one of my closest friends. She is the administrative director of the naval school at Acre, named in memory of the Twenty-three.

Zvi was one of the first to pilot a Piper Cub in Palestine; his son too has distinguished himself, for he holds an outstanding record of service in the air force. Though he never knew his father, he has qualities that seem to stem directly from him. I had not seen the boy for several years; then we met by chance in connection with a film in which he had a role—hardly an expected pastime for a young officer. But Zvi had loved the theater too, and always wrote our school skits. The film dealt with the Bedouin—those same tribes that were the background for our youthful adventures. Zvi's son knew nothing about his father's poems and stories; those were part of his life that had been connected with me. When I showed them to the boy, they opened up a whole new aspect of the father he never knew.

This is a poem Zvi wrote when he was nineteen, seven years before his death at sea:

I will row on, and with my hand hold back this wave,
And thrust my brow into the stormy tide,
For not in darkness shall I rise, and not in shade,
Not these will end the desperate tatters of my mind.
I will go on, and in my skull will smash
The knowledge of defeat, the basalt wall and iron gate;
And if the terrible wave's too wild to pass,
The gate too massive and the stones too great—
Then I will break my arms in its proud waterfall,
On iron crush my skull, and down the abyss I'll leap;
And to the battle—a stubborn one, though small
And mocked—these arms shall silent witness keep,
And a stain of blood will mark the grave forever
Of the boy who burst all bonds, and lived and died a dreamer.

4 · Shimron

It began early in 1936 with the letter that came to us in England from Moshe's cousin, describing the new outpost just being established on the hill overlooking Nahalal. It ended in the autumn of 1938, when the Shimron commune broke up and several members went north to establish the new kibbutz of Hanita.

What happened in between, during two years at Shimron, is full of paradoxes, and I doubt that anybody could write a "true" and complete history of our little group—which was a commune in the best sense of the word. What little I remember, perhaps because I prefer to forget the others, are the beautiful things, and there were many. But the evidence from our letters of that period points to conflicts and despair. As always, I went from extremes of joy to extremes of sorrow, and I was more inclined to sit down and write letters when I was miserable than when I was happy. On joyous nights at Shimron we danced barefoot to accordian music—and who writes when one is dancing?

I remember the fun of nights when Moshe and I would go down the hill to steal fruit from the orchards of the agricultural school for our communal dining room, and how the more high-minded members of the group were against our immoral behavior. I was completely happy during such escapades; and again, you do not write long letters when you are stealing fruit by starlight.

Shimron seemed an utterly beautiful place of green peaceful-
ness—even though later, shots rang through the hills. An ancient
spring bubbled at the top of the hill, wildflowers sprang up
after the rains, and thick grass covered the slopes.

Moshe was delighted to be home again where everybody spoke
a normal language, Hebrew. He helped me understand the
beauty in nature, the mixtures of practicality and emotion that
dominated our lives—the colors of fields of young wheat that
signified either a good or bad year, the shriveled leaves of thirsty
grapefruit trees. The shapes and colors of the clouds were beautiful in another way, and today when I climb the deserted Shimron hill, I see double rainbows in the sky, and the sunshine
breaking through the clouds is not silver, as the saying goes, but
a pure gold.

The idea behind Shimron was entirely practical: to provide
the framework for a new settlement for the sons of Nahalal. The
next generation, Moshe and his classmates, was growing up and
becoming restless. Land and facilities at Nahalal were limited;
only one son could take over the parents' farm. Those of us who
crossed the road, climbed the hill—about half an hour's walk—
and settled in five huts on the crest were sons of Nahalal farmers,
with a few girls from the Nahalal school, a few from neighboring
settlements, and, later on, new immigrants from Europe.

We were all young. Nobody in the group, which started with
six founding members and never had more than twenty-five, was
older than twenty-two, and all of us had the deep convictions
and emotional intensity of youth. Boys outnumbered girls—and
all the boys seemed to me very handsome. Five of us girls did
all the housekeeping chores—cooking, laundry, mending, kitchen
garden, and caring for the pine seedlings in the forest we
planted.

Shimron means "watch place" in Hebrew and is mentioned as
"Samana" in Egyptian writings of the fifteenth century B.C.,
when the earliest historical battle was fought at Megiddo (Arma-
geddon, about nine miles south). A nearby Arab village retained
the name in "Simunya." The name Shimron does not often
appear on modern Israeli maps, but, like Nahalal, it was an
ancient Canaanite town. Both were in the area given to the
tribe of Zebulon and are referred to in the Book of Joshua.

One of my jobs was to milk a herd of seventy goats. Those
hours just before dawn alone with the goats in the dark stillness
were completely beautiful and satisfying, much as the milking at
the school dairy had been. But the first time I faced my goats, I
realized I had a terrible problem: how was I ever going to
keep track of which ones I had milked? Nobody had explained
to me the technique of managing a whole herd of goats whose
names you did not even know.

Fortunately, they turned out to be extremely clever. They

stood patiently in line, each stepping up in turn to be milked
and crossing over to join the group already milked, and so out
to graze. "In two days, each one knew her name perfectly!" I
wrote to a city friend. "They always stand in exactly the same
order, and nobody ever takes anybody else's place in line!"

In contrast, the sheep were stupid and filthy, nothing like
the charming goats. Their pen was always filthy, and you worked
up to your armpits in the mess cleaning it out. The sheep put
their filthy feet into the bucket while being milked, something
goats would never do. And the smell was awful. It stayed with
you for days; when you were not assigned to them, you could
not bear being near anyone who was.

The recipe for goat or sheep cheese, Shimron style, was simple.
Into each bucket of milk we dropped a pepsin pill—the same,
more or less, as is used for indigestion. The milk immediately
curdled into a kind of sour jelly. This was cut into squares;
each square was removed with a sieve and left to drip from a
cheesecloth bag. When the moisture had dripped out, the bags
were placed under stones, where the cheese became hard in
three or four days.

Shimron was organized around two main huts. One served as
dining hall and kitchen; the other was for our guns and ammunition. As the first married couple, Moshe and I had our own room.
Our furniture was of natural oak—made by Moshe.

Moshe did some cooking, too. He finished guard duty, his
assignment during our first three months at Shimron, at three
every morning when I got up for my goats. Moshe would put
away his gun, go to the communal kichen to fry himself some
eggs, and prepare my favorite 3:00 A.M. meal—an onion omelette
with potatoes on the side. Then he woke me, gave me my
omelette, and turned in for some sleep while I went off to
milk.

We took whatever jobs were available nearby—picking or
packing fruit at Nahalal, guard duty—and pooled our earnings.
Our best income came from planting the "King George V
Forest," today a sweep of pine stretching above the highway,
and Shimron's main support. The girls started the seedlings
in the kitchen, tending them with forks till they were ready for
transplanting, and joined the boys in the actual planting. It
was satisfying work, like everything in which you can see your
efforts grow, except when trouble with the neighboring Bedouin
flared up. They would creep into the area at night and uproot
the seedlings, or sometimes herd their goats into a newly planted
area. Planting paid well by the standards of the day, but Shimron
was hardly an affluent society, and individual expenses were
carefully checked by a committee.

At the start, the only troubles Moshe and I had were of minor
housekeeping dimensions, with a little communal ideology

thrown in. "Bad news," Moshe wrote to me when I was briefly away in Jerusalem. "The committee on supplies wouldn't authorize the purchase of the coat I wanted to get for you, because coats aren't bought in the spring. And you have a jacket, the one Eytan [Moshe's cousin] gave you. Well, we can't argue with them. I just wanted to get you a nice present. But if they don't authorize it, I don't want to try to get money outside of Shimron. Let it be this way. If we're at Shimron, we have to obey the rules."

Archeologists deal in broken jar handles, and from these build their theories. Letters are more revealing, and Moshe and I wrote many during our Shimron period. But letters can also be misleading, since they record only the mood of the moment, and my moods, particularly, were always changing. Yet the fact that we wrote so many letters points to a problem. (I never threw away a single letter from Moshe, though very few of my own still exist.)

The trouble was that, except for those idyllic first months of my 3:00 A.M. onion omelette, we were seldom together. Moshe started going off to training courses for the British police and I, left alone for increasing periods, began going home to my parents, feeling very sorry for myself. I too started taking courses away from Shimron; one in practical nursing was the first. The goats were very nice, but to sustain myself I had only a certain dream of life. Moshe, at first, felt completely a part of this dream. In an early letter to me from a British police training camp, where he was enrolled in a course for sergeants, he wrote, "We both know that I've agreed to be a sergeant and to do the job as best I can, but my home will always be with you." It was difficult for others in defense work to manage to stay at home, but Moshe told me he was sure he would be different. "I'll work, more or less, but I'll certainly not move from home. If they want, let them install a telephone at Shimron. If they want, let them buy me a motorcycle. But I won't, under any circumstances, live anywhere else but with you."

Moshe did not like Shimron. For one thing, he was not in charge of security; Nahman, who slept in the ammunition hut with the guns, was in charge of the commune's defense and of most other things as well. Tall and self-contained, he was, like Moshe, the son of a founding family of Nahalal. Nahman knew me from Nahalal schooldays; Moshe, of course, he knew from early childhood.

Also, Moshe was hurt by the group's insistence that he and I pass a period as candidates "on approval," the rule for new members. This was ridiculous, he said, for all the members knew both of us and many had grown up with him. But it was no use, rules were rules.

"Moshe would agree to kibbutz living—provided the kibbutz

developed according to his views," said one old Shimron friend. Differences of opinion about the degree of collectivization were a frequent subject of conversation at Shimron. As a moshav son, Moshe was against any veering towards the close social organization of the kibbutzim. I had been brought up in the kibbutz tradition, and it was Moshe who deflected me from that aim. Shimron was set up along the looser, more individualized moshav lines, but unlike Moshe, some moshav sons rebelled against their parents' ideas and inclined more to kibbutz aims. When Shimron disbanded in 1938, some members went to newly established kibbutzim, while others, including Moshe and me, returned to Nahalal.

To my mother, Moshe expressed another of his complaints about Shimron. "Your generation, and my parents', has already built up this country," he observed unhappily thirty-five years ago. "What is there left for people my age to do? Here where we're sitting now, right next to Nahalal, everything is already civilized. The best we can do at this point is to go to some unsettled point near the northern border. Or else to the Negev. . . .''

Then there was the affair of the chicken coop and the hundred-pound-sterling gift. The father of my Jerusalem friend Zelda, a member of the wealthy South African Jewish community, wanted to make a contribution to Shimron that would enable us to buy a chicken coop to start an agricultural branch. Moshe was obstinately against accepting charity from such a capitalist source, while I, though a good young socialist, thought it silly not to accept. Serious arguments broke out in the dining room on the chicken-coop question and, quick to lose my temper, I shouted at Moshe. In the end, the money was accepted.

My election to this or that committee, and my delight in the bustle of the meetings, was something else Moshe did not approve of. He found committee life distasteful, and did not like his wife seeming to enjoy it so. And while I liked dancing, social life, and saying whatever came into my head, Moshe liked tranquillity, mental effort, and choosing his words carefully. In this conflict in temperament I gave way to Moshe and gradually bottled up my feelings.

Kibbutz views on bringing up children also annoyed Moshe. Of course, we did not have any children and there were none in sight; in fact he did not look forward to the prospect. But he was even more against the theory of collective child-raising. His children, if he ever had any, were to be brought up by himself and nobody else.

I badly wanted a child. We had been married for three years and there were no signs of pregnancy, a situation Moshe considered satisfactory. Always honest with me, he had told me from the outset that he was not interested in fatherhood, and that he was unlikely to provide the kind of stable, normal home most women want; and though he might wish to be a loving, kind, and thoughtful husband, he doubted whether he had the capacity for it. On the other hand, some of his letters show that, at least in certain moods, what he longed for most of all was a quiet home of our own where we two would always be together.

Meanwhile his world was widening. Moshe's first officially documented defense appointment is dated March 26, 1937. A short mimeographed form headed "The Palestine Police Force" and signed by the British officer in charge of the Supernumerary Police of the Nazareth District certified that Moshe Dayan (address: Shimron, Colony: Shimron) had been appointed to the "specific duty" of "protecting the lives and property of all persons within the Colony."

His identity photograph is far from military-looking. It shows a suntanned young man in an open white shirt, sleeves rolled up and clean, though wrinkled, looking calmly at the photographer. The background appears to be a haystack.

Unlike many of the girls I knew, I never actively joined the underground defense, though I was given various tasks informally. My Jerusalem girl friends who settled on kibbutzim found themselves more involved in the Haganah and joined their men at meetings in Tel Aviv cafés for discussions of plans with the leaders.

This was something I came to resent. These adventurers seemed to be having all the fun and glory while I dutifully went on cleaning out sheep dung, and I also had doubts about their effectiveness. In any case, they made me feel very much on the fringe of things.

Mother was at the center of Haganah activity from the start, driving her car on assignments, smuggling ammunition, and doing it all in her particular, cool, practical way. She even enrolled for training with hand grenades, though she was not very good at it. "They usually fell backwards, on my friends," she said. Mother was very different from the girls I resented; she considered this grenade training highly impractical, since it was obvious that she, personally, was never going to be throwing one. In the same year that Moshe was appointed to the police, Mother was asked by Dov Hos to learn to pilot a plane. The theory was that this might be useful when civil aviation became a reality. "No, it's ridiculous," said Mother.

In a note from Shimron to Jerusalem in the spring of 1937, when I was at the short nurses' training course, Moshe wrote, "I know you want a home, and a warm stove, and Laba and Leset there with you. But our destiny is different."

Laba and Leset were not names for unborn children, but two boxer dogs who occupied an important place in our correspondence and affections. As a farm boy, Moshe was less sentimental about animals than I, who had been brought up in the city with an English attitude towards pets. Still, he wrote to me about Laba's recuperation from an injury in practically parental tones: "Yesterday she crawled a bit and opened her eyes. . . . And now she's taking a bit of milk. . . ."

Laba was also a point of friction in my attitude towards the group. From Shimron I wrote to Moshe, away at a training course: "They want to shoot Laba just because she bit somebody! It's not fair! Two other boxers were accepted at Shimron. I'm going to leave, and I'm going to take Laba with me."

My moods were petulant, and Laba was not really the issue. For Moshe was not warmly appreciated at Shimron. A friend who was a member told me many years later that I, seeing the resentment against Moshe, decided that I was the cause of his unpopularity.

Minor rounds of guard duty were not for him, Moshe decided, and he was accepted for further Haganah training, where his abilities were soon recognized. I went off on courses too, but these were unsatisfactory efforts to alleviate Moshe's increasing absences.

My course in dog training was a comedy of errors. I arrived to find that I was the only girl; the other settlements had all sent men. Each participant was supposed to arrive with one dog; I came with two, Laba and Atida, both boxer bitches and sworn enemies. I was given a room without a human roommate, sharing it instead with the two dogs, for you were supposed to spend every moment of the course in intimate contact with your animal. My two were tied up at night, but once Laba slipped her collar and attacked Atida. The men in the next rooms had to help separate the animals by prying open their locked jaws.

Training included simulated attacks by "marauders." I had to do each exercise twice, once with each dog. It was exhausting, but I enjoyed the intense involvement with animal psychology. And for us, trained attack dogs were often the difference between life and death. Laba once saved Moshe during a Bedouin ambush.

With all this, I felt far from strong and had serious backaches. The doctor suggested that the backaches might be helped if I had a child. The fact that I was not yet pregnant, he assured me, was no cause for worry; eventually a child would certainly come and everything would be much better. Mother was dubious about this and took me to a specialist in Jerusalem, which Moshe considered a waste of money, and the specialist began a series of treatments.

Luxuriating in a feeling of guilt, I wrote from Jerusalem to Moshe at camp: "I feel like a terrible bourgeoise, sitting here in a warm room with tea and a cigarette. . . . How I love you, especially when you're sulky! . . . You make me feel like a dog, you're working like a beast and here I sit in comfort, eating, gaining weight, reading wonderful books. And all I want is to help bring you your dream. . . ."

Now it was I who disliked Shimron: "It can sink into the ground for all I care. Come and have a hot bath! When I think about Shimron from a distance it seems like a home for abnormal types. Among twenty-five people, to have so many strange characters! And I don't care for the whole approach. You think of me as a bureaucrat, but how can one sit in those meetings and be interested? It's not interesting, it's stupid and you know it. . . . Come to me!"

I returned to Shimron; Moshe wrote me from camp in a fit of depression: "I miss you so much and I'm miserable and I so much want a home of our own and for you to be happy. But this seems so far away—who knows when it will really be? I practically don't believe it myself any more. And will there ever again be peaceful times? And if they do come, where will you and I be? We've already finished with so many things and there's really nothing we want. It doesn't bother me that everything's filthy here, that I don't have a change of clothes, that there's a stink of beer in the room. The main thing is that I want to know what's going to become of us."

And so, at twenty and twenty-two, we were looking back on the lost days of our youthful happiness. We knew that when we were together we fought; it was when we were apart that we were joined by romantic longing. Love by separation, as we were to know it when Moshe was in prison, was powerful for both of us, but it was not a rule, because later we were truly happy at our own farm—together.

"It's terrible, my dearest Ruth, I've never had such a feeling of having no place to go," he wrote, for in those days Moshe was capable of feeling vulnerable and lonely. "I don't believe in groups or communes. Maybe we can adjust and maybe not, but in the final analysis the people are strangers to us. Ruth, I'm scared to say it, but at this point I almost think we should go back to Nahalal. Even though it's awful there, and it's bad to be with my mother and father, and the farm is bad and the moshav is bad and the work is terribly hard for you. But still, everybody has to get along with bad people and adjust to difficulties. All farm work is hard. And even if a moshav is a bad place, at this moment I can't think of a better. At least at home the house will be ours and ours alone. I feel so strongly that I must have my own home. We are a family and I must take care of you." Moshe realized, as I often failed to, that life requires compromises.

"And what if we just don't get along with a group? Will we move on again? And you don't want to go to Migdal. . . ."

Migdal was another communal settlement, which later became Kibbutz Ginossar. This was the only time Moshe ever considered joining a kibbutz-affiliated settlement. For him Migdal was a possibility only because it was a distant, challenging outpost founded by some of his Nahalal schoolmates.

"And nothing will come of our plans to go to sea," he continued sadly. This was another much-discussed plan: we wanted to join the infant Jewish merchant marine, Moshe as deckboy and I as a stewardess. But even with help from influential friends, we were turned down—Moshe for being overage.

". . . And I won't join the police, especially not now, when there's no call for Jews on the force," he continued his elegy of unemployability. "My dearest, I so much want a home of our own, yours and mine, where we'll be together morning and night, and I see no alternative for this but Nahalal. We've been drifting for so long. I don't care that people have contempt for us, in a way they're right. We must settle down and work and be together. . . ."

In another letter, he wrote about the possibility of a job abroad, but immediately explained that nobody could think of leaving the country just then; besides, he would never consider a job where I could not be with him. The news was that "Sikriga had a calf. She's quiet as a kitten and seems fine. And Fabia had eight puppies. I've taken one and am trying to raise it on a bottle with a bit of rubber, but I'm not sure it will survive. . . . The riots will be over one day, so it seems. . . ." Bloodshed and terrorism were increasing; this was the period of Arab gangs, but Moshe concluded cheerfully with the pedigree of the new puppy: "Greetings from Leset, daughter of Fabia, daughter of Dita, daughter of Satan."

A few days later, still optimistic, Moshe was concerned with two problems: "Come. It's hard to find work here but everybody else manages and so will we. Even if we have to go into debt, we'll get our own place. Come, that's the main thing. But before you come, do find out from some experts the answers to a few questions: A. What do you feed a puppy for the first few weeks? B. When do you clip the tail and ears? C. At what age should he start being trained?"

From a training camp he described the military routine and approved of the instruction methods in terms that foreshadow his later analytical approach: "Basically, the problem in learning is not the content of a subject, but the organization of the way it is taught."

What was not foreshadowed was his own future: "You'll laugh, but I'm certainly going to find an opportunity to leave all this soon. With honor or without. A man usually does just what he wants . . . and as I see things, it won't be long before I'm a farmer again."

"Sticks instead of rifles," he wrote in another letter. "An indication of the state of military preparedness in this country. Well, there's nothing to worry about. I won't emerge from this as an officer. I'll finish this course, and that's that. Because geniuses like me, there are plenty of." Then he added the enigmatic comment, "At least, that's what they say."

He sneaked time off to write to me in Jerusalem: "Dead tired. I'd like to take a day off to take care of Laba but I just can't. There's a big maneuver tonight and I'm very worried that I'm going to be in charge, and it's hard to make it come off right. It's not so important whether I'll succeed; all I want is to be finished with all this. It's so boring. . . . When will there be peace? All I want is quiet, and all there is is terror, terror which we must fight. What will be the end? It's better not to think about that. Whatever happens, the main thing is to love one another. How awful it is when we fight! And we'll love Laba too. It's not her fault that she's so fat."

We made endless efforts to arrange meetings. To get to Moshe's unit at Afula from Shimron I went by bicycle—three hours by dirt road, balancing Laba at the rear of the bicycle. I did not like to take her by bus, which cost only a penny or so, because she usually vomited; on bus trips between Jerusalem and Shimron she rarely failed to throw up, to the annoyance of other passengers, and in those days I was not a personage whose carsick boxer would be forgiven.

On that twenty-mile bicycle trip, Laba fell off every mile or so. After trying Laba across the handle bars, which did not work either, and crying for most of the trip, I finally arrived at Afula and checked in at the small, dreary hotel. I managed to send a message to Moshe, and at midnight he arrived for a very brief leave. At dawn I pedaled off again to Shimron for the morning chores, with poor Laba across the rear of the bicycle.

"Do you remember those dreams we had of a peaceful life?" I wrote Moshe from Jerusalem. "Do you remember, you wanted to be a watchman in the forest? Alone, alone? Not one of those dreams remains. Now it's just a question of keeping going, like thousands of others. . . . Why am I going on like this instead of encouraging you? Don't pay any attention to me. . . ."

More measured and realistic, Moshe answered:

I know you don't want to come back to Shimron. There was a time when things were different. But since then time has passed. There was a time when everybody at Shimron would have accepted you gladly and liked you, and chosen you on committees, and you would have had a good feeling. Since then, I know, things have hurt you and that is why you don't want to feel any closeness.

I have my doubts whether other arrangements would please you better. At this point we're at Shimron, members of Shimron, and be-

long to Shimron and have a stake in it. What do you suggest we do?
Leave the group and start studying something now? That I should
be a clerk? Ruthie my dearest, I won't do it. I won't give up the life
of the group. It has cost me far too much effort to become adjusted
to it. If you remember, it was once just the opposite. But now I won't
leave. Because really, there is no alternative.

My notes usually ended, "I can't wait any longer. Come, come
somehow. . . ." Moshe's typical answer would be, "It's almost
impossible to get either time off or money. I'll come as soon as
I can. Meanwhile, write every single day. Every day, and nicely.
So that at least each of us will have something more real than
all this tension, this shooting. . . ."

One view of our lives at Shimron is through the eyes of a
cocky English corporal who wanted to join our commune. His
name was Tom Tucker; he was with the Essex Regiment stationed in Haifa, and he was desperately anxious to bring his
wife, Nancy, and his baby son, Shirwen, from England to Palestine. He actually managed this, after endless plans and correspondence, and Nancy and Shirwen were with us at Shimron.
Nancy soon came down with malaria and I was busy taking care
of her; Moshe ended up as Shirwen's baby-sitter. Moshe does not
like all children, but he became tremendously attached to the
little boy, who was a charming towhead and soon mastered the
basic Hebrew sentence, "Moshe, I want peepee."

In Corporal Tucker's long correspondence with us from his
Haifa barracks, he complimented Moshe on his English. But
his main concern was with my moods, because Nancy, who
knew no Hebrew, was dependent on me, when I was so un-
decided and petulant. "I do hope you will put things right,"
he wrote me during one of my absences in Jerusalem,

and that this little cloud will pass away. I have the deepest respect for
you and cannot believe that you can do anything really wrong. You
are just like a little child in your ways, and so, like a child, you have
gone away to sulk, at the same time showing your independence.
Why you should run away from Moshe, or what Moshe is doing to let
you go, I fail to understand. So please do not be silly and return to
Shimron. I, like everyone else, like you very much and how anyone
could hurt your feelings to such an extent as to drive you away
beats me.

Anyway, what is the trouble? Please make an effort at reconciliation
and return to your husband who, even if he won't say it, misses you
very much. You say you have been offended. Do you mean insulted?
The world would be a funny place without a spot o' bother now and
again. . . . You are only making yourself and everyone else, myself
included, unhappy by your desertion. So make an effort to return to
Shimron and your husband. As things are now I don't know what your
attitude is. I would like to talk it over with you, but I hope you will
be frank in your next letter and tell me all about it. Perhaps I can

help. You love your husband, don't you? Well, go to him and your differences with the others will melt away. . . .

He wrote to Moshe on the same day: "I have received a letter from Ruth, who tells me she may go goodness knows where. I cannot have my wife out here if Ruth is not at Shimron; her inability to speak Hebrew would make her life unbearable. What is the matter with Ruth? Why is she so discontented?"

Early in 1938, the First Battalion of the Essex Regiment was posted to Egypt, ending Tom Tucker's dream of life in a commune.

There was more and more shooting around Shimron. During another of my absences in Jerusalem, always a dangerous place but by 1938 the scene of serious riots, Moshe wrote from Shimron in an affectionate and thoughtful tone: "Here we're expecting an attack any day, though probably that's just bluff. Don't worry, it's really nothing; Jerusalem is where it is really dangerous. Here, by comparison, it's a garden of paradise. Write every day, that's the main thing, and don't worry. There's no reason for concern."

A few days later he brought me up to date in a model of understatement: "Yesterday we went out on an action, about seven of us, and met 80 Arabs. Our boys were a bit nervous and so didn't shoot absolutely straight. But don't worry, it's not dangerous. . . . Really, don't worry. I'm writing you about this only because you may read about it in the papers and be alarmed. Captain Wingate was here and will be coming for a week. Otherwise nothing new. I haven't slept for 48 hours and must go out again tonight. But just don't you worry."

At the close of this considerate and modest letter a note of pride slips through, and no wonder: "Everybody thinks our action was quite good. Captain Wingate praised the operation and we may be getting a citation. After all, we were just seven and there were 80 of them. Our boys behaved wonderfully."

During one of Wingate's visits to Shimron, I was assigned a small task by the Haganah, one whose nature distressed me. "Go through his overnight bag when he leaves it in your hut," I was told. "We can't really trust this Englishman yet. See what he has in there." I had met Orde Wingate and his wife earlier and, as always with English guests, our place had become their center. The idea of secretly inspecting his belongings upset me, but these were Haganah instructions. So, behind Captain Wingate's back, I went through his small bag. It contained no pajamas, no toothbrush, no change of shirt. It was empty—except for a Bible. I was terribly ashamed of what I had done, and never confessed it to Wingate's wife, Lorna, even after she became a good friend.

Moshe was now a fighter, but he continued to long for solitude and peace: "Every night I go out on duty, and I don't understand it. Why is all this necessary? Will it always be like this? Will we never have a home, and quiet, a room of our own?"

My letters to him were about how much I loved him, how meaningless life was without him, how much I missed him: "I miss you so much I even miss our fights!" We both lived for each other's letters, and the mails were terrible.

"The age of miracles is not yet over," Moshe observed, "since I write every day and you write every day, and each of us receives one letter a week." He had good advice to cure me of my irritability: "Why do you fight with everybody? Don't pay attention to people, you can always read books. Don't be so nervous, calm down and act like everybody else."

Watching all this from the side in characteristic silence was Nahman, Shimron's acknowledged leader. Nahman has been described as "the conscience of Shimron," and that is just what he was. Everybody came to Nahman with his troubles, though he was barely older than the other boys, and few decisions were made without him: he held us all together.

Nahman watched my miserable moods in Moshe's absence; I seem to have impressed him from the time of my arrival at the Nahalal school three years earlier. During my days at the school, for instance, we had a race down from Mount Tabor that I barely remember but which Nahman recalls distinctly. A few girls from the school and boys from the village had driven the horse and cart to the biblical site of Deborah's prophetic command. We raced down on foot; I was the only girl who took part, and I won in seven minutes flat. Nearly forty years later, Nahman remembered that winning time; he did not remember whether Moshe, whom he had known practically all his life, was along that day. He was.

Nahman also respected Moshe's growing military success. He has always held Moshe's special military genius in great esteem, volunteering for Moshe's commando group in 1948 and later following him to Jerusalem. He himself has devoted much of his life to the army as an officer; and of his five children, four served simultaneously once with the defense forces.

For some reason Nahman had not been at our wedding and at Shimron he noticed that the honeymoon seemed to be over. It was something nobody at Shimron could help seeing. "Why don't you two keep your quarrels to yourselves and not spill them out in front of everybody?" was a frequent question in the dining room. These quarrels were practically always about ideological principles—the old kibbutz-versus-moshav debate—on which Moshe and I disagreed. At these group meetings our public arguments turned into private quarrels, with me shouting furiously at Moshe. But right afterwards, I could not wait till we would be together again in our hut.

In Moshe's absences, I finished my work assignments with

bitter thoroughness and none of my earlier enthusiasm. Nahman's shoulder was there to cry on; he was a pillar of security for everyone and on friendly terms with all.

The group sent me to Tel Aviv for a three-month bookkeeping course so that I might have an alternative to physical work, for my backaches were growing worse. My lodgings turned out to be a rat-infested shack where, filled with loneliness and self-pity, I wrote Moshe long, sad letters. That group of shacks, just off Dizengoff Circle, was not torn down till thirty-four years later, and my particular hut was the last to go.

Nahman sent brotherly notes from Shimron: "We're working on the forest and wondering when we'll be hearing from the Arabs, who have terrorized the whole neighborhood. We hear shots but from the hills; they haven't got to us yet and it's getting boring to wait for them. . . . No girls around . . . Shirwen is an adorable child, he's learned to sing 'Cucumbers in the Garden' and 'Cookie, Cookie, Cookie.' The black bitch had two pups and the ewes have started to lamb.

"Oh yes, the main thing. As you suggested, we sent Officer Ring the season's greetings with a fat baby lamb." (Officer Ring was the British District Police Officer and I thought it might be wise to remember him at Christmastime with a small bribe.) "But what happened?" Nahman continued. "He arrived the next day in his car with the lamb sitting next to him. It bleated all night, he said, and his wife doesn't like lamb anyway. I think a turkey might be a better idea."

During Moshe's absences I began walking with Nahman on his nightly guard rounds. We talked about ourselves and grew close emotionally. For me it was nothing new to open my thoughts to someone else. For Nahman, famous for his silent nature, it must have been some kind of revelation. I needed his presence and relied on his strength; I loved those qualities in him because I was lonely and miserable. At the same time I knew—and I later wrote to Nahman—that I felt "caught in Moshe's iron grip," and there was nothing to be done about that. I was both egotistical and moralistic: on the one hand I let Nahman come close, and on the other hand, because of Moshe, I made him keep his distance.

For Nahman I was unattainable. I told him, moreover, that "I might as well be his grandmother" as far as sophistication and experience in life were concerned. This was perhaps true in a way; I was, after all, married. But I was far from sophisticated, just as I was far from sophisticated twenty years later.

Guilty and depressed, I spoke to Moshe of my split feeling between the two men and my mixed emotions; and I wrote that I would never leave him. I already knew that Moshe was having flirtations with many Haganah girls; I was jealous, of course. But I refused to take them seriously.

One day Nahman's brother Moshe—who was lost at sea during World War II with three hundred Palestinian soldiers on service with the British—came to see me. A born leader and as articulate as Nahman was silent, he told me that I was being unfair to his brother and that I must choose between him and Moshe. But I already had.

"I've never been so alone in my life," I wrote to Moshe from Jerusalem. "I must write to you, but I know I won't mail this letter. Sometimes I, too, must be proud. If I didn't love you so much I wouldn't behave like this. I'm always apologizing as though I were guilty, or I pretend that I'm not hurt and talk about other things. . . .

"If you don't believe me, that's the end—what can I do? You've made me not know what to do about Nahman, whether to write him or not, or send you the letter first to be censored. No wonder I cry. You wouldn't certainly; I know what you're like. And yet I love you to distraction. But why write all this? I know you won't believe me. Probably you think I've found myself a boy friend here. . . . My relationship with my mother is rather cool and I doubt whether we'll ever be close again. I don't want to upset their lives as I have yours. . . . I won't go back to Shimron. Why do I write all this?"

Moshe and I had already had it all out, but because I was so intent on having everything in the clear I sent two letters to Shimron, one to Nahman and one to Moshe. Moshe saw both envelopes in my handwriting and acted in a characteristic way: he opened both. In my letter to him, I explained that I loved him completely and belonged to him alone, but that, in a way, I also loved Nahman. Nahman's letter contained the same message. Moshe sent both letters back to me, with a cool note saying that Nahman's was warmer and more lyrical.

I was deeply hurt that Moshe did not immediately believe me when I assured him that nothing had happened that I could be ashamed of: emotional though I was, I was also very moralistic. To Nahman I wrote unhappy letters saying I had purchased peace for my family at a high price. And I begged his forgiveness.

He left Shimron soon after; without Nahman, morale sank. Everybody discussed this triangle—it really was an innocent one, though our emotions were intense—and everybody blamed Moshe and me jointly for the loss of Shimron's leader.

Because we were young, Moshe and I recovered fairly quickly. Nahman, soon after leaving Shimron, joined Wingate's Special Night Squads, British-trained commandos who set up a defense against Arab terrorists. One of the first to volunteer in May 1938, he served with distinction until the units were disbanded in October. Not long after, Nahman married a girl from a nearby settlement. His silent character, great courage, and high moral standards gave him much in common with Orde Wingate.

"After much thought," I wrote Nahman after he left us, "I'm glad you went. It's good for you, and it's good for the group. Now we'll all have to learn to get along without Nahman."

Nahman himself has told me, "I left because, among other reasons, I couldn't stand what amounted to the hero worship of the group—who, really, were children. It was something I didn't deserve, and it was a relief to be with Wingate's men. There I was exactly like everybody else."

About a week after Nahman left, Moshe wrote him a friendly note. It mentioned that "the new immigrants are settling down well, and we are starting to sow corn. . . . There is talk about a possible Arab attack nearby. . . . We had no special celebration at Passover. . . ." It ended, "Please do write." Moshe took the opportunity of sending this little piece of lined notepaper with a friend who would be seeing Nahman, and it did not have the tone of a desperately hurt rival.

When I now wrote to Moshe from Jerusalem, it was largely about Laba: "I stayed up with her till three in the morning and will take her to the doctor today." I still complained that "nobody understands me at home." Again, there was that old question, What does the future hold? "Have you no wish at all to go back to farming? It's true that our aims do seem so far apart. And I love you so tremendously. . . ."

To Nahman, with Wingate, I wrote a gay note describing a "close escape from death" when my father and mother and Reumah came to Shimron to drive me to Jerusalem. Arab attacks in 1938 were frequent and dangerous, and we had a wild ride, including pursuit by an armed Arab on a motorcycle who tried to force us to the side of the road where more armed Arabs stood. My description tells more about my mother than about our earlier relationship: "Mother wanted to stop and talk to the Arabs," I wrote, "but the rest of us insisted on driving on as quickly as we could."

By the end of the summer there was a new and happy note. As usual, I was romantically happy but, at the same time, unsure of myself. I had finally become pregnant, and I wrote to Moshe, "Our child isn't making a sound yet, and maybe we'll never hear from him. But if we do have a child I'll be so happy! I don't want anybody but me to take care of him. . . . We'll be alone in a forest somewhere, with our child running barefoot over the rocks. . . ."

When Shimron disbanded in 1938, I traveled north in the truck that took several members to the Lebanese border, where they helped establish Kibbutz Hanita. My friends thought I should sit in the front with the driver because of my condition, but I insisted on sitting on top of the truck with everybody else.

It was a gay trip and, although I was six months pregnant —but barely noticeably—and the drive was bumpy, I laughed and joked all the way; and when we arrived I danced all night.

Moshe and I returned to Nahalal, but not to Devora and Shmuel. First we rented a tiny one-room hut and then, three months later, arranged to rent a larger one—our very own at last.

5 · Trial and Prison

One morning early in February 1939, I was standing on a ladder scrubbing down the walls of what was to be our new hut in Nahalal. That year was critical for us in many ways. Yael's birth was just a week away; Moshe was to go to prison. And, of course, World War II was to start.

But that morning, scrubbing the walls, I felt cheerful, for we were moving into what we thought was a mansion—two rooms, a closed-in veranda, a kitchen, but of course no bathroom or toilet. I had been six months pregnant when we left Shimron and rented a one-room hut at Nahalal; now, three months later, we were about to move into our very own, very grand home.

Seeing things come clean has always been very satisfying to me, and scrubbing wooden walls and plank floors with hot water and soapsuds was one of the things I'd learned from Devora. We always did it once a year, before Passover, standing on ladders and crawling on the floor. To this day I'm rather unhappy watching people clean house with a mop. Perhaps what many women consider a chore has always been for me a pleasure —watching the dirt vanish and clean surfaces emerge.

So I felt happy thinking how nice everything was going to be now, with our vegetable garden and a place for the dogs.

"You must be mistaken," said my mother-in-law, who had just dropped in to see me. "You can't possibly be in the ninth month." It was true; I looked very thin and barely pregnant, let alone almost ready to have a child. As usual whenever

Devora and I spoke, there was an undercurrent of conflict. She was convinced that the baby was not yet due, and this time I did not argue the point.

The next day, as I was doing the laundry, I had terrible pains. But my mother-in-law had said that the time had not yet come; and since she was always right, I assumed it was a false alarm. But the pains were sharp. To ease them, I stood with one foot on a chair while holding the washboard in the basin —that was how we did it, by hand and on a board. I wanted everything to be really clean because the baby was coming.

At the same time, I couldn't believe that I really would have a child—that I would actually do something properly. I've always had the idea that I couldn't finish anything. I hadn't finished high school; I hadn't finished the Nahalal school, because I married Moshe; we hadn't stayed at Shimron. The only things I had completed were the bookkeeping course and the dog-training course—both short ones.

I felt shy about telling anyone about the pains. Finally, though, I left the laundry and went next door to the Nahalal doctor. He was a typical old family physician who knew everybody, and everybody's health, intimately.

"You'd better get to the hospital," he said. "To Afula." When I arrived, the doctor, who also knew me, started joking.

"Why are you playing games?" he asked. "You must be about in the fifth month."

"No, I'm serious," I said apologetically. "And I have terrible pains." He examined me and agreed I ought to remain.

In those days patients weren't pampered. I was simply put on a cot in a hut and had pains for two and a half days. When Moshe came to visit on Saturday I said, "You see, Moshe, I can't even have a baby."

To make things worse, I overheard the staff talking about someone who needed an operation, and I thought they were talking about me. I was so frightened that all I wanted to do was get to a telephone to tell everyone that I was going to die, and that if they wanted to see me once more they had better come quickly.

At six the next morning no doctors were on duty, and I asked the nurse to call one. "Why?" she asked. "There's nothing unusual here."

I told her about the operation I thought was intended for me; she laughed; and a quarter of an hour later that morning, February 12, Yael was born—healthy, weighing more than six and a half pounds, and really beautiful. Her size surprised the doctor, who had been sure the baby would be tiny.

"Are you sorry it isn't a boy?" I asked Moshe when he came. Of course he said what was expected of him. But he adored Yael from the beginning.

Mother came to help and went with Moshe to buy all the baby's things; in line with the old Jewish superstition, we had bought nothing before the birth. Mother drove us home after eight days—the usual maternity stay then—to our new "mansion." It was pouring rain and since the road did not go to our hut, we walked the last portion through the knee-deep mud.

The baby's room was beautiful. Mother had bought a little bed with string netting in place of the usual wooden rails because she thought the baby might hit her head against them. But as it turned out, poor Yael was always getting her head stuck behind the netting, and Moshe used to pull her out regularly.

That first evening everybody had a try at diapering the baby; at eight days she was already an expert at getting herself unwrapped. The next morning the doctor showed us how, and it was Moshe who became the most expert. Mother had already left to make her remarkable drive across the Sinai Desert.

For help, I had the neighbors. At Nahalal, as at all moshavim, there was an excellent and well-organized system of mutual help. Whenever anybody was sick or needed assistance, someone from a neighboring family came to help with the chores. We had a regular plan of rotation; everybody took turns helping.

The first night Yael cried without stopping, and nothing we did helped. She cried fairly constantly for three entire months, and the local doctor had no useful advice. Finally I took her to a private children's doctor in Haifa, who diagnosed the trouble as malnutrition. We started her on a bottle and everything improved.

In those days you were not supposed to touch babies when they cried. I would hear her in my sleep and hold myself back from picking her up. Moshe decided that was ridiculous. He would take command, tell me to be quiet, and to pick her up. She was the one baby he worried about, cared for, and diapered. That is, when he was home.

By now he was away at courses more and more. I was alone with a crying baby, growing increasingly bitter about the Haganah, feeling out of the mainstream. I kept our little vegetable garden, took care of our rabbits, and made clothes for Yael—lovely little smocked dresses, and batiste ones with embroidered or appliqued flowers. The other babies of Nahalal had simple, functional clothes; but Yael's always had some pretty decoration, which I loved making. And Yael always did everything so much earlier and developed so much more quickly than any child I've ever known.

I also knitted sweaters—sweaters for the whole family. I think there is a whole "archeology" in sweaters; they contain the thoughts and events knitted into them by women everywhere.

I feel the same thing is true of the rugs woven by the immigrants I later worked with—lives embedded in handwork.

Sometimes we had guests in our little hut, though by far the most exciting event for me was the sound of the wheels of a car bringing Moshe. Among our visitors were several British officers of the Royal Dragoons, one of the units stationed nearby. We had met them in 1936, when they had been cavalry; now, in 1939, they were a tank unit. We first had become friendly when the soldiers came to the Nahalal general store to buy beer. Then we got to know two of the officers, Major Joy and Lieutenant Makins, and we became close friends. They often came to tea, and I liked baking special little biscuits for them. Geoffrey Makins came from a distinguished family and liked playing with Yael. The officers felt that our hut was in a way their home. We had English books, and our bed-sitting-room was a cozy place. (The bedroom was Yael's. That was our arrangement for years—the bedroom was for the children, and the pull-out sofa in the living room for us.)

On Sunday, September 3, Major Joy and Lieutenant Makins came to visit. We turned on our radio—one of the few in Nahalal —to hear Neville Chamberlain announce that a state of war existed between Germany and Great Britain as of 11:00 A.M. that morning. Our British friends left in great excitement and, that afternoon, took part in the first British operation of World War II in the Middle East—the "occupation" of two nearby German villages, Waldheim and Bethlehem.

Waldheim and Bethlehem, which is not to be confused with the Bethlehem near Jerusalem, were picturesque, long-established little places settled about sixty years earlier by German Christians who wanted to live in the Holy Land. We had always admired their skill as farmers, but they were unfriendly to Jews, especially after the rise of Hitler.

The British soldiers came back from this operation rather drunk, and with quantities of pictures of Hitler—every house in the two villages had one. The Germans were arrested soon after by the British and interned in Australia for the duration of the war.

On October 3, a month later and just before the holiday of Simhat Tora, I planned a dinner for our British friends, with a fine roast turkey and cake. Moshe didn't come. It was getting harder and harder for me to explain his absences; he had not been home for the previous holiday either.

The next morning he sent a note saying that he hoped to be home from camp for the next holiday but he was not sure, and that he could not telephone. The reason for all this I did not learn till later: two British officers had visited the camp where Moshe and a group of Haganah boys were training illegally. The boys tried to camouflage things, but they knew they would be searched the next day. They had to move to another location, and were afraid the telephones would be tapped by the British.

Meanwhile, knowing nothing of Haganah secrets, I was roasting turkeys and making tea for British officers. Moshe was always on guard duty or at some course. I was resentful of the whole Haganah business, and I think most women who were not part of it found it hard to understand and accept. I was jealous of other girls my age who wore dashing uniforms and rushed about in jeeps. When you are on a moshav, the birth of a new calf seems the center of the world.

Not until years later could I appreciate what the Haganah did for the state. In fact, I felt towards the organization much as I did towards my mother-in-law. In those days I quarreled with her practically every day, not realizing how much she had given up for her ideals. With her background and education she could have had a wonderful life anywhere in the world; instead she gave it up for what any common laborer could have done. In the same way, I could not appreciate the Haganah because to me it was simply the thing that took Moshe away.

Watching Devora hold the farm together while Shmuel was so often at Zionist meetings—they were what took him away—I promised myself that I would never repeat Devora's pattern of life. And Moshe agreed that I was never to stay behind at the farm if he was to be absent for long fixed periods.

Now, for Simhat Tora, I spent the day baking cakes that would please Moshe. Perhaps he would come! I scrubbed the hut, and in late afternoon dressed Yael in a beautiful smocked dress. Then I put her in the pram—bought from the neighbors for a few pennies, and the one that held practically every baby in Nahalal—and walked the mile-long dirt track to the main road to meet Moshe.

The road down from Nazareth, the road by which he would come, winds in curves down the hill to the valley. I began to count the buses as they came in sight around those curves. It grew darker and cooler. I told myself, "Another two buses . . . Another three . . . Another four buses."

Finally I gave up. Miserable and furious, I imagined taking the baby and running away from Nahalal. I pushed the pram back to our hut feeling that I couldn't go on like this, with Moshe never home and the baby growing up. I took the dry and overdone chicken out of the oven and put the baby to bed. And then I cried, as I so often did in those days.

The next morning was Saturday October 6. Yael was playing under the tangerine tree with her second cousin Dan, and I was going to take a photograph of the two children playing. Then Shmuel and Devora dropped by, to see if Moshe had arrived.

Just as I was about to snap the picture of this happy family group, a man from a neighboring village ran up to us with our dog trotting after him. He gave me this note on a small piece of crumpled paper:

Ruth. We have been arrested and taken to Acre on a—seemingly—minor charge. I hope it will end well. Kisses to you and Yael. See you soon—

Your Moshe.

A group of our boys, it seemed, had been put in lorries and taken to prison. Moshe had one of our dogs with him, and when the lorry passed Nahalal he saw a man from a nearby village on the road. Moshe managed to scribble his note on a piece of paper, tuck it under the dog's collar, and let the dog jump out of the lorry. The man took the note from the collar and brought it to me.

I read it without saying a word. Still holding the crumpled paper in my hand, I snapped the picture of the two children under the tangerine tree. At that moment I resented having to share Moshe's fate with others, even his parents. But of course I could not keep this to myself, and immediately showed the note to Shmuel and Devora. We made endless telephone calls to find out more details. The general feeling was that it was not too serious. Forty-three boys had been taken to Acre Fortress.

The next day I went to Haganah headquarters in Haifa. "It's probably not too serious," I was once more told. The boys had been caught transporting arms. A distinction would no doubt be made, our people said, between forty-two of them on the one hand and one other, Avshalom Tau, who had been caught in the act of aiming a rifle.

Moshe and another boy, Mordechai Sukenik, had been ahead of the main group as scouts, and had been stopped by the police. But there was nothing against them and they were allowed to go on, for although they had one revolver between them, they also had a license for it. After the police caught the rest of the group, they returned for Moshe and Mordechai.

"Their case might be handled separately from the others," my lawyer father suggested.

A few days later, I arranged to meet a Haifa lawyer who was working on the case. It was a breezy, glittery night when I went to his beautiful home at the top of Mount Carmel, with stars in the dark sky, the lights of Haifa bright below, and the sound of the wind in the black trees. I arrived in shorts and sandals, the usual Nahalal outfit, but the lawyer nevertheless welcomed me to his elegant residence because of my parents, who had been schoolmates of his.

"Couldn't Moshe and Mordechai be treated separately?" was my first question.

"No," he replied without hesitation. "Ben-Gurion is against any such idea and thinks they should all be together." Then he

said, "You know, for something like this they can be hanged."
There was dead silence. "Well, maybe we can get them off with
ten years or something like that," he added charitably.

This was the first time anyone had told me how serious the
charge really was. I walked out into the night and past the
black trees. In my imagination, I could almost see the one picked
out for Moshe.

This is the first of the short official letters Moshe was allowed to
send me from Acre. It was dated April 12.

Dear Ruth,
Excuse my short letter but I hope you will visit me Saturday. If this
letter doesn't reach you before then, I am sure you will get in touch
with the "Community Committee" [the Haganah] in Haifa about
visits. Visiting hours are approximately from 10:30 to noon, and from
1:30 to 3:00. Visitors must arrive promptly and only two for each
prisoner. My Ruthie, I don't think it's a good idea to bring Yael
here, though I miss her very much. Every night I wake up with a
start and think of you two, my poor darlings. . . .
We are enjoying pre-trial rights. The food is good and sufficient,
and most of the day we are outside. Send regards to Mother and
Father and Aviva and Zorik, and ask Father to come to visit me.
Ruthie, don't worry too much and kiss Yael for me. If you can,
bring me an undershirt, a shirt, sweater, and shaving cream, because
we shave here with the cream used by the religious. And a suitcase
for my clothes, and a soap dish. . . .

It was signed formally: "Shalom and kisses to you, yours, Moshe
Dayan." At the bottom he wrote, "The address is Central Prison,
Acre. Write the address in English. Letters must be short, and
you can send two a week."

My only really influential friends were the officers of the Royal
Dragoons. The war had already begun and they were stationed
in the center of the country. I decided to appeal to them.

I smile when I think of it today—how I did that, like so many
other things, on the spur of the moment. There I was, a Nahalal
girl of twenty-two in sandals, covered with mosquito bites, approaching the guard at the barracks gate asking to see Major Joy.

The guard looked at me and said, "You know, there's a war
on."

I said, "You must call the major and let me in." He called
Major Joy and told him a Ruth Dayan was at the gate on an
urgent matter. I was received kindly. In a certain way, I trusted
the British; even though for so long we had so much against
them, it was still part of me to believe that by talking to an
Englishman you could get an honest reply.

In the head office I was given a cup of English tea. Geoffrey
Makins was called in and I told the whole story. Our two officer
friends had, of course, known nothing about it. When I finished,

Major Joy said, "Well, now we know where Moshe was when we were eating that turkey."

I said, "Look, there's only one thing. You've known us for three years. Please, one of you come and give a good character reference for Moshe at the trial. It will make an enormous difference. You don't have to take any responsibility—just be a witness that you know us and that we are of good character. That's all I ask."

Naturally, Major Joy said, he would have to talk to his commanding officer; but anything he was permitted to do, he would do gladly. He and Geoffrey visited me at Nahalal and brought presents for Yael, and before long the wonderful news came that Geoffrey would be allowed to give evidence.

That Saturday, when I went to visit Moshe with Yael, both our families came too, although only two visitors were allowed into the fortress for each prisoner. Once again, there was the eternal friction between me and Moshe's parents, for the first problem was who would go in, Shmuel or Devora. Of course, I would have liked to speak to Moshe alone, but that was out of the question. Finally it was agreed that one would go with me in the morning, and the other in the afternoon. Each visit was from three to five minutes. We developed a sort of rondo—in one entrance, out the other, and back in again. And throughout the visiting hours all forty-three families waited in the courtyard, which was about fifty-five yards wide.

The visit was an ordeal. All forty-three boys were brought into the courtyard, where masses of barbed wire were piled; everybody had to shout over it, and I held Yael over my head so Moshe could see her. Over and over again we shouted, "How are you?" The Arab policeman on duty was pleasant—there were many Arabs in the prison—but the British captain was extremely strict. This was Captain Grant, who had a reputation for severity, and only one leg—the other had been amputated as the result of a shot from an escaping prisoner years earlier.

Moshe sent me a letter immediately after this visit:

My dear Ruthie, Today they told us the trial will be on the 25th. That means we have one more Saturday before the trial. I don't really believe this will reach you before then, but there are a few things that are impossible to say in a visit; what is more, it is probably even impossible to say them out loud. But now, when all around me people are singing and playing chess, and my head is ready to explode from all these thoughts, I want to write them. . . .

Almost every night I wake up—the air in the room is awful—and think of you and Yael. . . . My Ruth, if sometimes during a visit it seems to you that I'm not enough of a family man—if only I could pass on to you one thousandth of the love I feel for you both every night, if only you could know what you and Yael are to me. . . . That is what I wanted to write. Also, if I told you not to bring the little darling here, it's only because of the filth and because I'm not sure I wouldn't start to cry if I saw her over the barbed wire.

Moshe's strength of character, however, kept him from maintaining this tone very long:

Still, it isn't so bad. When I see the lonely men rotting here and compare them to us, who have behind us the Jewish Agency, the settlement, and most important the knowledge that is within us— then I feel I have the strength to endure. And I know that you, too, have the strength to accept everything as it comes and in a general way rather than just the effects on us personally. The day will yet come, and very soon, when we'll be sitting having tea, you'll be knitting, I'll be reading and asking you words in English, and the darling will be crawling on the rug. . . .

Moshe expressed his philosophy very clearly in this letter. "It is clear to me that life is divided into two categories," he continued, "that of the free man, and that of the prisoner. Anyone who hasn't experienced both has lived only half a life." He ended by telling me not to worry, to eat, to be healthy and strong.

The prisoners' parents formed a committee headed by Ben-Zion Dinur (later Israel's first Minister of Education). I often went with him to meetings with the authorities, as the wives' representative. There was resentment that I was permitted to go along, and this was not helped by the fact that my father was one of the lawyers. Still, there were very few of us wives, because most of the boys were so young—eighteen or nineteen. My Moshe and Moshe Carmel (later a military commander and Minister of Transportation) were among the oldest and were the leaders of the prisoners.

Avshalom Tau, the boy accused of pointing a rifle, had been married only three weeks. Laura, his wife, was an immigrant from Poland. We became friendly and she stayed with me at Nahalal. She knew her husband was more involved than the others, and yet she behaved with great dignity and calm. I envied and admired her capacity for this.

Moshe's third letter was dated April 29:

We will most likely see each other tomorrow, but who knows if we can talk. We have prepared ourselves for the sentence and the new conditions, but it will probably be a hard adjustment at the beginning. Ruthie, what can I write you in this letter? You already know everything. Even if there will be no more letters, there will still be visits every two months. And even if the Ramadan cannon doesn't wake you at midnight, Yael surely will, and you'll think of me just as I think of you.

But it doesn't matter. A man who knows how to say "A" must also know how to say "B" and accept the consequences.

He asked me to bring Hebrew and English dictionaries and grammars, "and serious study books on literature."

At the trial, thanks to the Royal Dragoons, I was the only civilian and the only woman allowed into the army court, which was set up in a large hut in the barracks with rows of wooden benches. I waited outside with Geoffrey Makins and we watched the boys arriving in a closed van, handcuffed together in pairs. Outside the gate were the families, come with food for the day, hoping for a glimpse.

"This is a show trial and the conclusion is foregone," Geoffrey told me. He would not say what the conclusion was, only that I must be prepared for the fact that nothing could help, and that it was immaterial whether he gave evidence or not. But he came every day, though he was never called to testify, and sat with me.

On the last of the trial's three days, Moshe and I had a moment for a joke. When the prisoners were being taken from the vans, I managed to stand at the entrance to the courtroom. Moshe, handcuffed to the next prisoner, said, "If I get a year, let me have *Gone With the Wind*." I had just finished the book, and it had helped during the waiting. At that point we all thought a year's sentence would be the maximum, and there was even hope for six months.

During the course of the trial I began to see the British in a different and terribly changed light. I had always liked them, and of course loved London. But now I began to hear soldiers—who did not know I understood English—talking about "those bloody Jews."

On the morning of the verdict, five days after the trial had begun, the judge rose and read a long speech on what the boys could have done, though they had actually done nothing and had only been caught carrying arms. He read out forty-two names, one after the other. As his name was called, each boy stood up.

Finally the judge said, "You are hereby sentenced to ten years' imprisonment at hard labor." There was not a gasp in the courtroom; everyone was too shocked. It was a hot day, and flies were buzzing in through the open windows. Two strange thoughts went through my mind: Yael as a girl of ten, and *Gone With the Wind*.

Then came the worst part. "Avshalom Tau," the judge read out. Avshalom rose. "You are hereby sentenced to life imprisonment." For a moment I forgot Moshe and looked at Laura sitting beside me, Avshalom's bride, in the courtroom that last day. Tears began to roll down my cheeks. Laura did not move; she was utterly dignified. I thought, Avashalom, you are in prison for life. Because he had dropped to his knee while holding his gun, and the witnesses, British and Arab, said he had been pointing it.

The "Forty-three" were handcuffed and marched out to the vans. All the times before they had joked and waved to us through the bars of the van. This time there were no jokes. I gave *Gone With the Wind* to the sergeant in charge to give to Moshe. And then I overheard a soldier say, "What a waste of good British money, feeding them for ten years! Put them up against a wall and shoot them."

The words would not leave my mind. The next day I wrote a long letter to the commanding officer, which is just the sort of impulsive thing I still do. I reported what the soldier had said, in his typical barracks vocabulary, and told my story in the most dramatic way I could: how a woman, brought up to admire the British, stood by with her ten-month-old baby and heard that. He never replied.

Since Laura and I were the only ones who had heard the verdict, we had to go outside the courtroom and tell the others. All through the trial, our lawyers' optimism had made a verdict of one year seem like the end of the world, and even six months had appeared terrible. Now I had to tell the others that the sentence was ten years' hard labor. I walked out to the dirt road where everyone was waiting and stood facing them, unable to speak. Finally I managed to say, "Ten years." First there was silence; then everyone started crying and talking. What could we do? Why hadn't the Haganah done more for us? It was decided that Dinur and I and a few others should go immediately to Ben-Gurion in Jerusalem.

I picked up Yael on the way and went to the Jewish Agency building that same evening. It occurred to me that I might start trying to get Moshe and Sukenik out separately. In Ben-Gurion's office I put Yael down on the floor and asked what was going to be done. Perhaps there was a case for handling the two apart from the rest?

Three times in my life Ben-Gurion has answered me in the same vein, though each time under very different circumstances. Yael was crawling on the floor and Ben-Gurion stood facing me. "Ruth, my dear," he said, "you have in your life only Moshe Dayan. In my life, I have all the Jews in Palestine." On no condition would he agree to treating Moshe's case separately. I picked up Yael, started to cry, and walked to my parents' house.

After a trial everything changes. Before, prisoners may receive food, clothing, books, and visitors once a week. Afterwards all this stops. Our lives began to revolve around smuggling in extra food, notes, and somehow arranging for a glimpse of the prisoners.

Our first aim was to get the sentence reduced before it was

confirmed. For this I was inspired to talk to the commanding officer at British headquarters; my friend Zelda agreed to go with me. We told nobody about our plan because we knew there would be objections. Instead we put on our nicest dresses and set out for the King David Hotel, whose top floor had been taken over completely by the British command.

The first thing we did, downstairs at the Regence Bar, was to have a stiff cognac each, for courage. Then we took the special lift upstairs and were of course immediately stopped.

"We have an appointment with the commanding officer," I said. Everybody was polite and very British. Outside the C.O.'s office, we waited. Nobody knew what we were doing there, but assumed that if we had gotten that far we must be on legitimate business. Finally the C.O. himself, a very nice old gentleman, emerged from his office. We stopped him, just like that.

"Excuse me, sir," I began, "I must talk to you. I am the wife of one of the Forty-three and I absolutely must see you before you confirm the sentence."

He looked at us as if to ask, What in the world are these two young ladies doing here? "I beg your pardon," he said, most correctly, "any requests concerning the trial should be sent in writing." He would not speak to me further and asked the lieutenant to escort us to the lift. There we met Reuven Shiloah, an important Jewish Agency official who knew us very well indeed. He glared at us as though he would have liked to kill us.

"I've been at a meeting upstairs, and working on this problem for weeks, and now you two, out of stupidity, are just interfering," he said.

"We had to," I said, "because not enough is being done." But I was more frightened of Reuven than I had been of the British commanding officer, for I am always more frightened of people close to me than of unknown officials, however powerful.

Feeling crushed, Zelda and I went back to the Regence Bar for another drink. We took some King David stationery from the lobby and composed a long letter to the C.O. When the sentence was confirmed soon after, it was reduced to five years for all but Avshalom.

Then I decided to see the Queen, because in all those books of my childhood the hero eventually goes to plead before His Majesty, and everything turns out happily. I also thought that I could appeal to her as woman, wife, and mother. My idea about the Queen was well received, at least among my friends. Lieutenant Makins promised to do everything to help, and even Moshe agreed I should try. I told him about the plan during a special visit I arranged after the trial. Officially, no visits were permitted for three months; but I did manage one, and was the first to see one of our prisoners.

The visit took place in the dungeon of Acre Fortress, a massive Turkish prison built on Crusader foundations. I was expected, and invited by a pleasant officer to sit down in a thick-walled room. The prisoner was brought in.

How enormously changed Moshe was, how different from before! His head was shaved and the uniform was a horrible brown affair with no buttons. But he was allowed to sit down, and we were left alone.

Earlier visits had been full of jokes; now it was deadly serious. How was Yael? Did we have money? Yes, I should try to see the Queen, but on no account must I do anything that did not apply to all forty-three prisoners. And that was that.

For the next eight months all our lives revolved around maneuvers, bribery, ways of smuggling letters and food, and arranging extra visits. Not surprisingly, I did not go to see the Queen, for I was refused a visa. But that was only one of the disappointments in the tangled network of arrangements.

The prison dentist and the rabbi were part of our chain for smuggling notes. Suddenly everyone had toothaches and became unusually religious. The dentist's nurse smuggled notes on tissue paper inside her brassière. And Zvi, who had learned to fly a light plane, once flew over the Acre Fortress and dropped a note for Moshe.

One evening that winter I received a phone call on the Haganah line in our house from an Arab who was working in a match factory in Acre. "Regards from your husband," the stranger said in English, "and don't worry." I had no idea what he was talking about and did not learn until later that Moshe had been caught with a prohibited tin of bully-beef, one of the food items we used to smuggle in, and his punishment was several days' confinement in a cell about one yard square.

Solitary confinement could be a mind-breaking process, and some boys took a long time to recover. Moshe was able to take it. He asked for a candle and a Bible, and his request was granted.

The first official visit after the trial came about two months later, on February 12, 1940. By coincidence this was also the date, on the Hebrew calendar, of Yael's first birthday. It is also the time of spring, and the hills of Acre were covered with crocuses. I wanted terribly to be allowed to take Yael inside the prison on that visit so that she might see her father directly and not across barbed wire.

I telephoned Major Wormsley, the officer in charge of the Acre prison, and explained why this was such a special day, that I believed in the significance of coincidences, and that I was eager for permission to take Yael inside. He was extremely kind as I went through this long story, and assured me that he would try to arrange it. He told me to see Captain Grant when I arrived at the prison.

Hundreds of people were milling around the Fortress hill on the day of the visit. I went up to Captain Grant and immediately made my first mistake, for I referred to Major Wormsley as "Colonel Wormsley."

"Madam, he is a major," said Captain Grant, irritated.

"I'm sorry—Major Wormsley. Have you heard from him about me? I'm the wife of the prisoner Moshe Dayan, and the major said my daughter would be allowed to pass through the gate to see her father."

Captain Grant looked straight at me and said, "If I had to decide about bringing my own children to see me in prison, I wouldn't want them to come at all."

"That's not the point, Captain Grant. You are not in prison. My husband is."

"It's not educational to bring children to prison," he answered.

"And if I were in your place, I wouldn't need to ask permission for my children to visit me," I went on with the argument.

"We'll start having kindergarten classes here if we let everyone's children come through the gate," he said nastily. Yes, he had heard from Major Wormsley but he was not going to allow any such nonsense in his prison.

As usual, I couldn't help crying, though I think this time it lasted only a few minutes. We were in a crowded courtyard, with the boys lined up on a lower level. I held Yael, and Devora and Shmuel tried to decide which one of them would go in with me. It was a madhouse—everyone wanted to get in just one more word, to be the very last to see just a little more.

A huge Sudanese policeman was on guard at the gate that day, counting the prisoners and making sure that they had not received anything from us across the barbed wire. I was standing at the gate with Yael when all at once, on his own initiative and without a word or a bribe, that Arab policeman opened the gate, took Yael from me, gave her to Moshe for a moment to kiss, and handed her back to me.

In his first letter after the first visit, Moshe told me that I must never again bring Yael; he could not bear for her to see her father under such conditions. So on the the next visit I left her home. Afterwards he was sure that something terrible had happened to her, and I could hardly convince him that she was safe and sound. All our life together was like that: he would tell me to do something, and then wonder why I did as he asked!

Yet in that strange period, we felt uncommonly close. Waiting from letter to letter can bring people together without the irritations of everyday contact, just one overwhelming emotion. We had one goal to look forward to, freedom, and the dream of our home and farm. I have more than one hundred and fifty letters out of the many Moshe wrote in the eighteen months that he was a prisoner; the others were destroyed for security reasons or eaten years later by the Nahalal mice.

It was Moshe, writing from prison, who took pains to cheer me up:

I imagine today was a hard day for you. I knew we would seem to adjust to imprisonment and recognize it for what it is. But then the day comes when I cannot hold Yuli [Yael], and you see me in these clothes. . . . But what can we do? This is the way it is and we can't change things. We must, we must accept it; there is no alternative. If only we could be alone a little longer, and you could get through that first moment of concern over clothing and external things, you would see that it isn't so terrible. I know that this "unfortunate" isn't me. Probably when you read this letter you think I don't feel your suffering, and am not hurt by our circumstance, cut off from family life, unable to kiss Yuli. . . . I know all this; but we have to accept it. . . .

His pride came through clearly in this letter on a subject about which he had strong feelings:

Also—I'm just not prepared to give Grant the satisfaction, so I don't want you to ask his permission [for bringing Yael] because I know he wouldn't give it. When he's in his office we never go to him, we ask nothing from him. . . .

Then he continued on quite another level:

By the way, how did the photo of me come out? Bring lots of pictures, and I hope they come out better. . . . If we can't live a normal family life, we'll create one of our own.

Even under these conditions, he trained himself to end, usually, on an optimistic note:

The most important thing is not to feel sorry, not to allow yourself to grieve. I don't believe we will really sit here all three and a quarter years. Besides, we are young, we have the strength, we can stand this. Ultimately, it's not only our private matter and we aren't the only ones. How many Jews are arrested every day in this country? How many others are here in Acre? Be strong, and raise our wonderful Yuli. . . .

Then would come the paradox of whether or not to arrange special visits:

I saw your mother and you and Yuli when you were sitting beside the ditch, and almost managed to arrange to go out to work; then we could have seen each other at the wall. But I couldn't fix it with the guard. I was in a bad mood too after the visit; but what can we do? Try to pull strings to arrange a special visit. . . .

By mid-February, after more than four months in the Fortress and much negotiation by our people, the Forty-three were moved to Mazra. This was a work camp not far from the Fortress and near a government experimental farm; today it is a mental hospital. The prisoners' duties included working at the experimental farm, which was a fine arrangement, since many of them, including Moshe, were farmers from birth. As prisons go, it turned out to be far from unendurable.

The men lived in barracks, sanitation facilities improved, and there were no criminals—only "politicals" of both the left and right. There were Communists, and there were Revisionists, a right-wing political group. In the spring, thirty-nine Revisionists were imprisoned for illegal training and were added to the Forty-three. Moshe wrote me, with a certain satisfaction, that "everybody—British and Arabs—likes us, 'the forty-three,' and nobody likes 'the thirty-nine.' "

There were also Arab prisoners, detained for illegal political activity, and relations between them and the Jewish prisoners were generally excellent. For the Feast of Ramadan that year the Jews ate in the Arab mess, and when some Bedouin prisoners from a tribe near Nahalal were also arrested, Moshe wrote with concern asking what had happened to those he knew.

On one visit I brought Yael, who at eighteen months was already walking. She managed to squeeze through the entanglements of barbed wire and throw her arms around her father. As they held each other, the child in a fluttering white dress and the kneeling man in a brown prison uniform, I heard the camp sergeant shout, "If you don't take that kid out I will shoot!" The scene haunted me for months.

As the days dragged on, it became hard even for Moshe to remain cheerful.

I know I'm not a diplomat and can't fully deal wtih such problems and maybe I exaggerate the importance of our matter. But I know that without continuing pressure, nothing will be achieved. There are prisoners who sit for years without a trial. . . .

But he always kept a rational balance, and concluded,

To every war there is an end. Take care of yourselves, be well, and send me pictures.

For my twenty-third birthday, in the spring of 1940, Moshe wrote me a poem. Writing poetry and playing with rhymes was always something that gave him pleasure; and these verses, which he called "Evening in Acre," had enormous meaning for me:

> From prison in Acre, a very small token
> On her birthday,
> To Ruthie, with Yulik alone in the hut,
> To Ruth, the girl and the mother.
>
> Evening, and letters have come from home.
> The guard moves along. Light the cigars . . .

Under the blankets, by flashlight alone,
Hearts pour out, like guitars.

From outside a golden moon steals in,
And the song of frogs and the smell of hay.
One single window, barred, crossed and thin,
Cuts all into quarters, quarters to stay.

In the rustle of paper, hearts pour out,
Pour out, for they know that boys they are not:
We have built strong walls and made fields sprout,
And fought for our souls on the dark mountaintop.

Then why, tonight, does the steel seem to melt? Tell
Why eyes grow so moist and reading so hard?
Mother, at home, is teaching Yael
To say "Father" to the face on the card.

The sounds fade away. Out goes the light.
Footsteps go by in the corridor. Then
By the wall like misty forms in the night
People huddle together there—children.

Political prisoners at Mazra had more privileges than hard-labor detainees such as the Forty-three. Politicals were permitted books and gifts and one visit every week with just ordinary barbed-wire fencing and not bales of it. The best arrangement of all that we devised for extra visits involved one of these politicals.

From a list that a Jewish police sergeant provided, I picked one—a nice Communist called Bayan, which rhymes exactly with Dayan. There was no Mrs. Bayan, and I decided to come as his visitor. During one of my regular visits, I whispered the idea to him—could I come to see him and leave books for my husband? —and he agreed. It was prearranged for Moshe to be working nearby. Shmuel sometimes came to prison pretending to be the cantor, and Moshe hoped that I might assume the role of the dentist's nurse; but the arrangement with Mr. Bayan was among the best.

When Yael started to talk she used to shout "Daddy!" at every prisoner she saw. If we were riding on a bus and passed prisoners working on a road, she would call out "Daddy!" and everyone on the bus would turn to see what was happening. At this time she barely knew who her father was; he did not, after all, have an eye patch yet.

On one of my Bayan visits, I brought Yael along in a beautiful white smocked dress with a bow. She was running ahead when two policemen came toward us with Moshe between them.

He was working in the bakery and was carrying firewood. Yael rushed to him, not knowing the difference between this man and any other prisoner. She scooted between his legs—he lifted one to let her by—and she ran off. He did not touch her or give any hint of recognition; she did not know him. I went on speaking to Bayan, Yael was running around, and Moshe kept going back and forth, finding reasons to return for another glance at Yael. Otherwise he would not see her again for a month. But he could not kiss her, or even touch her.

One of my letters to Moshe is dated May 1940, and refers to the increasing closeness of the war. "At Nahalal we have prepared to take in relatives from the cities if this should become necessary." Then I turned to our daily life:

The house has been full of guests from Hanita [our friends from Shimron who had gone north to establish Kibbutz Hanita]. But I have no patience for guests, though they come to play with Yael. In fact I'm thinking of putting Yael into nursery school, so she won't have to be with such a nervous mother so much. Also, that will give me more freedom for making arrangements about you.

Yael sees that I'm writing and keeps saying "Acre! Acre! Acre!" It's all perfectly clear to her. . . .

I'm getting you some mosquito netting. . . . Your English is excellent! Not a single error in style, though there are still some spelling mistakes. But these will pass, too. . . . I think of nothing but your being home; I even think of things for us to argue about! I love you. . . . And when will there be another little Yuli? And what about the war? And the petition for reducing the sentence? Any suggestions for more action we can take? Tell me immediately. . . .

As things became organized we became greedier. When the boys were first imprisoned, the most we could dream of was a glimpse of someone from the hilltop overlooking the Fortress. Then, one of those terrible official visits. Then extra visits. At Mazra better conditions, no bars. Finally, summer came and the prisoners were working in the orchards and vineyards of the experimental farm; I developed a really good system.

What I did was apply for a job there; after all, I was a trained dairy worker. An interview with the director was arranged, and when the day came the Jewish agronomist in charge of the dairy told me to come with him. We walked to a eucalyptus grove and and he told me to continue walking. I did . . . and there, in the center of the grove, was Moshe. That, of course, had been arranged by our people.

It was the first time we had seen each other alone for about ten months. We sat on a deep bed of eucalyptus leaves that crunched and crackled and gave off their strong, striking scent. Always, eucalyptus scent has had deep associations for me—once with Zvi at the scout camp; once when Moshe paid me his compliment at Nahalal; and now, after so long, at the Mazra prison experimental farm.

"You must never do this again," Moshe said when the time came to leave. His reason was simple: "How can I face all the other boys? I know you can arrange it . . . but this is something I just cannot do to forty-two other men."

Still, there were other ways. I decided, for instance, to start raising rabbits at Nahalal. And the best rabbits—beautiful white fluffy chinchillas—were to be bought at Mazra. "You can't stop me from buying rabbits," I told Moshe. "I intend to expand our hutch and I'm coming here to buy them. Of course, if you don't want to see me when I come . . ."

Eventually we arranged a regular roster for family members to come to the fields and be with the boys. It became a sort of "love among the vineyards" affair—the weather was beautiful, the green straight rows of grapevines gave a degree of privacy, and that entire summer had an intense, enchanted atmosphere. Sometimes, there among the fruit trees with children and baskets of food, it seemed that we could simply walk home, hand in hand, free.

The books Moshe asked for included Shakespeare, and he was also reading poetry in English for the first time. His special requests were for *Little Man, What Now?*, by Hans Fallada, John O'Hara's *Appointment in Samarra*, which all of us thought one of the greatest books ever written, and O'Henry's short stories. He also asked for *The Cloister and the Hearth*, the historical romance by Charles Reade about the background of the Dutch humanist Erasmus. Then there was something called *Century Book of Horrors*, with marvelous vampires, which Zelda gave us and which was passed around in prison.

Moshe also liked making things with his hands, and there was time for "art and crafts" in prison. He made beautiful necklaces out of peach pits for our friends by a technique he learned from the Arab prisoners, who made prayer beads of polished olive pits. Peach pits when polished have a fantastic grain. For my mother, he made an olive-wood frame to hold a photo of Yael, and a little pot decorated with shells, which she still has.

So it was not so terrible. But I was consumed with guilt most of the time—that I was free, and sleeping in a real bed, and able to go to a movie, while Moshe was a prisoner.

Because it sounded useful, I spent several weeks in Tel Aviv that summer as Nahalal's representative at a first-aid course given by the Hadassah Hospital. There the war suddenly came very close. Moshe wrote: "I've just heard that our daughter has been saved by a miracle, and the boys here want me to give a party to celebrate."

Our letters crossed, for I had written Moshe the details of this miracle. "Please return this, I want to keep it for Yael as a memento," I asked him in this letter, dated September 10, 1940.

"You once wrote that you visualize us among bombings and explosions, and now this has come true," I wrote. It happened one hot afternoon while I was at the hospital in Tel Aviv. Yael and I were living in a little flat with Tzippora, a cousin of Moshe's who took care of Yael while I was at the hospital.

Suddenly there was a series of tremendous explosions: Tel Aviv was being bombed by Italian planes. It went on for only about two or three minutes; then there was utter silence. The operating room was immediately prepared for emergencies, and casualties began to arrive. The British police did a superb job carrying in the dead and dying, among whom were a British major and his wife. Ninety-nine persons were killed and one hundred and twenty wounded, of whom eighteen died later of their injuries. Among the casualties were fifty-five children.

My letter to Moshe described the scene:

Bodies were brought in smashed to a pulp. I saw a policeman bring in a little boy and rushed to see if I could help. "No use, he's dead," the man said. Now I realize what it is to see children like Yael without arms, without legs, without faces. It went on for five hours, and I knew the injured were coming in from the neighborhood where Yael was. At eight in the evening I was asked to go to the surgery to help there; that was when I asked permission to see about my daughter, and naturally it was given.

Tzippora's street had been closed off. There were many casualties from the neighborhood; the windows of the houses were blown out. I was let through and raced to ours: between it and the next house was a six-foot-deep hole where a bomb had struck. The house itself had gaping shrapnel holes and no windows, but Tzippora was unhurt. She had been hanging up Yael's clothes when the attack came and fell straight to the ground, and so escaped.

Yael was nowhere to be found. Someone said that Reumah had come for her, and I soon found Yael in the room nearby where Reumah was staying, peacefully eating yoghurt on the balcony. She had been alone at Tzippora's and we never knew what happened. All her clothes were torn and there was a small shrapnel burn on her leg, but that was all.

I wrote to Moshe the following day:

When she saw me and called "Mother," I cried, and told her that her father would come very soon and take both of us for a trip. How absurd it is—you in prison, and us without you. Why can't we celebrate together, and kiss Yael together!

The *Palestine Post* of September 11, 1940, carried what was Yael's first newspaper appearance, though she was unnamed:

An infant girl, whose mother was acting as a volunteer first-aid nurse at the time, was in a room whose wall collapsed, almost burying her in debris. She was found with one shoe missing and plaster in her hair, but otherwise unscathed.

That night Yael ran a high temperature and I was given permission by the hospital to take her to my parents in Jerusalem. The doctors assumed she was in shock. She must have been asleep when the bombs fell and that was what saved her; if she had been playing and not been covered by a sheet, she would have been killed.

I was back at work the next day, busy with the terrible daily grind of cleaning and bandaging patients with shattered bodies. It was not the first time I had seen dead and wounded, for all through the thirties people had been killed in ambushes and attacks.

Italian bombers had pointlessly raided Haifa two months earlier, killing forty-six and injuring eighty-eight, practically all Arabs. British military headquarters in Jerusalem, in a communiqué announcing the Tel Aviv raid, noted that "bombs were dropped indiscriminately, far from any possible military objective." Less than two weeks later, on September 22, Italian planes struck Haifa once more. This time, in addition to the bombs, they dropped leaflets in Arabic claiming to be "Defenders of Islam." They hit a mosque and a poor Arab residential section, and in this raid all victims were Arabs—thirty-two killed and sixty-eight wounded.

But all this was a distant corner of the war, far from the decisive European and African fronts. To recall those days: the week of the raid, Myrna Loy, Robert Taylor, and Douglas Fairbanks were playing in the cinemas of Jerusalem, and the film at the Armon Theater in Haifa was *Gunga Din*.

Autumn went by, winter came. At Nahalal I worked packing apples and doing bookkeeping for the village. A very nice immigrant from Germany whose husband was taking agricultural training stayed with me at the hut to help with expenses. She was a wonderful housekeeper and cook, and taught me new recipes.

On Hanukkah, 1940, Dov Hos of the Haganah High Command visited the Acre prisoners. While hurrying to another meeting, he was killed in an automobile crash. His wife, who was the sister of Moshe Sharett, his daughter, her sister-in-law, and his niece died with him, as well as Yitzhak Ben-Yaakov, who was working with Dov organizing the Haganah's illegal air force. The tragedy hit everyone in our close circle, for he was also the brother-in-law of Eliahu Golomb; to me he had been like an uncle.

One night in February, two British sergeant-majors suddenly arrived at our place—Tommy Tucker, from the Shimron days, with a friend, both on leave from Cairo. This was the last time

I saw Tommy; he was killed on the North African front two years later.

About ten that evening, there was a phone call and a message: be at Kibbutz Ein Hamifratz the next morning at nine, with clothes for Moshe. The house, usually so spotlessly neat, was a shambles of beer bottles and cigarettes. We cleaned it up in a whirl of excitement and even baked cakes. I packed a black-and-white sweater of Moshe's I had knitted two years earlier, which he had never had a chance to wear. Somehow, he had had a fancy for a black-and-white sweater.

Buses were at the kibbutz the next morning to take all the families to Mazra. And there, on February 17, 1941, with no prior explanation, the prisoners were released. They had served less than two years of the five-year term. But with the war now taking a serious turn, the British were anxious to use all available manpower. After release from the British prison, most of the men volunteered for action with the British forces. Two of them began training almost immediately for the *Sea Lion* operation, and were among the Twenty-three lost with Zvi.

At first it seemed that Avshalom Tau was not going to be freed with the rest; Laura was with us and it hurt me to think of her. The forty-two others said they would not leave without Avshalom, but they were assured that in a few days he, too, would be released, and indeed he was.

Moshe put on his black-and-white sweater, and we went home.

6 · "Who Will Hire a One-eyed Man?"

A round of modest celebrations followed Moshe's return, with much cake-baking and visiting. These little parties disturbed Shmuel, who did not approve of people dropping in for cakes and tea. "Don't they have anything to eat at home?" he would ask.

Immediately after his release Moshe began looking for a job, and the best-paying one offered was driving a beer truck. But he decided against this in favor of driving a tractor, for this would keep him closer to home. He also took jobs building concrete stalls and troughs for the cowsheds, and worked as a night watchman as well. We were very happy, though knowing Moshe as I did, I was sure this peaceful period would not last. The war was coming close.

One evening in May, Moshe had just returned from work when there was a knock on the door. I was putting Yael to bed. She was a little over two years old, unusually lively and intelligent, and Moshe was fascinated by her. They were just getting to know each other. The cat was asleep, the dog waiting for her dinner, and all in all it was a cozy domestic scene. Then the door opened, and there stood Zvi and Yitzhak Sadeh, founder and first commander of the Palmach (the Haganah's striking arm).

The three men began a serious discussion, and I went to the kitchen to prepare tea. I didn't follow much of what was going on except to gather it had something to do with Australians. Many Australian soldiers were in our vicinity, for an Australian base was operating nearby.

Zvi stayed behind with me while Moshe and Yitzhak Sadeh went next door, where the Haganah office was located. He was now a high-ranking Haganah officer. He had studied in London for two years, married, and had a baby son ten months old.

"We need Moshe for an important job," said Zvi. I was expecting this, and answered him sulkily. Moshe had been home only three months after nearly two years in prison, and we were just settling down. We felt affluent, and our hut was the most luxurious one in Nahalal, with two rooms, a closed-in porch, a real kitchen, and extras like an inside shower.

Zvi looked around our room and said, "Look, you have everything. A beautiful home, a child, a real life. Moshe will go out on this job, but he'll be back. You'll have him."

In a nostalgic tone he continued: "I can't keep a home. I'm always away." His wife, Shosh, was also an officer in the Haganah and their baby was at a kibbutz. "When I go to visit there I hardly know which one is my child. Sometimes Shosh and I don't see each other for weeks, both our lives are so wrapped up in the Haganah.

"So what do you have to complain about? We need Moshe. You have your home and your child. Moshe will come back. And he has such a nice place to come back to." Zvi left later that evening; it was the last time I ever saw him.

Moshe and Yitzhak Sadeh came back from their phone call. The three talked a bit more and did the dishes. The next morning Moshe started planning his assignment, and after that was practically never at home. He told me the starting point of his mission would be Kibbutz Hanita, near the Lebanese border. Since this was where most of our Shimron friends had gone, I asked to go along. So on June 4 we left Yael with Devora and drove north, in a car that belonged to the Haganah in Haifa. When the Haganah man gave us the car he said jokingly, "If Moshe comes back from this, maybe we'll let you keep it."

A good friend, Zalman Mart, happened to be in Nahalal that day and when Moshe asked him if he'd like to come along on a mission, he got into the car. Casually, just like that.

On the way to Hanita we stopped at Naharia, on the coast. The German Jews who lived there had turned it into a miniature Riviera, with everything sparkling clean and neat. The whole population rode around on bicycles, there were lovely gardens, and delicious food. At Naharia you could get strawberries with whipped cream; strawberries were still rare, though not long afterwards we began growing them at Nahalal.

Moshe and I walked along the seashore hand in hand. "You know, Moshe," I said, "I'm dying to have strawberries and

whipped cream. It's so strange, but I have a craving for them."
I was, of course, pregnant with Udi, but that possibility never
entered my head.

We went into the town's most luxurious hotel and ordered
enormous portions of strawberries and cream. At that moment
Moshe had his thoughts on the coming military operation, while
all I could think about was strawberries.

At Hanita it was wonderful to see our Shimron friends again,
and there was excitement in the dining room where everybody
had gathered. Several groups were going out on different mis-
sions that night. Australian officers were there too, and I joked
with them. But now what I had on my mind was olives. After
the strawberries I had a craving for olives, so I had my tea with
a huge pile of them; and to this day that's how I like olives—
with tea.

I walked with Moshe and his group—our boys and the Australian officers—up to the Lebanese border, on a ridge overlooking a beautiful view. Moshe talked about Yael. Then he said
he'd be back in a few hours and that I should wait for him; in
the morning we'd drive back to the farm.

We said good-bye and I walked back to the dining room and
had more olives, talked for a while, and then went to the room
I'd been given and tried to sleep. But before long the sounds of
shooting began in the distance, and lasted all night. I felt as I
have so often in my life when Moshe was away and in danger.
Across the border the shooting continued. I went back to the
dining room and had a few more olives.

At about four in the morning the first group returned in high
spirits, driving two automobiles with Lebanese license plates
which they'd captured. I asked where Moshe was, and the men
in this group said, "We weren't together." There was nothing
to worry about, they said; Moshe was in a different sector. Everybody happily drank fruit juice and ate omelettes. More bursts
of shooting came from the darkness on the other side of the border. More groups returned and it started to grow light. Soon
practically everybody was back and very excited. Everybody except Moshe's group.

Much later in the day the Haganah man in charge of the
northern area came to me and said, "Moshe has been slightly
wounded in the hand. It's not serious, he won't lose his hand.
But he's at the hospital in Haifa and you'd better get there."
The only trouble, he added, was that all the roads were jammed
with British tanks and armored vehicles massing for the invasion
of Syria.

"But where are the others in Moshe's group?" I asked. "Where
are the Australians?"

"Oh, they're fine. They've done the job and they're on the way
back. Now you'd better get to Haifa."

The only car available was one that had just been brought back from Lebanon—a good-looking two-seater sports car. But I didn't know how to drive. I asked if there was someone who could take me. "It's hard to get a driver just now," he said. "Tanks are on the move, and there's fighting all along the north."

I said, "Look, I don't know how to drive, but I'll take the car and start. If I get somewhere, fine. If not, I'll hitchhike." I had driven a car a couple of times without knowing how. Once I couldn't get it out of reverse and a stranger had to help me.

So I started the car down the hill. Then somebody decided this might not be wise and somehow a driver was found. During the trip I began to be sure that I had not been told the truth. The driver, I felt, was concealing something. Devora and Shmuel and my parents were already at the Rothschild Hospital in Haifa, a dilapidated old building, when we arrived. Then I heard the whole terrible story. Devora told me my signature had been needed for the operation, which had been held up for some time. Finally they could wait no longer and had operated without it.

A bullet had struck the binoculars Moshe was holding to his eyes while standing exposed to fire on the seashore horizon. The binoculars became embedded in the eye socket. It took nearly thirteen hours to bring him to the hospital. The pain had been so great that Zalman Mart had tried unsuccessfully to remove the metal; that eye was completely lost. There was hope of saving the other. The hand that had held the binoculars was badly smashed; the other hand was slightly wounded.

It was a very hot summer night without a breath of air; vivid starlight made Haifa almost as bright as day. The city was completely still, so the boom of distant shooting—now far away across the northern border—came clearly to my bench in the eerie silence. The drastic change in Moshe's life completely eclipsed my own feelings, which not so long before had been unhappiness at his frequent absences. Now that dissatisfaction was dwarfed by an enormous event, as it would be again and again in the future. This date of June 5 was to be the eve of D-Day in three years; twenty-three years later still, it would be the start of Moshe's greatest triumph, the Six-Day War.

When I was allowed to see him that night, his head and both eyes were completely bandaged. The bridge of the nose had been shattered and there were countless fragments in Moshe's head. I noticed a gaping hole near his nose where a tube had been inserted so he could breathe. Another tube for breathing was in his mouth. There were safety pins in his nostrils to prevent choking. Both hands were encased in enormous bandages, from which came a horrible smell of fish oil. There was nothing that I could do. This is a terrible feeling of helplessness, and it has come often: Moshe wounded, or in pain, and nothing in my power to help. I begged to be allowed to stay in the room in case something happened; or if he might need something. But of course this was not permitted.

That night I did the only thing I could, which was to go to the home of the hospital's chief surgeon, whom my parents knew. When he saw me he became furious, shouting that no private visits from me were going to help matters.

I cried, of course, and said that I just wanted to know the truth. I wanted to know what was going to happen to Moshe's remaining eye, whether he would be able to see. And Moshe, I knew, wanted the truth too.

I spent the night on the street outside the Rothschild Hospital, on a little bench. I was terribly afraid of seeming forward, but I made myself go inside the hospital and tell the head nurse that I was there, and would be there until morning. I begged her to let me know if I could be of any help.

All that night there were sounds of shooting in the distance, and I sat on the bench and thought that Moshe might be blind for the rest of his life. Moshe, with his sense of humor, used to say later that I probably wouldn't have minded if he had been blind because then I'd have had the chance to prove my devotion.

When daylight came I was allowed to see him. He could speak a little, and the first thing he wanted to know was whether I had seen the doctor, whether he would be able to see. I told him that everything would be all right, that he would have the sight of one eye—this the eye doctor had told me. The staff had been worried about possible damage to the brain, for there were so many fragments in his head. But he was absolutely clear and rational.

By now all the family had arrived and Devora had brought Yael. I didn't know whether to take her to see her father. He looked terrible with his head in bandages, and naturally he would not be able to see her. And she was not yet two and a half years old. But I decided it would be good for Moshe, so I took her into his room for just a moment. He smiled when he knew she was there, and touched her with one bandaged hand. Yael had no bad reaction from this. Her only question was why her father had safety pins in his nose.

I was in and out of the room that day without being of any real help to anyone. The hospital seemed to me unpleasant, and I wished we were in Jerusalem, where the Hadassah Hospital on Mount Scopus was so much better equipped and where my parents had so many friends.

That afternoon Zelda came from Jerusalem to be with me, as she so often did when I needed her. That night and the next we stayed at the Zion Hotel. By now we knew the operation had been a success; I could accomplish nothing by spending another night outside the hospital.

In our room the second evening, just as we were getting ready for bed, Zelda and I heard a terrible noise. The bombing of Haifa had started again. The shelter turned out to be a gay place; in fact all of Haifa was lively at that time, teeming with sailors and British soldiers, and representatives of governments-in-exile of Mediterranean countries. So we spent the night in the shelter with various diplomats of exiled governments, and the bombing went on. Sitting there, it was hard to imagine that anything of Haifa would be left. The one thing on my mind was the Rothschild Hospital, which, I knew, had no air-raid shelter.

I tried to leave the shelter to get to the hospital but it was impossible, for the British did not let anyone move in the entire city. We had visions of nothing existing above ground any more, and of the hospital simply gone. Bombing from the air makes a terrifying noise, and there was no radio to let us know what was happening. The diplomats with us were having a good time; they were drinking, and seemed to think nothing could happen to us, even though the whole building was shaking.

When dawn finally came, I emerged from the shelter and there was Haifa, still standing! It seemed unbelievable. Of course, windows were shattered and some houses had suffered direct hits, but there were few casualties. The Italians had missed everything. They had dropped bombs into the sea and outside the town but actually caused little damage.

At the hospital everything was in order; though all that had been done was to remove the patients from their beds and put them on the floor. I was determined that Moshe was not going to spend another night in Haifa. We knew that Jerusalem was safe because of its status as a holy city; it was never bombed. I phoned Mother and said we must get Moshe to Jerusalem even if I had to carry him there on my back. We put Moshe into Mother's little Morris and drove to Jerusalem.

He stayed at the Hadassah Hospital for only three or four days and after that recuperated at my parents' house, though we took him to the hospital every day for treatment. The tubes stayed in his nose for a long time, and the shattered hand needed endless treatment. The smelly fish-oil bandage stayed, too, and had to be changed daily.

Moshe's conduct during the action in which he lost his eye became well known. The Australian officers came to visit him, and one of them said to Mother, "That boy scout son-in-law of yours, if there's anything he doesn't know about military matters, it isn't worth knowing."

Moshe's group of five Jews and ten Australians (three officers and seven soldiers) had been ordered to guard a bridge and keep

it open for the British advance into Syria against Vichy French
troops. But because the British were delayed and the group was
being shot at from a fortified police station manned by French
Senegalese troops, Moshe, on his own initiative, decided to try to
capture it. This he did, singlehanded and under fire, by rushing
the station with a grenade, the Australians covering him as he
had told them to. The arms carried by his group sound today
incredibly limited—five English rifles, one Tommy gun, one Bren
gun, and little more. They replenished their ammunition only
after capturing prisoners at the police station. Moshe's calm behavior, from the time he was wounded until he was finally
brought to the hospital, left a lasting impression.

One day at the hospital, while the bandage was being changed,
I fainted. That was how I found out I was pregnant again. I
was very happy, because I wanted to have many children. I knew
Moshe would probably not be pleased with the idea, but I was
not prepared for the degree of his reaction.

"Who is going to hire a man with one eye?" he said. "It's impossible! I'm not going to be able to support my family. We
can't have the child." He was in a terrible mood, convinced that
his future would be such that he could not possibly care for another child. But my doctors agreed that it was too late to do
anything, and Moshe gradually grew reconciled to the idea.
When I became pregnant with Assi three years later, he raised
no objections. By then we were back at Nahalal, living on our
own farm, and Moshe felt that on a farm one more mouth to
feed is no problem. But that autumn in Jerusalem he was seriously worried about his future.

The transition period from such an injury is a terrible strain
—learning to focus with just one eye, the continuing headaches,
the fragments that kept working themselves out of the wound. I
was unable to grasp the psychological difficulties at the time; I
was concerned with the daily changing of bandages, not the
long-range effects.

During his recuperation Moshe became involved in the higher
levels of political planning, and these began to fascinate him.
One plan was for a system of wireless transmitting cells that was
to go into operation in the event of a German occupation and
provide an intelligence network.

A training course for wireless operators was held in Tel Aviv.
Moshe and I moved temporarily to a rented room by the seashore, on the spot where the Sheraton Hotel now stands. In the
morning I took Yael to nursery school and attended the wireless
course, where I was not a good pupil. "All the rest are much
better than you are," the instructor told me, "but on the other
hand, you are good at English." I was five months pregnant with
Udi, and this time my pregnancy was obvious. It was only when

I worked on the farm that I stayed thin the whole time. So although I finally did achieve a khaki uniform, it did not look right with a big stomach, especially during morning drill. There were quite a few jokes about how the baby would be born holding a transmitting key.

When we returned to Jerusalem, we took a four-room flat of our own for Moshe's activities, and rented out two of the rooms. Our boarders were two British sergeants assigned to the intelligence plan, Frederick Allen, who was red-haired and nicknamed "Ginger," and Ron Langdon. They became very much part of our family. I cooked for Ron's girl friends and talked to Ginger about his wife, in London, whom he hadn't seen in four years. Both sergeants felt it was a pity I was not as good a radio operator as I was a cook.

I wanted Moshe to love Jerusalem as I did. I took him to my favorite restaurant, the National, just outside the Old City, to introduce him to the dishes that I—and Yael, aged three—liked so much, especially meat with rice prepared the Arab way. But in those days he preferred Nahalal cooking and was never as entranced by the smell of the old alleys as I was.

Udi was born at the Hadassah Hospital at three in the morning on January 31, 1942, a quick and easy birth. There was a big party to celebrate his *Brit* (circumcision ceremony). I continued with my radio transmissions, operating the transmitter with one hand and giving Udi his bottle with the other. Often, when Moshe was away, the sergeants would give him his late bottle.

By the end of summer the work with the British was over and we prepared once more to return to Nahalal. This time we intended to buy our own farm and settle down to a permanent life. I look back upon that year in Jerusalem with pleasure. Moshe was engrossed in new work that fascinated him, and our home, with two children, a dog, and many friends, was a happy place.

Our English soldiers thought so too, and kept in touch with us. Ginger wrote from Egypt:

Dear Ruth, your charm must still be percolating through the awkwardness of those afternoon teas. If you have to give less sugar in the tea or jam on the cakes, just plaster a little sweetness on your face, so to speak, that ingratiating smile of yours, the informal and easy manner of "take it or leave it." . . . When I get leave and come to see you, we'll get around to those places where Mosha [sic] won't be asked to wear a collar and tie!

In October 1943, he wrote:

There's no reason on earth why you shouldn't write. Husbands and wives are the only people who shouldn't write to each other. How can you so easily forget those long and pleasant months I spent looking after your baby, keeping you company whilst your loving but unappreciative husband was gallivanting all over Palestine, occasionally washing your dishes and saving your sanity. . . .

I can send you some farming journals from England, how to milk cows by candlelight. . . . You really ought to get a virile husband for your rabbit, Ruth—those my wife has at home seem to breed a litter every time she writes. . . .

Because I like to trace friends and find out what has happened to them, I made a real effort to locate Ginger when Moshe and I were in London in 1952. But there must have been about two hundred Frederick Allens in the London telephone directory and I gave up after a few tries.

Then, in 1967, Yael received a letter out of the blue, post-marked Portsmouth, England. With it was a snapshot of Yael at the age of three with our dog and Ginger; "1942" was written on the back, and the return address was Frederick Allen. Yael, of course, had no idea what this was all about. When I was in London later the same year—Assi was making a film there—one of the things I was most eager to do was to call Ginger. This time the number was easy to find, and when I rang Portsmouth a woman's voice answered.

"I knew your husband twenty-five years ago," I said.

"Of course! You're Mrs. Dayan," said a very pleasant voice.

We arranged to meet that evening, and we had a marvelous time. Ginger and his wife had an enormous collection of Moshe Dayan newspaper clippings, and kept apologizing for taking my time that evening. "But you must have so many more exciting things to do!" they insisted. It was hard to convince them that little could give me more pleasure than being with a very old friend who was now living a happy, normal life.

In contrast was the tragic telephone call when I tried to get in touch with Geoffrey Makins. He had written us from Egypt, congratulating Moshe on his release from Acre in the spring of 1941, and since then we had heard nothing from him. There was no trouble finding this telephone number, for Makins was a distinguished name. This time, too, a woman's voice answered the phone. I began eagerly, "I am an old friend of Geoffrey's and I'd very much like to get in touch with him."

There was a terrible silence at the other end of the line. Then the woman, composed but under great tension, answered, "My Geoffrey was killed at Tobruk in 1941."

7 · Four Children on Our Farm

One of the good parts of being Mrs. Moshe Dayan was that doors opened easily for me, and so I could try to help many people. But I have had my share of failures, and Tzippi was one of them.

We are all born with a certain character, and though wars or chance events or what is called "fate" can make life go one way or another, there is not much that can be done about one's character. With Tzippi, who lived with us almost as a daughter and whose life still crosses mine, I watched how something within her twisted her destiny in tragic directions. Perhaps, for all we tried, it was bound to happen.

Tzippi was a pale skinny child of about ten the first time I saw her, at Nahalal in 1943. Her head had been shaved because she had typhus. Five years later, living with me and Moshe and our children at our farm, she was a big husky girl with thick black braids. The last time I saw her, in Tel Aviv recently, her long hair was dyed a brassy blond; the month before, I had taken her to the hairdresser and insisted she have it dyed back to its natural black, but Tzippi, now thin as a rail, preferred it blond. While she was under the dryer I took her youngest boy to the movies. Tzippi named him Moshe, after my Moshe, and she named one of her daughters after Devora Dayan, and another son after Shmuel. But those names were only a helpless gesture: of Tzippi's six children, only two are legitimate, and their father is in a hospital for the incurably insane. Two other children were sold for adoption by the man who fathered them. Today Tzippi holds some simple job for a while, but never for long, and continues to be exploited by men. I believe that if she had stayed at Nahalal she could have become a good farm wife.

She and her little brother arrived in Palestine during World War II, two of the "Teheran Children"—several hundred young refugees brought from Eastern Europe by the Jewish Agency. Most were from Poland, but they have always been known as the Teheran Children because the last stopping point on their long voyage home was neutral Iran. In the spirit of the times, families throughout Palestine volunteered to take these children into their homes, and a group of forty was assigned to Nahalal for such informal "adoption."

"These two should be put into an institution immediately." This was the verdict of the psychologist who examined Tzippi and her brother, after their medical and I.Q. tests. The little boy did look backward, while the girl seemed frightened but otherwise normal. But Devora would not hear of putting the children into an institution. She could not bear the idea of this little girl growing up without a normal home environment, and insisted on taking her. Another Nahalal family agreed to take the brother. Though he was the one marked least able to cope with the world, he is today married and lives at a kibbutz. He refuses to have anything to do with his sister.

Moshe and I and our two children just happened to be in Nahalal the day the Teheran Children arrived, for part of that year and much of 1944 Moshe was on a special mission for the Haganah and we were living in rented rooms in Tel Aviv.

We had moved in with Shmuel and Devora after our stay in Jerusalem, thinking once more that we had returned to Nahalal for good. It is never pleasant to live with in-laws, and we began to think about buying our own farm. Moshe and I and Udi and Yael were in one small room; the other room was rented out. Rain poured through holes in the roof in that miserable winter of 1942, and we spaced our beds between buckets on the floor to catch the leaks. It would have cost very little to have the roof repaired, but Shmuel would not hear of such a waste of money. "Moshe will fix it," he said.

To earn a little extra money, I began making children's dresses with a sewing machine Mother gave me. Yael's clothes turned out nicely, but I used no patterns and never really learned properly. Shmuel was in a fury that "his daughter-in-law was a dressmaker," and when I spoiled a piece of wool trying to sew a dress for a friend, I gave up the project. (Ten years later, when we were living in Ramat Gan, I tried dressmaking once again and it was just as unprofitable, for I refused to take money from friends and ate up any profits feeding lunches to my clients during fittings.) But I did make little rag dolls out of scraps in our cramped room at Nahalal, and these at least were a success.

Whenever we discussed buying our own farm I ended up in a pessimistic mood, because I was distrustful of happiness. "It won't last," I said to Moshe, though he had every intention of being a serious, full-time farmer. "You think you are always right about everything," he would answer. The things I have been right about often made me miserable; I would dearly love to have been wrong. "I wish I weren't always right" was my sulky answer.

Sure enough, one afternoon in 1943 Eliahu Golomb knocked on our door and walked into our room, much as Yitzhak Sadeh had come to call Moshe away for the Syrian operation two years earlier. Eliahu Golomb, my parents' friend from their secret-society days, was now commander of the Haganah, and Moshe was needed for a dangerous, and this time spiritually trying, task. The "Saison," as it was known, was a terrible assignment, for the Haganah was tracking down members of other underground organizations. It was a time of divided loyalties, of old friends on opposite sides of the political battleground.

For this new job Moshe had to be in Tel Aviv. He wanted us to be together, so I brought the children to the city and we lived in a series of depressing hotel rooms. Udi started nursery school and Yael, who at five already knew how to read and write, began her school career in the second grade. People sometimes think Yael skipped at school, because she was always two years younger than her classmates, but the fact is that she just started earlier and never had the slightest trouble keeping up.

To keep busy I enrolled in a French course, but most of the time I was depressed by the Saison. There were lists of "most-wanted men," and the drop of a word could mean a hunt. It was like a detective story, but we were living within it; actual human beings were involved. One dreadful evening I met a good friend from schooldays on the street, one of the nicest boys in the class. But he was now of the enemy, politically. I wanted to invite him to our room for a talk, but I knew this was impossible: Moshe was in a sense at war with my friend's group, just as my friend was with Moshe's. It was a tragic time of suspicion, a condition we lived through more than once, and are now living through again with the Arabs.

Everyone was relieved when it was over. We returned to Nahalal at the end of 1944 and took the great step of buying our own farm with the help of my parents. It seemed such a sign of permanence when we bought Number 53 on the Nahalal Circle, where Udi lives today. Curiously enough, the Nahalal album that lists the history of each farm notes that Number 53 belonged originally to a pioneer from Russia who came to Palestine in 1909. But his Russian wife, whose profession is listed as dressmaker, was one of the very few Nahalal women who took the step of leaving their husbands; this she did in 1931.

Tzippi had been with Devora and Shmuel for about a year when we began working our own farm, and Devora's way had turned out successfully. She had put the little girl to work, and at eleven Tzippi was busy with farm chores. It was a big help to Devora, but it was also exactly what the child needed. Devora, typically Russian, had that unique combination of great compassion and extreme toughness. She was full of emotion, but it was bound up with the strength to overcome that emotion when necessary.

I was fascinated by the change in Tzippi. She had put on weight, turned brown from the sunshine, was learning Hebrew and forgetting her Yiddish. Moshe was fond of Tzippi and found time to play with her; he invented her private nickname— "Pippa." She was devoted to Udi, and got along well with Yael, even though, at five, Yael was more than the intellectual equal of much older children.

Tzippi soon asked to move in with us at our farm. She was an eager worker and proud of her achievements, especially when I could teach her something like milking, which Yael, however precocious, was too small for. But she was a poor student at school, and she was sulky, something I am capable of myself. For a time she stole toys from Udi, but this passed. I purposely made dresses for her that would outshine Yael's, and she was the first to get a bicycle. She tried to show her independence, and she invented a defense against me: "If you discipline me so much I'll go straight to the Jewish Agency and complain that you are cruel." At the same time she was devoted to me, always staying by my side at home and in the fields.

"I was often jealous of Yael," Tzippi told me twenty-five years later. "But you and Moshe were like my real mother and father." Then she added, "The years have done their work."

Like all the Teheran Children, she had her dreams of what the future would be when her parents found her. They would be rich, and she would live in a beautiful villa. Another little girl who came to Nahalal with Tzippi had the same dream; she decided her father was an architect, and planned her reunion with her real parents. In 1947 Devora was in Germany working among refugees and found them—two broken wrecks of human beings. Their daughter committed suicide when she was twenty.

Assi was born on November 23, 1945, at the Afula Hospital. I had wanted to have the baby at the farm, and at first the local doctor agreed. On Friday evening I felt the pains beginning. I finished the cake I was baking and asked Moshe to call the doctor, who insisted that we go to the hospital. We broke the night curfew imposed by the British and drove to Afula in the Nahalal milk lorry. I was furious, because I had everything carefully organized at home for the birth of a baby and for the chores to continue. I wanted this baby to be born at 2:00 a.m., the same time that Udi had arrived; in this I was successful and Assi arrived right on time.

I spent only four days at the hospital, and four days after that I took the baby to our doctor for the *Brit*. But he said the day was not suitable.

"I've been picking grapefruit all day and my hands are shaky," he explained, "and besides, this is my first *Brit*." So Assi had his much later, when the doctor was not involved in agriculture.

Tzippi adored Assi. She loved to hold him and fold his diapers exactly as I showed her. She and Yael were both a great help, for in those days at Nahalal there was no question about young girls helping with the housework. Even Udi helped, more or less, and Assi was brought along to the fields and put in a fruit crate, where we all kept an eye on him. Taking care of babies was quite simple; they took for granted things like being put into packing crates.

In the winter of 1946, five of us Dayans had an interlude in Switzerland. The event was the Twenty-second World Zionist Congress in Basle, to which Shmuel was an authorized delegate. The plan was for Devora to stay in Nahalal with the children, but as it turned out only Aviva, just back from Egypt, stayed at home. Yael, Udi, Assi, and Tzippi were left in care of the shoemaker's daughter, who had eleven brothers and sisters, and so knew all there was to know about children.

As an official observer to the congress, Moshe was entitled to a second-class ticket. This was also a chance for a necessary and long-delayed eye operation by a plastic surgeon in Paris. I was to go along to care for Moshe at the hospital, and with help from my parents we changed the second-class ticket for two third-class ones.

Zorik, who was with the Jewish Brigade in Germany, was anxious to see his fiancée, Mimi, and wrote asking whether money might not somehow be scraped up for a ticket for her. But at the last moment Devora decided that she would go too, for she was anxious to work with refugees in the UNRRA (United Nations Relief and Rehabilitation Administration) camps. My sister, Reumah, was also abroad, supposedly studying in London but in reality enjoying herself like any twenty-year-old girl, and she came to meet us in Basle.

The first disappointment was poor Zorik's. At the Basle railway station, arriving from Germany on leave and looking anxiously across the crowds, he saw his father, mother, brother, and sister-in-law, but no Mimi. It reminded me of the days at the Acre prison when Shmuel or Devora would join me during the visits to Moshe.

Still, it was gay at the small hotels and pensions where the congress delegates were staying. I had an official pass, beret, and arm ribbon certifying me as an usher to the proceedings, which had no particular interest for me. For Reumah, one evening at our hotel turned out to be important. Into the dining room walked a tall, handsome R.A.F. officer radiating charm and self-assurance.

"Where's my uncle?" he asked at the first table. "I've got to get some money from my uncle." His uncle was Chaim Weizmann and this was Ezer, his dashing nephew, the pilot. He came to our table—everybody knew his uncle but none of us had ever met Ezer—and smiled at Reumah.

"Anybody want to go back to London? I'll fly them back for fifteen pounds." He had just flown his small plane across the Channel in a storm in search of a loan, a frequent occupation of Ezer's in those days. Reumah did not accept; Ezer was described as "not Reumah's type." They were married four years later.

When the congress ended, Zorik returned to his unit in Germany, Devora also went to Germany, Reumah returned to England, and Moshe and I traveled to Paris for the operation. The hospital was in a convent and all the nurses were nuns. France, just after the war, was a country of shortages. There were no sheets on the beds, so at the Galeries Lafayette I bought what was available—a huge, elegant linen sheet with embroidered monogram: all sheets in those days came from castles.

The doctor was a specialist who operated on French soldiers with war wounds similar to Moshe's. The day of Moshe's operation he performed about eight others, all successful. Moshe's alone did not respond; the bone graft was rejected.

While Moshe was still unconscious I received a cable from Devora in Rome: "Shmuel seriously injured, inform Zorik." There had been a car accident and Shmuel's companion, the brother of Kadish Luz (later speaker of Israel's parliament), had been killed on the spot. Shmuel was badly injured, and returned to Nahalal on a stretcher.

Moshe's reaction to the operation was poor. He ran a high fever for four days and could not swallow food. Once again I sat by his bedside, this time on an uncomfortable chair in an unheated convent room.

"I can't understand why you remain in that chair, madame," said one of the nuns, a young and pretty one. "Why don't you get into the bed and keep Monsieur warm?"

Moshe's mood, when he finally began to recover, ran along other lines. He was cross and uncomfortable, but refused to let me out of his sight. "What am I going to do with all these nuns?" he complained. "You know I can't speak French."

Reumah arrived from London and was an enormous help, taking turns at the night watch. Almost as important, she had brought tea from London; after Moshe had his, the nuns re-used the tea leaves to supply the children's wards. And I gave Reumah advice, something I had already been doing for years.

"Stop wasting your time in London pretending to be studying. There are things that need doing. You ought to join UNRRA and help with the children in the displaced persons camps." Reumah did join UNRRA and worked as a teacher for two years. In 1948, on the eve of the War of Independence, she returned home on a ship bringing four hundred children to Palestine from the Bergen-Belsen camp.

As soon as Moshe was able to travel, we scraped together enough money for plane tickets home. Air travel was still something of an event, but seats were easy to get because crashes were all too frequent. At the airport, a plane for Spain left an hour before our flight to Cairo; by the time we boarded, the crash of the Spanish-bound plane had already been announced.

Not long after our return I received a letter in Yiddish from an unknown woman in Russia. A man at the factory where she worked, she wrote, was looking for his children. I replied, describing Tzippi and her brother, but heard nothing further for a year. Tzippi was rapturous with excitement when the letter arrived, and clung to hope through the silence that followed. We adults knew that holocaust survivors sometimes took the names of Jews who had died in order to be eligible for the voyage to Palestine and reunion with their families. I did not care whether the man was her real father or not; our feeling was that every additional immigrant was important regardless of his actual family ties.

The next letter finally came, and it was from a man from the Bergen-Belsen camp. "Sorry about the delay," he wrote, "but I've been busy doing business, and now I'd like to see the children." Tzippi was radiant again, but I sensed something abnormal. Still, I arranged with the British authorities to accept responsibility for him and wrote him that he was welcome on our farm.

A cable came announcing an arrival date, and when the great day came we baked cakes, put Tzippi into a new pink dress with a bow in her hair, and took the children by bus to

Haifa. Their father's name was on the list of arrivals, but he did not appear. "He was on the ship," an official told me, "but we have no idea where he is now."

We returned home and ate the cakes. I consoled the children and telephoned the Jewish Agency daily for a week. Finally a man telephoned and said in Yiddish that he was the children's father. "Why haven't you come?" I shouted in a language I barely knew. "How dare you disappoint your children?"

"Ah yes, the children," he said. "Well, I've been up north with some friends from the ship."

I asked the operator to tell the man in good rich Yiddish to meet us in Haifa the next morning or he would be in serious trouble. This time we baked no cakes, and I left Tzippi's brother at home.

After a long, tense wait at the Jewish Agency office in Haifa, a man finally appeared wearing a leather hat and leather breeches. He was tall and quite good looking. Tzippi clutched me. "That's him," she said, and rushed to kiss her father.

On the bus ride home Tzippi sat next to me, and I could feel her body stiffening as her father talked; she still understood Yiddish, though now she spoke only Hebrew. There was no doubt that it was the right man, but something was very wrong. He did not ask about the little boy, and his only concern was watches. "I have lots of watches," he said. "A whole crate. And broken sewing machines, and a great many screws. I've heard that in the Levant you can sell anything."

Survivors of the horror in Europe, I knew, responded in different ways; this was one of them. Tzippi understood nothing of this, and she only clung to me more and more tightly.

"The first thing I must do is see Ben-Gurion," Tzippi's father went on. "I have a plan to save the Jewish state. I need three hundred motorcycles and three hundred motorcyclists, and we'll take the British by surprise and sweep through the Arab countries. You must arrange a meeting with Ben-Gurion." Then he took a flask out of his pocket and began to drink.

When we arrived at the farm I asked if he did not want to see his son. Oh yes, the son. Tzippi brought her brother to meet his father. Moshe came in from the fields. Tzippi clung first to me, then to Moshe, desperately afraid that the stranger might want to touch her, though he showed no interest in either of the children. Moshe spoke no Yiddish. The situation was all mine.

It was time to milk the cows, and Tzippi's father wandered about outside. When we came back from the milking Tzippi hugged us both hysterically. "Please, please, you're my only family," she sobbed. "I don't want to be with anybody but you. I'll do everything you tell me, only don't let him take me." Moshe and I told her there was nothing to be afraid of, that her father had no legal right to take her, yet. The next morning he went to Haifa and disappeared. We made no inquiries. Tzippi behaved as though a cloud had passed.

Three months later we were all in the apple orchard. Moshe and I picked, Tzippi and Yael wiped the fruit and put them into baskets, Udi helped the girls, and Assi was in his crate. Through the apple trees I saw a man walking toward us. As he came close I could see the letters stamped on his shirt: GEHA, the name of a mental hospital.

"Let me tell you what happened," he said. "There I was in Haifa, just starting to make a speech about my motorcycle plan, when some British policeman took me off to jail." I had been reading *The Snake Pit* and this sounded familiar. "Now I must go get some of my watches," he said, and walked off again without another word.

The diagnosis of the doctors at Geha was, "Suffering from hallucinations but absolutely harmless." Moshe and I signed papers taking responsibility for Tzippi's father. He was discharged from the hospital, and the Jewish Agency provided him with two goats and a hut near Haifa. There he lived in peace, eventually marrying a widow who was also a survivor of the European holocaust.

When we left Nahalal for Jerusalem after the War of Independence, Tzippi was a husky girl of sixteen who looked as though she might soon marry a farm boy. The best thing, I thought, would be to enroll her at the Nahalal Agricultural School, which was then geared to lower academic standards than in my day. Devora would keep an eye on her, and when she graduated Tzippi would make a fine farmer's wife.

After a few months, we heard that Tzippi's father had arrived at Nahalal for a visit. He saw a big, strong girl "going to waste on agricultural studies" and asked if she would like to live with him near Haifa. She had had quite enough of school and left in the middle of the term.

Devora called me in Jerusalem a few months later to say that Tzippi had been caught stealing from a grocery store; a police file was opened against her. Nevertheless, she was accepted for army service. "If you're ever in trouble, come to us," I told her when she turned up at our home in uniform. She came once again, stayed overnight, and disappeared; by then we knew she had been dishonorably discharged from the army. A year later, Devora heard that Tzippi was married and living in Tiberias with a daughter and a son.

In 1957, when my own world crashed about me, Zelda telephoned to say that Tzippi had tried to kill herself by slashing her wrists. She was in the hospital in Jerusalem, eight months pregnant by a man serving a jail sentence for dealing in drugs. I arranged to take Tzippi to the home of an elderly couple far from Jerusalem. "After the baby comes, we'll get you a job and you can start a new life." We drove by way of Nahalal, to make her feel nostalgic for the past, and had breakfast at Aviva's, who gave her clothes for the baby. Three days later Tzippi ran away and returned to Jerusalem.

Tzippi's husband spent years in a Syrian prison. At first it was believed he had deserted, for during the sixties his voice was heard on the Syrian radio, broadcasting against Israel. After he was returned in the prisoner exchange following the Six-Day War we heard that he had been kidnaped by Syrian infiltrators. Today, like practically everybody who has endured years in a Syrian prison, he is a human wreck and confined to a mental hospital; of the eleven Jews returned in that exchange, only one came home sane. Under Jewish law, Tzippi cannot divorce her husband for insanity. But I think, given her weakness of character and the fact that men so easily exploit her, this may be for the best.

Tzippi did not receive the financial support due her from the government while he was in Syria, because he was thought to be a deserter. For many years she lived with the family of a man who fathered four of her children and who is a criminal; she became the drudge of his parents.

She and I were discussing her complex past a few months ago. "No, I never thought of going back to Nahalal," she told me. "It was a period that was finished, though while I was there I was happy." Her Moshe is now at boarding school; I arranged that, and this is the most I can do for Tzippi today—to be there when she needs me.

Watching my own children grow up at Nahalal, I was sure that the experience of farm life and our closeness as a family would have a lasting influence. And I think it did, basically, though they spent important years of their youth away from the farm. But being a child is never easy, and it is especially hard to be the child of a famous person. It did our children no good to see that their father felt he was entitled to break certain normal rules of behavior—starting with traffic regulations—and it left its mark, having a father who is larger than life.

All this was still in the future when we were on our farm during the forties. Tzippi was just one of the elements in our lives, for by far the most important thread that ran through those days and made them so happy was our closeness as a family. We were all completely involved in farm work, which was nearly endless, and we were all practically always together. On the days that we thinned the rows of young corn, for instance—and those were days that began at dawn and ended with nightfall—all of us, Moshe and I and our children and Tzippi, would go down the rows to remove the excess seedlings with a special quick twist of the wrist. It was hard, repetitive work; and when you have twisted corn seedlings from dawn to dusk for four days, you find that your wrist motion goes on automatically, even after you have gone to bed.

After work we had hot showers and supper, rewards you feel entitled to after a day of such physical labor. Suppers were simply many good things set on the table—hard-boiled eggs, lots of greens fresh from the garden, farm bread and butter, and quantities of cream.

Life was interesting and crammed with ingenuity. When we wanted to enlarge our chicken coop, for instance, Moshe decided to take our horse and cart to a deserted British army camp. He dismantled a few corrugated tin roofs while I stood watch, we brought them home, and he built new coops from them. We did quite a lot of stealing in those days.

The birth of a calf was always profoundly exciting. It usually happened at night, and as soon as we heard the cow beginning to low seriously, Moshe would leap out of bed and run to the cowshed. I would follow, and while Moshe handled the crucial assistance, my part was to gently oil the head of the calf as it was emerging. There are few more miraculous sights than watching a newborn calf, already bleating, wobbling on its legs a few moments after birth.

I loved learning things from our neighbors, though Moshe also had arguments with neighbors about things like water rights. Both women were fine farm wives and taught me many things. Making soap, from an old Russian recipe, was tremendous fun; soap was rationed during the war, and we needed quantities for washing farm clothes on our washboards over big basins. Over an open fire, we would boil for hours quantities of lard from the butcher, resin that I bought at a musical-supply store in Haifa, caustic soda, and finally a touch of eau de cologne. When the cakes hardened in wooden molds I made, the children decorated each one, and we had a supply for a year.

Our farm was first in many ways. We were the first with foot-and-mouth disease in our cowshed and so were quarantined for three weeks. Moshe sat for hours in the shed trying to relieve the swollen, sore, and kicking cows, though the milk was unusable. Food was left outside our door, and we had no visitors; it was really an extreme form of togetherness.

We were the first to raise Japanese cauliflower; Moshe practically slept in the fields with them, personally picking off each worm. He has a determinedly one-track mind, and was very serious about being a farmer.

And we were the first at Nahalal with turkeys. Today, Udi

raises thousands in huge sheds and incubators with automatic heat and light control. I just bought a few eggs and put them under some broody hens to hatch. The idea of baby turkeys emerging from under ordinary hens was very exciting, and I have never been able to resist the temptation of helping things along. So as soon as I heard the chicks starting to peck inside the shells I could not help giving a few helpful pecks from outside the egg.

"You leave those eggs alone!" Moshe would say indignantly, and of course he was right, for this was against all proper farming procedure. But I cannot bear not trying to help, even when I know it may not be wise.

It seems a very long time ago; we are so different today. Moshe was a farmer, and I had what I wanted. We were living a normal family life, and we were all together.

Moshe was sometimes away on Haganah duty but he always returned, and basically we were part of each other's lives. We got up together at four-thirty in the morning, when I lit the primus stove to warm water to wash the cows' teats; we milked together at five. We were together in the fields when I would walk out to bring Moshe a hot meal and help load the wagon with sheaves of wheat, bales of hay, or wonderful-smelling alfalfa. I would stand on top of the wagon and arrange the bales to balance the load as Moshe, who has always been unusually strong, tossed them up to me. When we had finished we would lie on our backs on the very top, almost falling asleep from exhaustion as the horses, who needed no guiding reins, pulled us back home. The tickle of the stems, the wonderful sense of complete fulfillment at a day's work done, the soaring happiness of being young under the blue sky—that is the strongest and most beautiful reality of my past.

Coming back from the fields on the wagon loaded with sheaves, I used to hum the beautiful melody of Rachel's poem, "And perhaps these things never happened at all. . . ." Whenever I hear it today those moments come back to me; I remember exactly how Moshe used to wake me up from my daydreams by tickling my ear with a stalk of wheat as the wagon jogged along. It is so far from today—but these things must all have happened, otherwise how could I remember them so clearly?

8 · The War of Independence

Around midnight of November 29, 1947, we woke Yael, Udi, and Tzippi and took them to the village community center where everybody had gathered to celebrate. Assi, just two, was left home in bed, but the older children saw the excitement. This was the date the United Nations General Assembly voted to partition Palestine between Arabs and Jews.

The singing and dancing that night worried me, for I was already suspicious of celebrations. There is nearly always a price to pay, a sweep in the opposite direction. The next morning there was a mood of unrest but no anticipation of war. Today it is easy to say that if the Arabs had accepted the plan they would now have a far larger portion of Palestine and the bloodshed and misery on both sides would have been spared. But at the time, as a farmer and a woman, I knew only that I was worried about our cows and our celebrations.

We continued to plow, collect eggs, and do the chores, but we heard the sounds of shooting more and more regularly. We could not know that an entire generation of boys was about to die. I believe it was a generation like no other in history, born and brought up with love and idealism; they were joined by newcomers who came almost straight from the refugee camps and were flung into battle. Their whole way of thinking was unlike anything I have encountered since.

The day after the U.N. vote, eight Jews were killed. By the

end of the week, the figure had risen to thirty-six. Arab armies were gathering on all fronts and terrorism increased. The road to Jerusalem became increasingly dangerous. By the middle of March it was closed, and stayed closed until the alternative "Burma Road" was built in June. For nearly three months I had no word from my parents; the telephone lines were down and our only contact with Jerusalem was the radio, which announced the day's casualties. In our village, as everywhere else, there were fewer and fewer young men.

Moshe was gone a great deal but came home every night. We usually did the 5:00 A.M. milking together; afterwards he would leave, I would get the children to school and see to the rest of the work. We dug trenches around our homes. Devora wrote of those days, "There was no front line and no rear area. They were both the same."

Itzhak Halevy, the son of Moshe's elementary-school teacher, was the first Nahalal-born boy to die. His father, Meshulam, whose Tolstoyan ideas of education—freedom and individuality for the child—sound strikingly contemporary, had a profound influence on all the early classes in Nahalal. Itzhak, handsome and sensitive, was an outstanding student at the Hebrew University, with a deep love and knowledge of nature; his collection of plants and stones was organized for its scientific value. He was killed on January 15 with thirty-four other university students who set out to relieve four settlements under siege near Jerusalem. Their mutilated bodies were found two days later by the British.

The following week a baby boy was born to Moshe's brother, Zorik, and his wife, Mimi. They were living near Haifa, close to another young couple, Erella and Ben-Ami Pachter. Ben-Ami, an old friend and a founder of Kibbutz Hanita, was in charge of the defense of isolated settlements in Western Galilee. Zorik idolized him for his qualities of leadership and character. The two young wives were also close friends. Erella was the beautiful daughter of Devora's brother. Ben-Ami was so handsome that the large number of girls who fell in love with him was something of a joke among us. They were married in November 1947, and Ben-Ami returned to his command the following day.

My cousin Yossi was the first member of our family to be killed. Yossi was the son of my mother's brother David and his wife, Tzippora. They had two younger children, and their Haifa home was a "town house" for all of us. My aunt Tzippora has always been a wonderful homemaker. She would feed us and listen to our troubles. Zorik, especially, used to rush to Aunt Tzippora when he needed consolation. Yossi joined the Palmach after finishing high school (the equivalent of a college education today) and was put in charge of the cultural program at several settlements. He was to be married in April and had just joined a northern kibbutz.

One evening in March, Uncle David telephoned and asked us to come immediately. Moshe drove me to Haifa. When we arrived we learned that for three days the police had run a notice in the newspaper that the body of an unidentified young man with blond hair was in the morgue at the Rothschild Hospital. Aunt Tzippora had told Uncle David, "You must go to the hospital. I'm sure it's Yossi."

"Nonsense," said my uncle David, "there's no fighting, and he's at the kibbutz." Yossi, it turned out, had been absent from the kibbutz; everyone there assumed he was at home.

Uncle David went to the hospital, and discovered that the body was indeed Yossi's. Identification was easy because of a childhood scar behind his ear. He had been found hidden in the Arab market in Haifa. He was not yet twenty years old.

As the police reconstructed the case, Yossi had been in a hurry to get from the lower part of town, near the seashore, to the center, where his parents lived. The Arabs ran taxis on this route, but Jews considered them unsafe and no longer used them, resorting instead to armor-plated buses with Jewish drivers. Witnesses among those waiting for a bus that day, March 10, recalled that some had tried to discourage Yossi from taking an Arab taxi.

"No, that's silly," he had answered. "I was born in Haifa and I've grown up among Arabs. One shouldn't be afraid."

Aunt Tzippora never recovered from the shock of the manner of Yossi's death. I have always thought that he died because of his own brand of heroism. He paid with his life for trusting his neighbors and believing in friendship; this kind of belief is as necessary as our eternal military vigilance.

Now the funerals came so quickly, one after another, there was no period of adjustment between them. We went to few outside Nahalal, but in our village of seventy-five families, twelve sons were buried. We could not go to the funerals of friends in Jerusalem, for the road was closed; and we did not travel to other parts of the country because conditions were so unsettled and one cannot leave a farm for long, even for death. I must have known hundreds of the five thousand boys who lost their lives between November 1947 and March 1948.

After Yossi's funeral I went to our neighbors', for Pnina Dromi was to be married in a few days. I had made dozens of coconut-cornflake cookies, all the while thinking of Yossi. Pnina's mother was famous for her pickles, and there were rows and rows of pickled eggplant and tomatoes and cucumbers in the kitchen, near the stacked baking tins of my cornflake cookies.

This was to be a rather elaborate wedding, with a beautiful

white dress for Pnina. Mine had been the first "big" wedding at Nahalal, but bridal gowns were by now more elaborate, and Pnina's was most impressive, for the father of the groom was Itzhak Ben-Zvi, the head of the National Council (and later the second President of the state of Israel).

Eli Ben-Zvi had been one of the boys in my charge in the Jerusalem scouts, and his parents, Rahel and Itzhak, were friends of my parents. He was a dreamy, idealistic boy and an outstanding student; yet he had joined the Haganah at the age of twelve. Now twenty-four, he was a member of Kibbutz Bet Keshet near Nazareth, the first Palmach settlement. He was in charge of its defense and concerned with the seemingly hopeless task of trying to improve relations with the neighboring Arabs—just as his father, as President, was to be dedicated to the problems of our minority communities.

From my neighbor's kitchen, among the pickles and cakes, I heard our telephone ring. It was Moshe. He told me that nothing was yet certain but that seven boys from Bet Keshet, including Eli, had been attacked by over a hundred Syrian Arabs in the nearby fields. They were presumed killed, Moshe said, but the bodies had not yet been found. He told me not to tell Pnina or her mother; for, until a body has been identified, the army does not consider it a casualty. I went back to their kitchen, leaving the door of our house open so I could hear the phone ring, and continued to bake and joke. I knew Eli was dead; but I was not going to be the one to stop life. Let there be another hour or two of happiness.

When Moshe came home much later, he said, "Yes, they found the bodies." One of the seven, badly wounded, had managed to escape and make his way back to the kibbutz. They had fought to the last bullet.

Every bride and wife took her tragedy in a different way. Pnina sat holding her wedding gown, alternating between tears and hysterical laughter. Now there was the problem of how to notify Eli's parents. Somehow, word had reached Jerusalem, where all communication lines were down, that Eli was missing. I waited near our telephone for a call from his father; the British would allow one call to go through, in view of Ben-Zvi's position. It was a terrible moment when the phone rang and I heard Itzhak Ben-Zvi's voice.

"Where's Eli?" he asked. I could not speak. There would be only this one call; at the other end of the line I saw the father of a boy I had known since childhood, my parents' friend. I did not have it in me to tell him his son was dead. I heard the father saying, "What, what?" and finally I said, "He's gone." Then I shouted, "Give me Amram."

Eli's brother came to the phone and I told him that the funeral would be the next day at Bet Keshet. I stayed behind on the day of the funeral and with a few neighbors removed traces of the wedding preparations.

Ben-Ami was killed on March 27. His assignment, one of the most dangerous, was to guard the poorly armed convoys that were keeping the roads open to our settlements. Forty-seven of Ben-Ami's men and girls were killed in a battle in the north. As he was retreating to Hanita with the survivors, they were ambushed and all were killed.

A night in April about a week later became one of the most terrifying of my life; I had a presentiment of death, but it pointed to the wrong brother. Moshe was called to Jerusalem, under heavy siege for months, on a special assignment; he was to fly up in one of our few Piper Cubs, and I was pleased that he would see my parents, from whom we had had no word all this time.

I gave Moshe a basket of eggs and a jar of farm cream for my family, luxuries long absent from rationed Jerusalem, and off he went. The flight was by way of a kibbutz on the Dead Sea. The next day we heard on the radio that it had been captured by the Arabs.

There was no word from him for two days. During all our wars I have always worried about the men under Moshe; this time alone was I convinced that he had been killed. The battle for the Kastel, an Arab hilltop village about five miles west of Jerusalem, lasted from March 31 to April 9, and the village, whose position was considered impregnable, changed hands three times. When I heard on the radio that it had been captured by the Palmach at a cost of two hundred and fifty men, my usually good intuition left me and I pictured Moshe lying dead on the battlefield. Actually, his assignment had nothing at all to do with the Kastel, but I could not stop crying all night. The next morning, I asked one of the Haganah people at Nahalal to phone Ben-Gurion to learn if there was any news.

Ben-Gurion answered, "No, and tell Ruth there's no need to worry; if anything had happened I would have been notified." The next day we learned that the Piper could not fly out again, and Moshe returned three days later with one of the last motor convoys out of Jerusalem.

Afterwards my mother told me about Moshe's visit. She and Father were using the back entrance of their house rather than the front, which was under almost constant sniper fire. If my mother agreed to do this the danger must have been considerable. When Moshe saw them use the back door, his comment was, "Defeatists!"

The city was sealed off until the secretly built "Burma Road" was completed six weeks later. On April 13, the nurses and doctors in a convoy from Hadassah Hospital were murdered on their way to Mount Scopus. Zorik was killed the following day. Devora wrote later, "Zorik was killed on a Wednesday. That day I could get no rest. I thought it was because the convoy to Mount Scopus had been ambushed and Dr. Yasski [the head of the Hadassah Hospital] killed. I remembered Dr. Yasski with gratitude from the time my son Moshe had been injured."

The battle for the Kastel overlapped in time the battle for Kibbutz Ramat Yohanan, near Haifa, which was fought from April 4 to 14. From the Haifa suburb where Zorik and Mimi lived one could hear the shooting at Ramat Yohanan. A battalion of Druses belonging to the Arab Liberation Army was advancing from Syria and attacking the settlement. Few of us knew much about the Druses then, though men of Druse villages within Israel joined our new army as soon as it was founded. But we did know that they were valiant fighters. They attacked with daggers between their teeth, armed with pistols and sabers. Our besieged settlements, each one on the front line, had practically no ammunition but were still able to send fire against the approaching Druses. Each side came to appreciate the bravery of the other.

Early in April, Mimi arrived at our house with the baby. She often came to stay with me since Zorik was away so much and there was more room at our house than at Devora's, where Aviva was living with her two children. Zorik turned up later that day, driving an armor-plated lorry. He was on leave from his platoon-command course and had a few days to be at home. Uzi, the baby, was about two months old and feeling cranky, and Mimi was grumbling because Zorik was hardly at home. I watched these little scenes and they seemed understandable and familiar. But Zorik was in a good mood, joking and optimistic as usual, though he was deeply affected by the death of Ben-Ami.

As Mimi and Zorik were leaving Nahalal to drive home, I decided to ride with them to a certain crossroads, for I wanted to go to Haifa. Zorik's armored lorry meant safe travel through a dangerous area; at the crossroads I would take the bus. I wanted to see Aunt Tzippora, in mourning for Yossi, and also to find out about arrangements for Reumah's arrival. My sister was expected in Haifa Port soon with the four hundred refugee children she was escorting from the Bergen-Belsen camp. They would be the first children to arrive legally in the new state of Israel.

So I drove to the crossroads with Zorik and Mimi and caught the bus for Haifa. All our buses on this route were protected with plating and had only slits for windows—too small to throw grenades through. Shooting was constant in Haifa, and the lower Arab sector was cut off from the Carmel

above. Zorik joked all during our drive. It was the last time
I saw him alive.

Later, Mimi told us about Zorik's last days. When he heard
the distant shooting, he said he could not enjoy the leave due
him while a nearby settlement was under attack. He was
convinced that he knew exactly what Ben-Ami would do in
such a situation if he were still alive, and how he would plan
the defense of Ramat Yohanan. On Wednesday morning, April
14, Zorik told Mimi that he was leaving because he had to
volunteer. He was going with three friends, also young officers
on leave. Mimi buckled Zorik's dagger to his belt; Zorik kissed
her and Uzi good-bye and left.

The next day Aviva's husband, Israel, arrived at Devora's
house. He was attached to Moshe's unit and there was no reason
for him to be home that day. Devora later wrote a description
of the moment she saw Israel and knew that one of her sons
was dead: "Which one would it be? Moshe, the older one? But
he had suffered so much already, had done his share in the
war. Zorik, the younger? God, but he had hardly begun to
live yet!" Somehow she felt it was Zorik, and it was his name
that she cried out.

Moshe phoned to say that he was going to Ramat Yohanan,
and Mimi and the baby were brought to our house. Mimi was
hysterical with grief and kept screaming, "I know he's alive.
I must go to the field where he's lying." Moshe returned. The
fighting around the settlement, he said, was so heavy it was
impossible to recover the bodies of our dead. He had seen them
through his binoculars, and it was clear they were no longer
alive. Mimi continued to scream; I slapped her to try to calm
her. Devora was extremely brave. She worried about how
Shmuel, who was not home that day, would take it; the older
generation had already been through so much. Aviva wrote
of Zorik's death, "With his life, and with his death, he gave
us life." Devora wrote, "There is no more terrible thing than
parents who have to bury their children." Years later I had
a dream in which the phrase came to me: "In order to save
these boys, we would have to commit national suicide." The
overwhelming odds against this generation of Israeli youth
made each of their deaths a kind of suicide; but it was their
sacrifice that allowed us to survive as a nation.

On Friday, Mimi was still hysterical. I left her with Devora
and went with Moshe to Ramat Yohanan to see if the bodies
could be recovered. But the shooting was still too heavy.
I stood on the veranda of a kibbutz building and looked
through the binoculars at the black dot we knew was Zorik. It
was difficult to see because I was crying so hard. It seemed
impossible that he was dead. Zorik was like a son to me. He

was nine years old when we first met, arguing about my macaroni. Zorik never seemed to me a "typical Dayan," for he was not a lone wolf and not silent or withdrawn. He loved people and loved to laugh. He was not devoted to farming, perhaps because he had to take over such a burden when he was young: he was only eleven when Moshe and I went to Shimron. He enjoyed literature and had been writing poems since childhood, like so many boys from Nahalal and throughout the country who fell in the War of Independence, the Sinai Campaign, the Six-Day War, and in all the troubled years between. The number of posthumously published poems by boys in their teens and early twenties—boys who joined the Haganah when they were twelve or thirteen—surprises even us. In other countries poems about young men dying in war are usually written by older survivors. With us, the boys themselves wrote their poems not long before their deaths.

When we returned to Nahalal, we telephoned my aunt, for Reumah was due the next day with her four hundred children. We could not telephone Jerusalem, so my parents still knew nothing of her arrival or Zorik's death.

Saturday we went again to Ramat Yohanan, but it was still impossible to approach the field where the bodies lay. That day we took a small car and drove to Haifa, going by a round-about route through the Carmel Mountains, for travel on the main road was almost impossible. We reached Aunt Tzippora's and telephoned the Port, which we saw below under sporadic fire. Nobody was permitted to come down, we were told; the children would be taken immediately to their new homes in armored buses, and Reumah would be brought up to us. And I had to tell my aunt and uncle, who had just buried Yossi, about Zorik.

Reumah arrived in a happy mood. On board ship and in Europe, there had been no news of developments at home; there was no war yet, Haifa Port was still open, the British were still here. She had found toys in Europe for our children, and was delighted to have brought the refugee children to their new home without, as in the case of earlier refugees, having to run a blockade and land illegally and secretly on some deserted beach.

I had to tell Reumah about Yossi, Ben-Ami, the other boys from Nahalal and Jerusalem, and Zorik, her childhood play-mate. So our meeting was overshadowed by tragic circumstances; the excitement of the return was stifled by the atmosphere of death. We put Reumah and the toys in our little car and returned to Nahalal. Ours was the last car that made it safely along that road. The following morning, four passengers driving the same route were all killed—not by irregular Arab forces, but by men from the Trans-Jordanian Frontier Force under British command.

The next day was Zorik's funeral. When he was finally brought home, we stood beside the black-draped coffin; candles were burning, and the weather was terribly warm. It was impossible to remain very long in the small room, for his body had lain in the field for three days. At the funeral, Mimi held a volume of poems that she had intended to give him. In Devora's house, a photograph of the trees in the field where Zorik fell hung on the wall until she died.

About two weeks after the funeral, an old friend brought up among the Arabs and the Druses came to Moshe on a strange mission. His object was to try to bring over to our side the Syrian Druse battalion that had fought at Ramat Yohanan. He made contact with the Druses and persuaded them to send representatives for secret talks with Moshe. At this dramatic encounter, Moshe spoke to them in his usual unemotional way and convinced them that it was in their interest to defect from the army of Syria, in which they had always been an insecure minority. The Druses could not understand how a man whose only brother had been killed by their fighters a short time earlier could be speaking to them of peace, for blood revenge is a tradition among them. Yet Moshe did this, and has been a hero to the Druses ever since.

For years now, at Maskit, I have had visits from Druse villages practically every day of the week. Sometimes it is about the baskets they weave for Maskit, sometimes it is about university education for their younger generation, for their traditions are now changing. I never associate my friends among the Druses with Zorik's death. Shmuel used to be disturbed by these contacts and told me he could not bear them, but Devora never held this attitude.

The battle at Ramat Yohanan was revived during a conversation I had with a Druse a few years after the war when I was visiting a Druse village where carpets were being woven for Maskit. I was having coffee with the sheik and was introduced to another Druse, whom I had never met. I asked where he was from. "Jebel Druse," he replied, referring to the high mountain in Syria that is the Druse homeland.

"How long have you been in Israel?" I asked my new Druse acquaintance.

He smiled and said, "Since 1948." Then he made a joke —a good one to anyone who knows a little of our history— "I'm a Mahalnik." Mahal is the abbreviated name of the organization of Jewish volunteers from abroad who came to fight in the War of Independence; this Druse soldier had taken part in the battle for Ramat Yohanan—but on the Arab side. "We all talked about your brother-in-law," he said to me, "as one of the bravest men we had ever seen. We remembered him especially, because he was on the verge of death, yet reached for his dagger when we came near him." Such a gesture was exactly the one a Druse would have made. I think this feeling of mutual respect must have been in Moshe's mind when he talked to the men who killed his brother. The Druse, whose religion is secret and whose bravery is a tradition, are a fascinating people.

Today, when I open the heavy volume *In Memoriam*—nine hundred and ten pages, each one with biographies and photos of our young men who fell between November 1947 and March 1949—I notice something unusual. The listings are alphabetical. The very first is Amnon Akhar, born in Tel Aviv, died at eighteen in the Negev. The second is Yaakov Abutbul, born in Haifa, died at nineteen in Galilee. The next three are Druses.

Less than two weeks after Zorik's death, another Nahalal boy was killed: Aryeh Slutzky, volunteer on the dangerous convoys to the settlements, this time in the Jerusalem area. On April 16, Moshe Zaharoni died in the battle for Safed. He was a member of the Nahalal family circle. Four days later, Eliezer Shvat of Nahalal died at the age of eighteen; his brother Menahem was to die six months later in battle.

A day or so after our forces captured Haifa, I stood looking at some fried eggs congealing on a row of enamel plates at the Haj Amin Arab Hospital. The patients had fled with the rest of Haifa's Arab population. Those cold fried eggs represented my first view of the enemy as ordinary human beings.

I was in Haifa that day with Moshe, who had come to inspect captured sites and to prevent looting—of which, I am sorry to say, there was some evidence, for some Arab shop windows had been smashed in. It would be absurd to claim that every Jew at every moment is capable of complete self-control. Considering what the city had been through, sporadic acts of looting were understandable, though never justifiable.

But another part of the truth was revealed that day in Haifa that our side has never adequately announced to the world. This is an issue I have often argued about with Arab friends who live abroad; Arabs who were in Israel at the time know what happened, even though they do not always choose to recall it: Why did practically all of Haifa's Arabs—forty thousand men, women, and children—run away during April 1948, and become refugees? The Arabs have always loudly maintained that the Jews forced them to leave. Nothing is black and white in this complex issue, but this accusation is simply not true. The case is especially clear in Haifa, where the largest Arab evacuation took place.

Proof lies with British police documents later found by the Haganah—and the British police have never been accused of being pro-Jewish. For instance, a memorandum dated April 26, 1948, marked "secret" and signed by the British Criminal Investigation Department, reads in part: "Every effort is being made by the Jews to persuade the Arab population to stay and carry on with their normal lives, to get their shops and businesses open and to be assured that their lives and interests will be safe."

Another memo of the same date states: "An appeal has been made to the Arabs by the Jews to reopen their shops and businesses. . . . At a meeting yesterday afternoon Arab leaders reiterated their determination to evacuate the entire Arab population and they have been given the loan of ten 3-ton military trucks as from this morning to assist the evacuation."

In other words, the Arabs, aided by British transport, saw to it that their own people left Haifa; they were convinced they would shortly be returning with their victorious armies. Wealthy Arabs had little trouble making new homes; it was the poor and uneducated who suffered. Where there was responsible Arab leadership, as in Nazareth, most of the population remained.

Some people in Israel believe that life would be simpler if there were no Arabs here. But the fact is that they are here, and many families trace their roots back hundreds of years. What our wars—our victories and the Arab defeats—prove is that both sides must learn to live in peace. And this will happen only when the Arabs, even those who believe that endless wars bring nothing but endless suffering, learn to reread history.

My own actions during our visit to Haifa were on a housewifely, and not entirely honorable level. I stole half a sack of sugar. Among the establishments Moshe had to visit was a sugar factory, and I could not resist looting a little. Sugar had long been rationed at Nahalal; when I saw a half-empty sack, I took it. I gave in to the same weakness after the Sinai Campaign, when I happened to be with Paula and David Ben-Gurion and saw a small ceramic jar that had been made in China. Paula gave me a terrible talking-to, for she did not approve of these lapses of mine.

In Haifa that same day I joined Lorna Wingate for breakfast. She was a widow—Orde had been killed in Burma in 1944 —and came often to Palestine to help our cause. We sat on the veranda of the Zion Hotel and looked out across the blue bay. The shooting had stopped, and it seemed like the morning of any normal day.

. . . . .

Our War of Independence did not start officially until May 14, 1948. On that day the state of Israel was proclaimed by Ben-Gurion in a broadcast from Tel Aviv as bombs fell on the city and as the armies of six neighboring Arab countries invaded the borders set by the U.N. Our army was not officially established until June 28, when our soldiers pledged allegiance to the new fighting forces; this was when the Haganah officially became "Zva Haganah L'Israel," or "Zahal," the Israel Defense Forces. All those who had died before, like Zorik, who fell exactly one month earlier, were killed before war was declared.

Moshe was assigned the defense of Kibbutz Degania (where he was born) with a Haganah unit. The decisive fighting there took place between May 15 and 20. I spent one night with Moshe at Degania, for our combat operations were still informal and this was another civilian settlement that had become the front. I went with Moshe whenever I could, getting there however I could. The atmosphere was still not that of a regular army; our men rushed from one crucial point to another, coming home whenever possible for a bath and to see how their farms were going.

The dying continued. On May 18, David Lis was killed in the fight for Degania. He fell trying to rescue a wounded friend and his last words were, "Don't worry, I'll get you out of here." He left a wife, a Nahalal girl, and a baby daughter. Seven months earlier, his wife had lost her brother, Eytan Avidav of Nahalal, killed in Austria in an operation rescuing Jews from Europe. Eytan, too, left poems behind; one was called "My Quiet Village" and recalled the happy times of Nahalal as seen from a distant country in wartime.

When you walked through our village now, you wondered which family would be next. And the Nahalal Circle made it even worse. You walked around it and passed a house in mourning; then you repassed it. There was no getting away from it. You remembered all the boys and their pranks. "If only he were here to steal another car," I thought to myself of Zorik. I remembered how he would take Yael for a ride around the Circle on his horse, and how Yael used to say "Once more round the Circle!"

On May 31 death struck Amos Fine, born to Nahalal parents —and grandparents, who were among the first guardians of our settlements. (His cousin, Mordechai Hod, born in Kibbutz Degania, is today the commander of our air force.) Amos was killed while mining a bridge; yet his view of war was not what you would expect from a demolition expert. Among his writings he left an essay called "To My Revolver." In it he wrote:

The good years, when Moshe was a farmer and we worked together

Gevaey

Zvi at the age of 15,
the time of his diary and
our romance

With Moshe in Venice,
en route to London soon
after our marriage

The wedding party at Nahalal: Moshe and I, my sister Reumah, Moshe's
parents Shmuel and Devora, my parents Rahel and Zvi Shwarz

Delta Studio, Yeo

Gevaey, Fürst, Haifa

Giving Yael her breakfast
at Nahalal, after milking
the cows

My temporary home in Tel Aviv
in 1937. It was pulled down
in 1971.

With Yael at our farm. The children all had chores—
in the henhouse, vegetable garden, and orchard.

Assi, Yael, and Udi, 1962

On the opposite page: This little boy lived with his parents in the leper village at Albert Schweitzer's hospital in Lambaréné.
Clara Urquhart

Yael and Assi in the Zahala garden

Entertaining one of the four wives of General Idi Amin on a visit
to Israel, not long before he expelled all Israelis from Uganda

During Eleanor Roosevelt's visit to Israel, I watched her pleasure
in human encounters, as with this immigrant from Arabia.

Prior, Tel-Aviv

Above: Inspecting raw wool drying in the sun in the village of Porat. It was settled in the early 1950's by immigrants from the Libyan Desert, where they had lived in caves deep underground.   *At right:* Checking rugs of weavers from Bayhan in Southern Arabia, where a small community of Jews had lived in peace with the Arabs.

Below: With Moshe Ben David, born in Bayhan, who has been working with me as a silversmith for twenty-three years. Today he is in charge of Maskit's jewelry department and, with equal skill, works both modern and traditional designs.

Prior, Tel-Aviv

With an Arab potter in Gaza, nearly five years after the 1967 war

Udi's son on a visit to Zahala, surrounded by Moshe's collection

© *Isaac Berez, Tel-*

You are evil! . . . I hate you, I hate you exceedingly. I am ashamed to carry you but I have no choice, and so I hide you beneath my coat that no one may see my shame. . . . But there will come a day when man will no longer seek the life of his fellow, and waves of security will envelop all mankind so that I will no longer need to rely on you for my safety or ask the help of you, there on my hip. Then I will take hold of you and break you into pieces. . . .

Like so many others, he came to terms with the likelihood that he would die. Some time before he was killed he wrote to his wife, preparing her for what could happen. "I could almost cry that I have left you alone, but I would have contempt for myself if I did not do my duty toward you and toward those who come after me."

I think the men were perhaps happier than the women about the May fourteenth proclamation. We mothers were too busy for much rejoicing; in the months following the departure of the British we rushed about keeping track of our children like hens after their chicks. We were not sure whether the British were still in control of the nearby airfield; there was bombing by Iraqi and Syrian planes, and Nahalal later had its turn. For us women, I think the physically hard farm work was a saving factor.

On June 9, two days before the first truce arranged by the U.N., I was again baking for a wedding. One of the three daughters of our neighbors the Liebermans was to be married that evening to a Nahalal boy, an officer in Moshe's unit.

This time I had one of my premonitions and so chose to bake in my own kitchen. I made an eight-egg torte, the standard Nahalal offering brought to friends' weddings. The phone rang that morning, too, and I learned that Itzhak Livneh, the husband of the Liebermans' older daughter, was dead. Itzhak had a remarkable character. He chose to work with immigrant youth, and his love of nature and knowledge of the land made him an outstanding tracker. He was a pianist, and he also wrote poetry:

I would like to be
As the echo of the field's breathing,
As the play of light in the empty space,
Winged with wings of Song,
Swept along like the running wave,
And driven like the wind;
As a joy that forgot its cause,
As a festival moving on and on
Like everlasting youth. . . .

Like so many others, he too had a premonition of death:

So clearly do I see the final day:
The morning smiling as it always smiles . . .

I'll gaze with the same clear look at the tranquil blue skies
Wondering, I'll see that I am twenty years old,
And with no pain I shall leave life, and all,
And you as well. . . .

The life of the Liebermans' son Oded also ended in tragedy.
In 1943 a horde of Iraqi soldiers stationed at a nearby British air
base stormed into Nahalal. Our boys drove them off, but in the
fight Oded's spine was injured. He seemed to recover, but a
few years later he had to be sent to an American hospital. He
died in October 1949.

I was to see Oded in America, for in the closing days of June,
Moshe and I were preparing for an almost surrealistic trip
abroad. Moshe was to accompany the body of the American
colonel Mickey Marcus to West Point for burial, and I decided
to go along. Reumah was still with us in Nahalal, so the children were in good hands.

Our lives were unpredictable then. Just before we left, I spent
fifteen hours in a café in Natanya, waiting for Moshe. We had
been on our way home from Moshe's headquarters, near Tel
Aviv, when he was called to take part in the affair of the *Altalena,*
a supply ship that tried to land arms. "Wait for me at this café,"
Moshe told me when he received orders to go to the *Altalena.*
I had no idea what was happening, but I stayed at the café with
an officer from eleven in the morning till two the following
morning. We heard shooting; the whole town of Natanya was
under curfew, so no one could move. Finally a car arrived to
take me to Tel Aviv, where we had breakfast on the veranda of
the Kaete Dan Hotel (forerunner of the present Dan). Everybody
was sure the *Altalena* would explode—it did not—but we watched
it sink. Then we went home to Nahalal and packed for America.

If I were to pick the ideal moment to see the New York skyline
for the first time, it would not be during the interlude of an
uneasy truce in a terrible war. Since I really had no business
being along, I stayed out of official sight. This was to be the way
I usually felt later on, when I accompanied Moshe on public
occasions. They were always awkward for me, even when I was
properly invited. There are practically no photographs of the
smiling wife at Moshe's side. I stayed out of the picture.

During the twenty-six-hour flight with Colonel Marcus's coffin,
I spent my time embroidering colonel's "pips" on Moshe's uniform. I don't know how I turned them out to look reasonable,
though I had seen enough British insignia of rank. Nobody in
our own army, barely a week old, had thought about such
trimmings.

Emma Marcus was at the airport when we landed, but I did
not meet her until years later. I was not allowed off the plane

until everybody else had left, because I had no reason for being along except to be with Moshe. We stayed at "Hotel 14," the United States headquarters for our arms-purchasing mission. I had no idea that the Copacabana was a famous night club; to me it was just the place downstairs in the building where we bought armaments.

I stayed away from official activities, preferring not to know what was going on. There were other things for me to do. From his mother in Nahalal, I had brought a jar of homemade olives for Oded Lieberman, who was in a hospital for the incurably paralyzed in Brooklyn. It was a horrible, depressing place; Oded was by far the youngest patient. A few months later he was brought home, where he died the following year.

I met many of Moshe's American cousins, several of whom were doctors, and started my usual practice of inquiring whether better medical facilities could be found for Oded. I also looked up my mother's American cousins. (In both my family and Moshe's, one set of grandparents went from Russia to Palestine, the other from Russia to America.) Some were charming, but one couple was not.

Wearing a perfectly nice skirt, and, I thought, quite properly dressed, I went to meet them. "Oh, is that the type of dress you wear in Palestine?" they asked. The husband took me to the top of the Empire State Building, and bought me a small souvenir penknife—a gift he did not seem to be able to stop talking about. When all three of us went to a posh restaurant, they treated me as though I had arrived straight from the jungle. I did use my knife and fork differently: the English way. They decided they would order for me since I could not possibly know how. An enormous chicken arrived on my plate, and they kept discussing this fantastic bird. I did not tell them I bred the things at home. I began to feel sick, partly because of the size of the enormous steaks all around me and the thought of my parents under siege in rationed Jerusalem. Finally I could not bear it any more, and went to the restroom and vomited. My cousins were worried about what the owner of the restaurant would think.

The racks and racks of dresses and coats at Macy's were also hard for me to take. There seemed to be millions of them. Still, this was probably the first and last time I enjoyed shopping, for I bought clothes for Aviva and Reumah and all the children with money my parents had given me; we were still using English pounds, whose value was good. It was stifling hot at Macy's; I was wearing a high-necked dress of Zelda's (our trip was on such short notice that I had borrowed some of her clothes) and nearly fainted. But I think it was mostly those endless rows of clothes.

On the drive to West Point for the funeral there was a stop halfway to the cemetery: suddenly our whole line of black limousines stopped at an inn and everybody trooped inside for a hearty meal. To me, coming from our funerals, it seemed terrible. But of course there is nothing wrong with eating, and no doubt I would easily accept such an interruption today. At the cemetery I more or less hid behind a tree on the beautiful grounds and was not introduced to anybody except General Omar Bradley, who was very kind and modest.

Moshe was anxious to get back home. As regular flights were not yet operating and none of our planes could be spared from defense duty, the only plane that could take him was one of the two chartered KLM's that carried our first paper currency, bank notes printed in America. Moshe was given the status of guard and flew home with the money. There was an unbreakable law against women on these planes, and though I cried a good deal, it was no use. I was stuck at "Hotel 14" with no money to buy a ticket and no commercial planes flying even if I had been able to afford one. Then Teddy Kollek (now Mayor of Jerusalem), who was in America purchasing arms, thought of something. He needed a document taken to Rome, a highly secret contract with a foreign government about using their flag to ship arms; this I was to deliver. I was also to take to Israel some special paper used to photocopy maps, and a little bag of radio crystals.

In Rome I bought a copy of the *Daily American* with a headline stating that General Allon had captured Ramleh and Lydda. Not a word about Moshe. Eager to get home I tried to find a berth on a ship, but chances were better on the plane bringing Mahal volunteers to Israel. I was squeezed into something with two propellers, jammed together with South African Mahalniks, and we flew to Israel. Lyyda airport was still under fire, so we landed at a tiny airstrip near Haifa. Here, in the middle of a war and at nothing resembling a real airport, a customs office had already been established. I was asked to pay duty on my baggage, not on any of my dresses but on those valuable radio crystals and map paper. Once again I cried, and as usual it was no help. I simply left the things there. Eventually the right persons would come to collect them.

I took a taxi to Nahalal, wondering where Moshe might be. I didn't know he had anything to do with the Ramleh operation, where in fact he played a dashing and decisive role. That evening we had a lovely coincidence, for Moshe just happened to come home from the south to see the children and take a bath. The next morning he was off again and I was back in my work clothes.

On July 9 the first truce ended. Israel had accepted the extension proposed by the U.N.; the Arabs rejected it. The Arabs made three air attacks on Tel Aviv and bombed Jerusalem for the first time in history. Moshe was in the Ramleh-Lydda area. There, in the hand-to-hand fighting for a small village, a Nahalal boy,

Josef Bentwich, made local history. He helped capture a heavy
Jordanian tank, which had been knocked out, and put it back in
working order, though he had never had any previous dealings
with such a vehicle. Labeled "The Nahalal Express," it became a
useful part of our underequipped army. In this still informal
war, Aviva and I were able to go and have a look at the tank at
the commander's headquarters in Lydda a few days later. The
"Burma Road" was opened and Reumah, who had been such a
help all these months in our home, returned to Jerusalem.
She joined the army immediately and was assigned to the press
office, for she had worked as a journalist in Europe.

On July 16, Assi and I were next door in the Liebermans'
kitchen. Yael was at home doing homework with a friend; Udi
had as usual managed to run off somewhere with a few other
children. The siren sounded, and bombs fell almost immediately:
Iraqi planes were over Nahalal. One bomb uprooted a tree near
our house. We just had time to run to the Liebermans' trench
and I fell on top of Assi, who began screaming. After a moment
or two I rushed out to find Udi, who turned up in the village
center in a trench with his friends, perfectly safe.

Yael was her usual cool self. With amazing presence of mind
for a nine-year-old, she rushed her friend out into our trench
as soon as the siren sounded. The tree fell across it but both
children were unhurt although a good many shrapnel holes were
made in our house; in fact, nobody in the village was wounded.
The other little girl was hysterical, but I did not notice the
slightest nervous reaction in Yael.

On July 18, the day the Arabs agreed to a second cease-fire,
Josef Bentwich was killed on the Egyptian front while driving
the tank he had repaired.

Moshe returned from the Negev to learn that he had been
appointed Brigade Commander of Jerusalem. The four of us
would be going with him to a new home, for this was unlike the
assignments of most officers, who did their military jobs and returned at intervals to their farms. At Nahalal, the wives and
children of such officers stayed behind to run things. This was
day-to-day work and Moshe would not be able to commute.
Shmuel was upset at our decision to move the whole family, for
he believed our children should be brought up on moshav ideals
and not exposed to city life. But Moshe thought otherwise, and
said, "We're husband and wife. Who knows what can happen
when you are separated. We are a family, and we'll stick together."

Whenever a Nahalal farmer accepted an "outside" job he had
to request permission to do so from the moshav council; this
Moshe did, and it was granted. We were lucky in finding a good
man to run our farm during our absence. Years later, after he
moved to another moshav, he turned up at my Maskit office to

show me a falcon he had carved out of wood. "Ruth," he said, "I've been looking over our accounts" (something our family rarely did) "and I find I owe you a heifer." So Udi, who was then running our farm, received a heifer with a long pedigree.

Moshe and I and the three children traveled from Nahalal to Jerusalem, taking the "Burma Road" for the final ascent. It was a wild drive. The road was barely visible and went down valleys and over rocks. We were to stay at my parents' home until we found a suitable house. They were away, but Reumah was there to help us get settled.

On the morning of August 3, when we had been in Jerusalem less than a week, Reumah and I were washing the floors, using bathwater, the accepted practice during Jerusalem's long water shortage. The children were all off playing. Suddenly we heard a strange noise. From the balcony we saw a small plane just taking off; it made a loud coughing sound, fell like a bomb, and crashed at a wooded spot near the Valley of the Cross, an area that had been part of my youth with Zvi.

Without knowing exactly what we could do, we telephoned army headquarters, the police, Magen David Adom (the Israeli Red Cross), grabbed a kettle of boiling water and some towels, and raced outside. Moshe's car was there with the keys inside; that morning he had been picked up by a driver. I had a vague idea of how to drive and we started off, making for the dirt road that led to where the little plane had crashed. The surrounding heights were still held by Arabs, so this area was exposed to enemy fire. We soon came to a military roadblock. "You can't pass," we were told.

"But a plane has just crashed," I said.

"And what do you intend to do about it?" asked one of the soldiers. "The right people will be along soon to take care of things." I started to argue with the soldiers, telling them I was the wife of Moshe Dayan, the military commander of this sector —the first time in my life I used that phrase—but it made no difference. More soldiers and officers arrived on foot. After much discussion one of them let us through and we drove close to the plane, which was in a clump of trees. No other vehicle was able to come as close as ours, because we had arrived by a different route.

Then I heard the name "Zohara," and knew whom death had picked this time. I thought immediately of Shmulik, killed just fifteen months earlier . . . death again in this incredible chain of killings in which we were living. This time the crash ended a love story that had something in it of Greek tragedy.

The two young people who had just been killed were Zohara Leviatov, a girl of nineteen who was an air force pilot, and Emanuel Rotstein, twenty-one, also an air force pilot. I had never met Zohara, but I knew a great deal about her because there were many threads connecting me to Shmulik Kaufman, the boy she planned to marry. Shmulik was killed in May 1947, at the kibbutz where he and Zohara were both in the Palmach. They had both just been released from the organization and granted permission to go abroad together to study. In the period before the establishment of the state it was possible to think of leaving home in spite of the tension. Once the situation began to crystallize, this attitude changed completely.

Friday morning, although he had been already released from service, Shmulik was asked to go out on a brief training exercise. He waved good-bye to Zohara, busy packing their things in their tent, and was killed by an exploding grenade. Zohara was only seventeen; she had already taken part in a Palmach action and been wounded, but she wanted to study medicine. After Shmulik's death she agreed almost without emotion to her parents' suggestion she go to America to study: "I will be doing, alone, what we dreamed of doing together." She was admitted to Columbia University immediately, an unusual tribute to her record, and was outstanding in her studies.

On November 29, 1947, partition day, she intended to return home; instead she was the only woman chosen for a special course for pilots in America. She passed brilliantly and came home in the spring. On the morning of the crash she had just returned to duty after a short leave in Jerusalem. Lieutenant Rotstein was at the controls of the plane.

Reumah and I stood by our car. Finally an officer said, "Well, we can't wait for the ambulance." Soldiers lifted the two bodies and placed them in the back of our car. The plane had not caught fire, and the bodies were not disfigured. Zohara was wearing a bright green skirt and had long, dark, curly hair. She was not yet twenty years old. The doors of the car could not be closed with the two bodies in the back, so a soldier sat in back and held the doors, and we could see Zohara's shoes as the car drove off.

There was nothing for me and Reumah to do but start the long walk home, carrying our miserable kettle and wet towels. My mind was filled with Shmulik, and his sister, and his cousin, and how we all existed with death and with love. Young people today, of the age that Zohara and Shmulik were when they died, know nothing of how they felt and why they acted as they did.

In Jerusalem I knew Shmulik slightly as a young boy, and his parents and mine, as I must say often in this listing of the dead, were friends. His father, Dr. Yehudah Even-Shmuel, is a scholar who compiled one of the best-known Hebrew dictionaries. Although I did not know Zohara, I heard much about her from her family. In those days Jerusalem was small; her parents lived in the same house as Shmuel Dayan did when he stayed in the city.

Zohara and Shmulik's generation differed from mine. When

we were young, we deliberately turned our backs on higher education. These two, and many others like them, were eager for learning. But theirs was a genuine interest, unlike that of many young people today who often go to university because their parents want them to.

After his son's death, Dr. Even-Shmuel published a thick memorial volume containing his letters and writings. Zohara's family did the same after their daughter was killed. Unless one reads the volumes—and Zohara's alone runs to six hundred and fourteen pages—it is hard to sense the beauty of those two brief lives. Her letters to Shmulik, written whenever they were apart for more than a few hours, are full of plans for the future and a love of living.

Many were written to him after he had been killed, simply because she could not stop. After she went to America, in August 1947, she wrote home describing the autumn colors, supermarkets and football games, her job in a biological laboratory, and, during the pilot's course, "how you make a plane go into a tailspin," complete with diagrams. But the undercurrent of every letter is her desolate sense of loss.

In a letter to her parents, after a long poetic description of her first sight of snow, she reluctantly mentions her examination marks: "I've received very high grades. Pure luck. I'm not saying this out of false modesty but really, I don't know why I should have done so well." English gave her a little trouble, but in chemistry and physics she was outstanding: "Strange, because I always liked the humanities and thought science was not for me. . . ."

In America in the late forties she notes: "Life here is so secure and predictable. People look for sensations to arouse their interest, but by and large everything is ordered and safe, and personal plans almost always work out. This makes the American a very different type of person from the Israeli." She was hungry for news from home, and grieved at reports that one after another of her friends had been killed.

She bitterly opposed the sentimental view that the young people of her generation went joyously to their death, and the notion that it is a fine thing to die for one's country. In one of her letters to Shmulik written after his death she tells him:

Today I received the memorial booklet about the fourteen who died at the bridges. It disturbed me terribly. Who knows better than we, Shmulik, that we do not love death? Nobody goes to his death joyfully. Everyone who sets out believes he will return. You, Shmulik, didn't go to meet your death, and if you had been given the choice you wouldn't have gone to die, for you loved life. And the same with them. Not one of them wanted to die, not one went into this action with the thought that it would be the last, for nobody on earth believes in his own death.

Do you remember when we spoke about death? I always said to you, "How can I die? What does it mean, that I won't exist? How will the world be able to keep going?" We laughed at death because we didn't know its meaning. Now you already have some experience with it, so it doesn't seem so impossible to you. But to me it seemed some kind of invention, and if not an invention, at any rate something apart from us. And now . . .

A long letter to Shmulik's father, written on a rainy December evening in New York, closes with:

Despite the fact that everything is so beautiful, I find things without any rhyme or reason. It is precisely because everything is so beautiful, new, and interesting that I feel such great pain. . . . I still have not fully grasped the idea that Shmulik is part of the past. It is still not clear to me who could have taken him, where he has gone, and why it is impossible to wish to bring him back.

9 · Weavers and Silversmiths in Tents

All the fighting, all the deaths and tragedies, brought us our state. With the state came newcomers—displaced persons from camps in Europe and refugees from Arab countries. For me, the state of Israel began not with the War of Independence, but with the newcomers. The war was the price that had to be paid to build a nation that would absorb immigrants.

Our move to Jerusalem reflected this change. Life which had been grim became gay. Because of Moshe's position as Brigade Commander of Jerusalem, his political contacts with the Jordanians on border and armistice issues, and his appointment in 1950 as Commanding Officer, Southern Command, our house became a social center for diplomats and political leaders. And because our home turned out to be a sort of commune, these social encounters were lively and informal.

This was not, I must admit, what Moshe had in mind. When we started looking for a place, Moshe wanted something small. He did not like big houses and preferred being alone with his family in peace and quiet. We ended up with my having my way. I like people and like being with them, and when in the course of our house-hunting we saw the big empty mansion of Abkarius Bey, with its enormous rooms and bay windows, I decided to accept the challenge of filling it with life. We had looked at many others; house-hunting in Jerusalem was a problem, for few buildings had escaped bomb damage and the city was much smaller in 1948 than it is today.

Abkarius Bey, whose wife was Jewish, was a lawyer who had left Jerusalem. Both Moshe and I had a strange feeling about moving into a house taken over by the Custodian of Enemy Property. It was against our principles. I knew the owner was alive somewhere, but at least he was not penniless. The problem with furniture was the same. We had none, and the arrangement was to buy things from a warehouse managed by the Custodian. Everything was listed and the money put into accounts to await a peace settlement. I thought I could never touch property left by fleeing Arabs and now I was furnishing my house in this manner. But human nature is good at rationalization, and I thought, If I don't use these things, somebody else will. Everything is recorded and awaiting the owners' return.

We were entitled to an official residence, but I opposed that. Udi and Assi were boisterous children, and I refused to spend my days shouting at them not to ruin the official furniture. Educationally this may not have been the wisest thing, but I wanted to have a tranquil household. So, with a loan from my parents, we were free of worries about public property.

The day after we took over the house I found a woman there cleaning up glass splinters from the windows that had been shattered by shelling from the Old City. She had been sent by the authorities to do the basic cleaning, and this was how Simha became part of our family for twenty years. Simha changed our lives and she was in a way responsible for Maskit's existence. If Simha had not taken over as she did, I would not have been free to organize Maskit, starting on a shoestring in immigrant villages and ending doing international business in a modern skyscraper.

Simha was about fifty—to this day nobody knows exactly how old she is—and had been working as a maid since she was thirteen. She was of Kurdish origin, had married three times and had four children, the first when she was fifteen. The last of the three husbands, Simha later told me, was the one she really loved.

I had no intention of hiring a maid. Away from the farm, I thought, it would be hard to fill my time in a city house, even a big one. But I had decided to rent rooms to a few boarders. We now had six enormous rooms plus a huge living room and dining room. Downstairs was a kitchen and three more rooms (later made into two flats). When Simha asked whether I would hire her by the hour to wash floors, I looked around at all this space and said yes.

I later learned that she had arranged to be sent to our house. She was anxious to be close to a high-ranking officer because her oldest son had been killed in the war and she wanted desperately to keep the second out of the army. She thought that if she worked for Moshe this would not be hard. I never succeeded in explaining to Simha that the Israeli army did not operate on the basis of favors.

Almost from the day she arrived, Simha ignored my claims that I loved housekeeping, and I was soon not allowed in my own kitchen. If I tried to prepare a meal she would say, "What, you don't like my cooking?" in an offended tone. And she was a wonderful cook. Besides exotic Arab delicacies, she could prepare dishes like gefillte fish because she had worked for a German professor and his wife. Even today, over seventy and in poor health, Simha helps me prepare for parties and is still offended when I try to assist her.

She was soon making meals for fifteen people a day: our family, plus eight or ten boarders or visitors. People who rented rooms saw that the food was good and asked to eat with us; Aviva and Israel and their children lived in our house, university students and officers from Moshe's commando unit boarded and visited, and Shmuel and Devora were often in Jerusalem.

The children were in good schools. Yael was at my old school, and had several of my former teachers. She was even thrown out once for the same reason I had been—bringing frogs into the classroom. Even at nine she was a good student and spent much time reading. Udi, on the other hand, was never interested in studies, but he had a lively time with his friends. Assi, not yet three, went to a nursery school just down the street. In winter Simha used to carry him there so that the little prince would not get muddy. I disapproved, but we were all intimidated by Simha and there was little I could do. She fell in love with Assi from the start, defending him against Udi, who was inclined to hit his little brother. Simha slept in the same room with the boys because, for all her matriarchal power, she was frightened of sleeping alone. Bombs still fell from time to time on Jerusalem, and so did one early missile. At such times, Simha would sleep with Assi in the cellar. Snipers' bullets occasionally hit the street where the children played, and Yael once brought one into the house still "hot."

To say that our sons were high-spirited would be an understatement. Their adventures were unusual and entertaining, and we were occasionally involved with the police. Once, the daughter of our very proper neighbor (Eliezer Kaplan, the first Minister of Finance) was working in the garden and uncovered a skull, which looked suspiciously as though it had been recently buried.

"It's those Dayan children," the girl's mother said accusingly. "Who else could think of such a thing?" She was perfectly correct. Assi was annoyed at not being allowed to join his big brother and friends in their "secret society." The older boys had removed a skull from an Arab cemetery and hidden it in our house, so Assi took the skull and hid it in our neighbors' garden.

Nahalal was certainly the best place for the boys. I am convinced that when children have definite, useful chores, as they do in a farm village, everybody is much better off. But even at Nahalal it seemed to me that the boys were often about to kill each other. Moshe found it hard to understand my concern, because when he was around things were calm. The moment he left Udi and Assi were at each other once more.

Simha's bedtime stories for the children were a ritual that lasted for years. They were always about "Juha," an Arabic folk figure who constantly gets into trouble. After the children were asleep, Simha would return to her chores and work until eleven at night. She loved her family, took enormous pride in her work, and even insisted on washing all the bed linen herself because she claimed that the laundry was bad for them. I bought her a washing machine, which she managed to break in the third week; she did not believe in such gadgets. And Simha was the only one who could get Moshe to take his pills. She could not read or write, but she was an enormous influence on all of us.

Her deep feeling of family integrity became clear soon after we met. She had a little granddaughter, orphaned at three months when Simha's son was killed. The mother could not keep the child, and Simha's own money was enough for just her own children. The infant was placed in the Women's International Zionist Organization (WIZO) Baby Home. Zelda, who worked there, told me how this beautiful child was so different from a group of immigrant babies just arrived from the Arabian peninsula in a shocking state of malnutrition. A Jerusalem couple wanted to adopt Simha's granddaughter and Zelda asked me to try to get Simha's permission.

"Look," I argued, "it's the chance of a lifetime for the baby. When people adopt a child they love it even more than if he were their own. She'll have every advantage."

Simha would not be persuaded. "I don't care if she washes floors for a living. She must carry on my son's identity." She would not go to visit the child. "The moment they know I'm making a little money, they'll park her on me, and I don't want that either. I want her to have what the Home can give her." She turned out to be right. The child did get an education which Simha could never have given her and is today a trained nurse at Tel Hashomer Hospital.

With so little to do at home, I put a chicken coop in the back yard so we could have more than the ration of eggs. But as fodder was rationed too, we fed the chickens leftovers from the table and they did not lay well. I also brought some geese from Nahalal, and they wandered around on our street. We visited our farm often, though there seemed less and less chance of returning. I sometimes brought a turkey back for a festive meal, a rarity in those days.

Our regular guests were diplomats, professors, U.N. personnel, and officials connected with armistice talks. It was a closed circle, but a changing one. When anyone interesting arrived in Jerusalem, he was brought by one of the "regulars." My parents had always held open house on Fridays, and now I adopted the custom. We rarely had fewer than fifty for Friday tea. Simha loved these occasions and produced fantastic little hot dishes—fresh-baked *pitta,* the flat Arab bread, and *kubeh,* crushed wheat dough filled with meat and onions, and a whole array of stuffed cabbages, marrows, and other vegetables.

Yael, who helped serve, was picking up English well, and there was always a dog or cat or lively boy underfoot. Everything was casual. That was the way I entertained in Zahala too, and I think guests enjoy it more than elegant formality. For parties we always had a help-yourself buffet because Moshe could not sit next to the same person through a whole dinner, especially when the language was English. He liked to be free to roam around. Sometimes he would disappear, and often he would be the last arrival at his own party. When he left for the fighting in the Negev, we never knew when he would be home. My Jerusalem friends understood this, but guests sometimes found Colonel Dayan's sporadic appearances disconcerting.

Our entertaining was a kind of "public relations," but it was also spontaneous and genuine. Some of the diplomats became our personal friends, and we have corresponded for years. Those posted to Jerusalem, the consular corps accredited to the Old City, in many cases had been pro-Arab and resentful of the Jewish victory. Gradually they became so involved with our family that they learned to understand our side. Generally, it was a time of optimism; people believed that peace might come.

Not that young men had stopped dying. In the season of the diplomats' holiday celebrations, two more Nahalal boys were killed. Nahum Zarchi, a relative of Devora's, died in the Negev on December 23, 1948. Less than two weeks later, on January 5, Israel Semel fell in the Gaza Strip. He had been a founder of Shimron, one of the boys who sang so beautifully on those calm nights.

Yet during that holiday season we went to a U.N. Christmas party at Government House. There was dancing, and one of my partners was Wasfi Tal, the Jordanian diplomat who was murdered two years later in Cairo by Arab terrorists. Assi had been lost near the border the day before, which often happened when he wandered away from Simha, and as we were dancing Wasfi Tal said, "Don't worry, Mrs. Dayan, if he should ever wander over to our side, we'll treat him like a little prince."

We were still on good terms with the Jordanians. Moshe crossed to their side secretly at night to meet King Abdullah and discuss ways of achieving a real peace. On one of these occasions they arranged for the exchange of prisoners captured in the Old City for a group of our people taken at a point in the north. My

uncle Mordechai, Father's brother, was among them, and I went
to the Mandelbaum Gate to welcome the returning prisoners.
Colonel Abdullah El-Tel, one of King Abdullah's favorite advisers, who negotiated the Armistice Agreement later signed in
Rhodes, was there too, and we were photographed together by a
reporter. The colonel prevailed on him not to publish the picture. It was all right to be photographed with Moshe on business,
he explained, but to be pictured with his wife would be going
too far.

"It is a good thing to have an enemy like your husband," Abdullah then said to me. "We know that a word is a word." This
thread of belief in Moshe runs through the story of his dealings
with the Arabs, and forms a basic part of his historic importance.

Moshe and Colonel El-Tel had a "hot line" that rang in our
house whenever there was a border incident, and one would say
to the other, "What do you mean by shooting at me?"

During one of the Jewish holidays, when mopping-up operations were still in progress outside the city, Moshe decided that
our family would visit soldiers at an outlying post which was
under fire. We left Assi in the kitchen shelter with Simha and,
taking Yael and Udi, went off in Moshe's car, which was hit by
a bullet on the way. We sat in dugouts with the soldiers and
sang songs; after a full moon rose, we returned to the car.
Moshe insisted on walking along the horizon at the top of a
ridge in full view of the snipers. Our soldiers called to him to
get down and not to expose himself along a moonlit skyline.

But Moshe would not think of complying. And because we
couldn't let him walk alone like that, the children and I joined
him, hearing the ping of bullets striking the rocks around us.
Moshe adores his children; yet he considered it perfectly natural
to have them up there with him in the line of fire. His courage
is unconscious; he feels no fear for himself or his children, who
are those closest to him.

Moshe and I had been farmers. Whatever else happened, we had
worked together in the fields and in the cowshed, partners in a
way of life. Now all this changed, but Moshe did try to involve
me with his work. When a new cannon was being tested near
Jerusalem, for instance, he asked if I would like to see it, and
I spent most of the night at his unit. As soon as the Arabs got
our cannon in range, they opened fire from somewhere on the
road to Bethlehem. Early in the morning a car took me home
and Moshe stayed with his men. Warfare is something I could
never be professional about.

We had coffee together every morning at a little café, for
Moshe's office was just down the street from our house. Then I
would go on to another café for another cup with a friend. I was
becoming a lady of leisure, something I would not bear for long.

An intelligence course was organized by the army and taught by an American officer who was often a guest at our home; I never knew his real name. He suggested I enroll, and I did. The lectures were intriguing, but I was a hopeless pupil and would never have made a decent spy. I have far too much trust in people and want them to trust me; I could never interrogate anyone, and even if I could, I would never be able to pass on the information I learned. So it was a waste of time, and I wrote a terrible examination.

During this period Devora asked me if I would help her in her work. She was in charge of the moshav movement's program of women volunteers who went from veteran settlements like Nahalal to help immigrants being organized into new moshavim. They were still living in tents on the sites that would become their village homes. Devora's section came under the Jewish Agency's settlement department, headed by Levi Eshkol.

Moshav women were performing one of the most important tasks in the country: showing families who came from the Arabian desert and European camps how to live in their new homes as Israelis. Under Devora's direction wives left their comfortable moshav farmhouses to live in new villages, often for as long as a year, taking their children along; their husbands, who were often army officers, went "home" on leave to tent villages. This was a form of national service whose purpose was to teach newcomers about such things as our vegetables—tomatoes and radishes were unknown to the people of North Africa —how to eat well without much meat, and even the basics of cleanliness and personal hygiene, for we had no organized home-economics service at that time.

Putting these newcomers into a kibbutz framework would have been the simplest and cheapest arrangement, but it would not have worked. Family ties were too strong and extended for that; the orientation was actually tribal. So a form of moshav became the best compromise, though the new farmers were usually people who had never seen a farm.

Devora asked if I would help with a settlement near Jerusalem, and Moshe agreed with my decision, because this kind of service was in the moshav tradition he had grown up with. Anyway, unlike other volunteers, I would be coming back every evening to my children, for Moshe's position and our social obligations required a Jerusalem home. It was Moshe who thought up the name for the project as it then functioned within the Jewish Agency—"Eshet Hayl," a biblical phrase meaning "Women of Virtue" (Proverbs, 31):

Who can find a virtuous woman? For her price is far above rubies. The heart of her husband doth safely trust in her, so that he shall have no need of spoil. . . . She seeketh wool, and flax, and worketh willingly with her hands. . . . Her husband is known in the gates, when he sitteth among the elders of the land. She maketh fine linen, and selleth it. . . .

"Your assignment will be Kfar Uriah," Devora told me. I had no idea that what I was getting into, the project of teaching people how to grow tomatoes and radishes, would snowball into something entirely different.

Kfar Uriah was a village with a history of defeat, settled and deserted several times since its founding. It was about twenty miles from Jerusalem, not including the two-mile walk up a dirt path from the main road to the ramshackle huts of Bulgarian Jews recently assigned to the place. Unlike newcomers from North Africa or Asia, they came from a high standard of living and were frustrated by their new home.

"Show the women how to grow vegetables in little back-yard gardens, and how to raise a few chickens" were Devora's instructions. On my first visit I went with a Bulgarian woman from the established moshav of Beit Hanan. That was the arrangement: a woman who had come years earlier from the same country and knew its traditions helped the newcomers. Those old-timers did a wonderful job. I spoke no Bulgarian, and they knew no Hebrew; we got along somehow through the Russian I knew from my parents. But their complaints were clear in any language.

"Everything here is terrible," they said.

"All right, now let's start growing tomatoes," I replied cheerfully.

"But there's no water in this awful place." And it was true. And they spoke of the magnificent rivers that flowed through the beautiful hills of Bulgaria. I was always received pleasantly in their depressing little houses. I met the husbands, nearly all well-educated men (in many cases dentists or dental technicians) trying to be farmers under impossible conditions. These families eventually left Kfar Uriah and the men returned to their professions. Today many of Israel's dentists are from Bulgaria.

The worst plague was the rats. When I walked down the path to the main road to catch the bus home, the fields were alive with them. From everywhere came a sound like people sucking air through their teeth—a sound I cannot bear anyway, and which I knew well, for it was not as though I had never seen any rats; I had been bitten in Nahalal more than once. But this invasion was on a giant scale. Deserted Arab villages had been taken over by rats. Seeds we planted were eaten overnight. Rats nibbled the wooden window sills to get into the houses. I did not need to understand Bulgarian to appreciate these people's feelings.

Inside their homes I noticed beautiful things—lovely curtains and tablecloths with hand-drawn lacework, trousseaus, delicate embroidery, and stitching in bold, peasant style. I was delighted, for I have always loved needlework, and the women saw that I admired the beauty of their craft.

Here was something unexpected. If rats and water shortage made agriculture impractical, why not do something with this talent? I thought that the women might be able to earn a little money selling handicrafts. Fine fabrics were unavailable—textiles were still rationed—but I could get sacking without ration points. The following week I arrived with piles of jute and scraps of knitting wool. We cut the sacking into round shapes, sewed them onto carry-all bags, added bamboo handles, and embroidered bold woolen patterns. We exaggerated and enlarged the traditional designs so that with less work more impact was achieved. I sold the bags to friends in Jerusalem and to the WIZO shop, which had from time to time bought the rag dolls I made out of scraps back in the Nahalal days.

I also gave the Bulgarian women a short course in Yemenite embroidery. Articles decorated with this stitching have always been popular, and I knew how to do it—though not as beautifully as the Yemenite women, of course. Somehow I have always been able to look at a piece of needlework and copy it. There are two types of Yemenite embroidery: a chain stitch, and an "overstitch" in which one thread is worked over with another. Soon the Bulgarians were turning out handsomely decorated collars and cuffs. They did not earn much money, but it was a help.

At the next meeting of women directing work in villages throughout the country, I displayed samples of what we were doing in Kfar Uriah. Here might be an idea to help in other villages too.

And suddenly, leaders in other places discovered handicraft talents. Bits and pieces of strange and beautiful things—weaving, jewelry—turned up at meetings, brought by astonished moshav women and social workers. It became a craze and was entirely new for us, because the Jews who had come earlier, and voluntarily, to Israel, mostly from Eastern Europe, came as "intellectuals." They never did anything in the way of handicrafts, for the more highly developed the background, the less there is in the way of craftsmanship.

But few of the new immigrants, who lived a life based on handwork, had dreamed that they would ever find work as weavers or silversmiths in Israel. Perhaps they thought this was the land of milk and honey, where everything would be different. They came wearing their own cloth and jewelry, but brought hardly any tools with them, though this was no serious problem: the instruments they used were primitive and easily made on the spot. One type of loom, for instance, was nothing but a tripod made of three lengths of wood.

Instead of concentrating on one village, I traveled to any

village where a handicraft project could be organized. Soon I was criss-crossing the country, going south as far as the Negev and north into Galilee, working with about twenty new settlements widely separated by language, background, and often by an absence of roads. There were countless obstacles and frustrations, but I also met many fascinating people, uprooted from distant traditions.

A sample of silver jewelry came to us, for instance, from the Jews of Hadhramaut in Southern Arabia, who were now settled in a village near Lydda. The men of Hadhramaut had a long tradition as silversmiths: when one of their brides married, she wore forty-five pounds of silver jewelry, and for an ordinary workday a belt of ten pounds.

The name "Hadhramaut," designating the region formerly under the British Protectorate and bordering Yemen, is related to the Hebrew *Hazarmavet*. In their striking robes, the Jews of Hadhramaut, with long, matted, unwashed hair, looked exactly like the Arabs from that area (and also like the hippies of two decades later). The more I came to know Jewish immigrants from exotic spots, the more clearly I saw that they resembled the other inhabitants of those countries: it is almost impossible to distinguish between an Indian Jew and an Indian, a Moroccan Jew and a Moroccan, or a Russian Jew and a Russian. That is why I always feel uncomfortable talking about "racial purity": there is no such thing; our world is too mixed up. The same is true of the Arabs in our area. I have seen too many Arabs and Druses with blond hair and blue eyes to be able to speak of ethnic separateness. Yet wars continue to be fought as though it were a reality.

To add to this mix-up, I learned that the silversmiths of Hadhramaut needed for their work the silver in the Maria Theresa thaler: not sterling, but the softer mixture in this old European coin, long preferred as currency in the region.

I found an elderly, one-legged silversmith from Hadhramaut in a little hovel in the new settlement, hammering away on his small supply of Maria Theresa thalers, and prevailed on him to make things for us. His specialty was a fascinating heavy box used to hold charms, which we still sell at Maskit. But I had a hard time getting these people to work. Their superstitions prevailed and they saw no point in changing their traditions just to supply us with merchandise. Some talked of sending back to Hadhramaut for more dollars for the jewelers, but nothing came of this.

There was endless trouble, as well, with sophisticated immigrants like the Bulgarians, who were full of arguments and complaints. Perhaps in the long run it was more interesting and challenging to work with those who were emerging from a culture of superstition and age-old tradition.

I received a monthly salary from the Jewish Agency. I would rather have received nothing; we were all "volunteers" in the sense that we were doing the work at all, but the families who had left their own homes used the salary to pay those hired to run their farms in their absence. Levi Eshkol was wonderful about helping, finding funds here and there for essentials. I ran things casually, buying the scraps we needed out of my pocket, paying myself back when we made sales, and measuring the lengths of woven cloth in Simha's kitchen. We employed more people in those days than we do at Maskit today, when our turnover is six million Israeli pounds a year (about one and a half million dollars).

Transportation was my main expense. I went by bus when possible, but some villages were a long walk from the nearest road, so I tramped with bags of wool. Often I hitchhiked, standing by the side of the road in my usual state of tears as cars passed me by. Once Moshe's car drove past; he was reading a newspaper and his driver did not notice me. It was always a strain to get home before Moshe, for he wanted me there when he was, though he was glad I was working.

"Well, and who's offended you today?" was Moshe's way of teasing when I began describing my adventures. I was nervous about the boys, too, because their talent for trouble was unbelievable. Assi used to greet me eagerly at the door, as I finally arrived with my bundles of embroidery, with pieces of news such as "Udi has just fallen off the roof!"

One incident on the road gave me nightmares for some time. I was trying to get back to Jerusalem from a settlement in the south—today it is in the center of the country but then it was considered part of the Negev. There we had found some women from Yugoslavia, superb knitters, who made beautiful girls' jumpers from wool scraps. That evening we were having a party for General William E. Riley, Chief of Staff of the U.N. Truce Supervision Organization, and his wife. Car after car passed me by and there were no buses. Meanwhile a policeman came along who wanted to hitch a ride to Rehovoth, and soon a green jeep pulled up. I was crying, of course, and explained to the driver that I desperately needed to get to Jerusalem, and that I had been waiting longer than the policeman and had a longer trip still ahead. The driver was nasty.

"Who do you think you are, telling me whom to pick up?" he said, and took the policeman. Tears streamed down my face as he drove off, with one seat still empty; but I managed to write down the license number.

I finally got home, nervous and miserable, and told everyone about the mean driver, including Ezer (Reumah's husband), who is a great help with such problems. Sure enough, the green-jeep affair had an ending of wonderful revenge. Not long afterwards,

a group of us went to the Negev for a Bedouin celebration—
Lieutenant General Yigael Yadin, then Chief of Staff, Moshe,
Ezer, Reumah, and I—and at the Military Governor's house in
Beersheba the first thing I saw parked outside was my green
jeep. I pointed it out to Ezer in great excitement.

"Ruth, now we're going to beat him up!" he said happily,
rolling up his sleeves. A few moments later he came back and
told me sadly, "I'm terribly sorry, but it's my cousin."

And so it was, a very nice person and an expert on the Negev
and the Arabs. I shouted at him that I didn't care whose
cousin he was, that nothing could ever excuse his behavior.

"But why didn't you say you were Moshe Dayan's wife?" he
asked apologetically.

"Why in the world should I? First of all, I'm sick and tired of
always being somebody's relative—either the daughter of Rahel
and Zvi Shwarz, or else the wife of Moshe Dayan. But that's not
the point. Why can't you behave like a human being and help a
woman in tears? Why does it matter whose wife she is?" Those
tears of mine were what had put him off, I suppose. He tried
hard to be nice and sent me a beautiful copper tray, but I never
really forgave him.

In the spring of 1949, Moshe went to Rhodes with the Israel
delegation to the armistice talks. Both the Arabs and the Israelis
were staying at the Roses Hotel, and negotiations went on for
weeks. I decided to take a few days' holiday from my village
work, because I had heard that Rhodes was a beautiful place
and I thought it would be a lovely opportunity to be with
Moshe.

By the time I arrived, the Israelis had already completed their
sightseeing and were busy with the working sessions. On my
second afternoon I hired a bicycle and went to see the Roman
baths. It took longer than I expected to get to the site, and when
I finally arrived, it was already getting dark. The place was
eerie, with not a soul around except the old caretaker, who
spoke only Greek but managed to explain that the baths were
closed.

A blue light, moonlight reflected on the blue tiles, held me
there a long time. I felt the desolation of personal loneliness;
yet the mystic stillness and beauty of the statues were absorbing.
I stood completely alone, far from everyone I loved, much
farther than a few miles from where the men I knew were making important decisions. But I was close to another dimension
of time. This was only the first of several such solitary, silent
experiences in distant places.

I stayed longer than I should have. On the way back my
bicycle tire went flat and so I pushed it most of the way. When
I finally arrived back at the beautiful Roses Hotel, I realized

that nobody had noticed my absence; the long evening work session had already begun.

Sixteen years later at Angkor Wat, I was alone in the Cambodian jungle, leaning against the stone statue of a huge dragon at the Wat entrance. I had walked out from the hotel for the once-in-a-lifetime opportunity to see this sight. It was almost too overwhelming an experience not to share. In the jungle at Angkor Wat, near the huge stone dragon in the moonlight, I was overcome by the strangeness of a situation repeating itself against a background of stillness, of ancient tales and legends. There again I thought about the quality of a life shared with a man who is himself a legend. Then I walked back to the hotel.

Russian-style blouses were still popular in Israel twenty years ago. The Russians had voted for us in the U.N. and the political climate was different then; so many of the early pioneers, like my parents, and Moshe's, were attached to Russian ways. This attachment expressed itself in embroidery, and it was suggested that we might take the simple Russian-style cotton blouses produced by Ata, our biggest clothing factory, to the immigrant villages and ask the women to decorate them. Julia Keiner, of the Bezalel Art School in Jerusalem, suggested that the simple kind of embroidery in which threads are pulled from the fabric and colored threads are then worked into the empty spaces be used instead of the difficult and time-consuming traditional cross-stitch.

Our first course, given at Beit Ha-Halutsot (Pioneer Women) in Jerusalem, was taught by a bright student from the Bezalel School's weaving and embroidery department. Our thirty students came from twenty different villages representing seventeen countries, from Persia, Tripoli and Algeria to Rumania, Yugoslavia and Poland. This made for considerable problems in language and just getting along together for ten days.

My difficulty was money; once again Levi Eshkol was tremendously understanding and contributed three hundred pounds from his budget. This, I am afraid, caused a quarrel with Golda Meir, then Minister of Labor. I asked her to speak at our "graduation"; I wanted a nice tea and a pleasant atmosphere and thought an address from Mrs. Meir, our woman cabinet member, would make a fine conclusion for these immigrant women.

But Golda Meir did not see it that way when I approached her. "If Eshkol doesn't give me the money I need to build roads, I'm certainly not going to help on this," she said in her forceful way, and I naturally burst into tears.

Money also brought an adventure with a thief, and a terrible *faux pas* on my part. At the end of the course I went to the bus station to buy tickets for each of the women returning to their villages. Suddenly I felt a hand in my purse—and my wallet with two hundred pounds was gone. But I caught sight of the thief as he ran toward a four-story building.

"Thief! Thief! Stop him!" I shouted.

"What does he look like?" asked the people milling around.

And then I said something I knew immediately was terrible, because I am so against this kind of national identification. "Moroccan," I said, because he had a dark complexion and black hair.

"Oh, he does, does he?" said another man with a dark complexion and black hair. "Aren't you ashamed to talk like that? I'm Moroccan myself, but I'll get your thief." And he started to climb to the roof of the building. Meanwhile, people in the crowd were heading for a nearby empty lot, on the theory that the thief had escaped and perhaps rid himself of the wallet too.

Soon two men came down from the roof: the Moroccan, holding my thief—who turned out to be of Kurdish origin like Simha. "He's all yours, lady," said the man who caught him, "but I'm not helping you any more." And off he went, leaving me to hold the man till the police came, which I did by keeping my foot firmly on his. Through all this I did not say I was the wife of the Brigade Commander of Jerusalem. At the police station my wallet with all the money was found in his pocket, and the man claimed it was his. In the wallet was a photograph of Moshe.

"And who is this?" asked the policeman when he came to the photo.

"That's my brother," said the thief.

Getting to isolated settlements and back home in time became too hard without a car, so I went on strike. Moshe supported me fully, and eventually a vehicle was produced. It was always getting stuck in sand or mud. Still, it was now much easier to carry my bundles. Not long afterwards I was given a jeep, and from then on I was far less nervous about getting home to Moshe on time.

My personal troubles, in any case, were nothing compared with those of people I was trying to help. Their living conditions were often shocking and their health terrible, owing to a combination of malnutrition and filth, superstition and fatalism. These elements varied according to their background. Refugees from Europe knew how to take care of themselves and their children; their problems were economic, professional, and temporary. But with immigrants from Asia and North Africa the philosophy was "God giveth and God taketh," and against this human beings were expected to do little.

There were 650,000 Jews in Israel in May 1948. During the War of Independence, 119,00 newcomers arrived. In the next year, 240,000 came. In 1950 the figure was 170,000, and in 1951,

175,000, so that in the first three and a half years of the state the Jewish population was doubled, and by 1964 we had absorbed 1,200,000 immigrants from all parts of the world. In the early years of the state everybody in Israel was poor, in terms of today's standard of living. We had limited resources to work with, although I saw many remarkable things done, especially by dedicated social workers. But this was rarely enough. Sometimes it was hard for anyone to set the right wheels in motion. I was lucky to be able to do just that because of Moshe's position, and because I happened to know so many key people and did not mind making a nuisance of myself on behalf of anyone I thought needed help.

Through handicrafts in one strange new community after another, I found myself learning about customs and beliefs and ways of life totally foreign to those of us who grew up in Israel. They seem distant and incredible today, and when I remind those same immigrants of the squalor and filth of their surroundings when we first met, they refuse to believe it was ever so. I can hardly blame them.

The worms and the little sticks, for instance, are an example of something I noticed in a dirty tent village of one group of newcomers from Southern Arabia and did not understand until later. Small sticks were tied with string around the wrists of many of the children, and one end of the string seemed to be tied to something else. When I tried to see what this was, the children ran off screaming, "You mustn't touch the worm!"

The string was indeed tied to a worm that lived in the child's body, with one end protruding. The stick and string were attached to the worm "to keep it from running away," one of the adults told me. This parasite, I later learned, was the *Dracunculus medinensis,* or Guinea worm; it can grow several feet long inside the human body. Immigrants from the Arabian peninsula told me that the worm "helped against another disease," which was why they were careful to keep it in and under control. A doctor friend showed me old woodcuts of the procedure as followed in Europe during the Middle Ages. Actually, the worm must be extracted without severing it, in order to prevent blood poisoning, and the device of string and stick makes possible a way of "rolling" it out a little at a time. Perhaps the idea of its value against some other affliction was suggested to make sure care would be taken to get it completely out.

With all the strangeness of this practice, I was fascinated to find history, even medical history, once again referring back to the Bible. According to the *Encyclopaedia Britannica,* the *Dracunculus medinensis* is the most ancient known parasite of man; the plague of "fiery serpents" visited upon the Israelites (Numbers, 21) is supposed to have been caused by it. Moses is thought to have set up the brass serpent to impress upon his people that need for complete extraction.

My introduction to the cave dwellers of Libya came in the form of an unusual, finely woven, and quite dirty little piece of cloth. I set out in my jeep to investigate weaving at the new settlement of Porat, in the dunes east of Natanya (this time I got stuck in the drifting sands), to meet an exotic tribe of Jews.

About a hundred families had been brought from a place called Garian, south of Tripoli in Libya, where the whole community lived underground in huge caves dug beneath the desert surface. I have never seen these caves of Tripolitania; those of Morocco, which I have visited, are quite different, being natural formations in the mountains. From my new friends' descriptions I understood their caves to have been hewn straight down, to a depth of twenty-five feet, and connected by a series of tunnels. A large air well was at the center. This form of living was a defense against both the wild desert wind and marauders. The people were tall, handsome, and far healthier than many other North African immigrants. One explanation for this had to do with how their children were raised. Until they were old enough to work, children were kept down in the caves, and the even underground temperature proved good for their health. The men of this tribe had been farmers in their native land and adapted quickly to farming in Israel, though they did try to dig caves when they arrived and were disappointed when our soil kept falling in. Their village, Porat, was one of the first to grow avocados, and today it is a prosperous community. Their weaving is now a thing of the past.

It was a sophisticated kind of work, not what one might expect from cave dwellers. The fabric was finer than the coarse textiles of other newcomers. The fibers were spun from the hair of mohair goats, both natural white and natural black, and cotton threads were woven into the pattern. The prayer shrawls made by these people were gossamer, with intricate triangles and squares. The only dye used was made from pomegranates; since the white mohair threads took the pomegranate color, turning rust red, and the natural white cotton threads remained white and the black remained black, the finished work was always in those three colors.

Their looms, too, were lovely. They were vertical, rather than the horizontal type often used by desert people. The women sitting at their work in their flowing robes were visible through the threads of the warp; they reminded me of harp players.

In some communities women did only the spinning, and the men were the weavers. Here the women did both. Perhaps because of their underground life, without the outdoor work of their sisters elsewhere, they had the time and inclination to develop a finer craft.

How could we sell this wonderful cloth? The human investment was beyond anything reasonable on a wage scale calculated by the day or week; this was a tradition outside the scope of financial value, with no relation to anything like "marketing." I decided to exaggerate and enlarge, just as I had done with the Bulgarians and their embroidery; so we shifted from weaving prayer shawls to rugs. I rushed to the Negev and managed to buy a supply of Bedouin natural wool, the best we have for rug weaving, and soon we were getting rugs from the cave dwellers of Tripolitania now living aboveground in Israel.

Lieutenant-General Sir Brian Horrocks (General Commanding Officer of the British Army of the Rhine and Gentleman Usher of the Black Rod in the House of Lords, a title that naturally fascinated me) was our guest in Jerusalem soon after I began working with these weavers, and was surprised to see a length of the traditional fabric in our home. "But the only place I ever saw this was in the caves of Garian!" he said, recognizing the unique texture right away. He asked about several of the men, having been down in the caves during World War II, and so I took him to Porat to meet his old friends. I also sent a rug to his London home.

Like most isolated communities, this was an extremely religious one. Jewish soldiers from Palestine with the British in North Africa who visited the people of Garian tell of having their uniforms kissed by these devout Jews, who had been under Nazi German rule and now saw Jewish fighting men for the first time.

Porat rugs were among our first exports. We sold them to several New York shops and arranged for two weavers to go to America and demonstrate their craft. Hanna Hagag—Hagag was the family name of the whole community—an older woman and one of our best weavers, flew off to New York with her niece Mazal. They were a huge success. Worried that New York food might not be sufficiently kosher, Mazal and her aunt took along food from Porat to be on the safe side—hard-boiled eggs and peanuts. Mazal returned with jewelry for the whole tribe that she bought, enraptured, at the dime store.

I became thoroughly involved with these families, their problems of love and health and money. Like everyone I have ever known, they called me—from the beginning—"Ruth," "Ruthie" or, most formally, "Geveret Ruth." They came to enjoy making rugs for us, perhaps because I was so enthusiastic about what they created. The following year, when I was abroad, Levi Eshkol visited Porat and asked where their rugs were, as production had dwindled. "Since Ruth Dayan has left," one of the elders told him, "we just don't like to make them any more."

Rugs of a different style and feeling made by Azerbaijan Jews living in the new village of Avdon in the hills of Galilee, are always connected in my mind with B. Altman, the New York department store. This was because a delightful Scottish gentleman, Mr. Keeler, then vice-president of Altman's, found himself in my jeep on a rough trip over rocks and canyons to Avdon, where he became fascinated by the Azerbaijan Jews and their rugs. They were already working for us by then, but the first time I visited Avdon I had been met by the stony suspicion of craftsmen committed only to their traditions.

The newcomers, living in tin huts, had brought with them much of the Persian culture of Azerbaijan. On the floors of their huts, cluttered with goats and chickens, they continued to hand-knot their carpeting on the traditional horizontal looms and use vegetable dyes. Made just for their own use, these rugs were simple rustic versions of the famous Persian rugs, with which they could not compete on any market. Besides, our standard of living, even then and even in isolated villages, was well above that of Iran's cheap labor. But I wondered whether we might somehow again translate this particular skill into a marketable product.

"See if they won't make rugs in simple, solid colors" was the suggestion of some interior decorators. I located some beautiful off-white wool—not easy in those days of ration coupons—and put it in my jeep together with some black wool for a decorator whose client wanted a plain black rug.

"I am quite sure nobody will do this work," said the elder of Avdon when I arrived with my precious wool and my ideas of plain, unadorned rugs. "But I'll try to convince them."

When I returned two weeks later, the wool was still standing in one of the huts and the men could not wait to pile it back into the jeep. They were not interested in making money and could not have cared less about the whole project. There was just one exception: a woman who had taken a bit of the off-white wool and made a small rug. It was plain except for a border of flowers.

"But what does it matter?" I asked. "You're just tying knots. What can be the objection to making it plain?"

"Ah, but it's so boring!" was the answer. And that was wonderful to hear, though it complicated my life. For these people had a real concern for the act of creation, the challenge of designing and executing new ideas. Something spiritual had to be added to each design; every rug made by a real craftsman, whether in Iran or India, always has an added "something," perhaps a color that does not belong in the pattern but adds mystic meaning. Later in India, I saw this same dedication among craftsmen who, on starvation wages, derived what satisfaction they had in life by figuring out new and intricate ways of printing block designs on fabric. As for the black wool, there was just nothing to be done about that. Dark blue or brown, yes; black, no.

During our bumpy ride to Avdon, Mr. Keeler was, in his way, just as suspicious of the whole thing as the weavers had been. But when he saw the looms, he knew immediately where they were from. He was on the way home from a buying trip in Iran, where fine versions are made, and was planning to stay in Israel only three days. He became so interested in what was happening that he stayed for ten. Altman's suggested that we hire designers to devise patterns for the rugs—plain backgrounds with vivid stripes. The artist Jean David, then a new immigrant from Rumania, worked out fifty different patterns in beautifully balanced colors. The Azerbaijanians agreed to the principle of stripes and we soon had some fine rugs.

Another kind of rug from Avdon is our "Yael" pattern. When Yael was fourteen, she spent her holiday on a dig in the Negev with the archeologist Nelson Glueck. Among that season's discoveries were some rock drawings several thousand years old. They included one of an ibex, and the name "Yael" means ibex in Hebrew. She drew a design of the animal, and this became a pattern for the weavers of Avdon. We paid her five pounds for her sketch—by this time we were paying designers properly for their work—and the "Yael" rug is still in production at Maskit.

Another piece of dirty but attractive hand-woven fabric was brought to me by a social worker in the summer of 1949, and she also described the terrible condition of the children in the settlement where it was made. Agur, in the hills south of Jerusalem near the old Jordanian border, was really nothing but a village of black tents, the temporary homes of new immigrants from Southern Arabia. The health conditions were shocking.

I went to the black tents at Agur with two women friends from Jerusalem (by this time I had something like a private army of women who helped in the villages). It was dark inside the first tent we entered. Partly from the smell, we made out that there were goats, chickens, excrement, dried figs, men, women, children, some army beds, and filth everywhere. The women were tall, their black hair worn in plaits and shaped at the forehead like a triangle; jewelry jangled on their arms. The children were lovely but sickly. The men wore boldly woven cloaks and sidelocks.

Something that looked like a small package of black rags lay on one of the camp beds, and from it we heard a little wail. We opened the package and inside was an infant boy, perhaps one day old, his hands tightly bound with a dirty cord, his face and body smeared with hideous bright colors, and his navel a festering sore. Next to him sat an old man murmuring sentences I could not understand. They were in bibilcal Hebrew, different from our everyday language. One of these strangers spoke modern Hebrew, a young man called Haim David.

"If the baby is ugly enough, the evil eye will not take him away. The colors are to make him ugly," he explained. "The cord around his arms is also against the evil eye."

Dr. Pearl Ketcher, a pediatrician who had come with me, quickly cut the cord. A great wail went up in the tent: "Evil eye! Evil eye!" Then a doctor arrived from the settlement clinic. He was a new immigrant, a Hungarian who spoke nothing but his own language. He and his wife did the best they could, but the people in the hand-woven cloaks did not trust him. They put their faith in their own healers. I prefer to call them "healers" and not "witch doctors," because at the source of many such superstitions is some evidence of real healing.

"The brands on her stomach are made by a hot iron, and are to bring down the fever," Haim explained in the next tent. Here was a nine-year-old girl with double pneumonia and festering sores on her body from the brands. It was terrible to see, but again I sensed somewhere a connection to medicine as we know it, for I remembered that when a horse has high fever, cauterization brings the fever down. Dr. Ketcher insisted that we get the child to a hospital immediately or she would die. There was a great outcry—many men and women, I noticed, had marks on their foreheads, scars from earlier treatment. But Pearl had her way and an ambulance came for the little girl.

As soon as I returned home I described the place to Moshe: "You must do something! This can't go on another day. You must talk to Ben-Gurion!" Moshe promised to speak to Ben-Gurion, then Minister of Defense as well as Prime Minister.

That night I barely slept, and when I did I had nightmares. My work was with embroidery and weaving; but these were conditions I could not ignore. Other people had seen Agur too, but not everyone was in the position that I was to start wheels moving.

The next day Ben-Gurion called me and asked whether things were really as bad as I claimed. Of course they were, I said.

"But this can't be!" he said. "We can't have things like this in Israel!" He told Moshe that the army medical corps should make an immediate investigation.

Then I began to worry. Perhaps things were not really so bad? Perhaps, in my imaginative way, I had exaggerated? But I need not have doubted; for when the army medical report was turned in, conditions were described in terms even stronger than mine.

So the army took over Agur and also, for the same reason, twenty-two other immigrant settlements, remaining nearly a year. Thus Moshe and I in a sense worked together during this period.

On my next visit to Agur I brought a bag of cotton that I thought might be woven into the patterns I had seen. "Where's your pass?" a soldier asked me at the entrance. I presented my identity card and entered what had become something like a regular army camp. The first thing I saw was the entire community, men, women, and children, lined up in rows three deep. With toothbrush in hand, they marched off to the hot-water tanks, which the army had brought in, to receive instructions on how to brush teeth. This was one of the early lessons given by the Israel Defense Forces to new settlers. On their first day at Agur, I was told, the soldiers had used more DDT in one day than the army generally uses in a year. Girl soldiers arrived to show mothers how to wash their babies—to this day one of the first special challenges for our women in uniform in the immigrant villages.

"If the mothers don't do as they're told and wash all that paint and filth off these poor babies," one of the girls told me, "a soldier pulls out the tent pegs and their whole home collapses. It's mean, but we can't bring about change without strict discipline."

I found some of the people I had met on my first visit. "Can you weave this cotton into patterns like those on your robes?" I asked. Yes, of course. "Then I'll come back for it next week."

"But it will be ready tomorrow morning," I was assured.

Haim David told me recently that they had been longing to weave once more: "We had stopped when we left home and thought we would never do it again. We wove the whole night through, and in the morning all the fabric was ready. That was one of the most beautiful nights I spent in Israel." The primitive horizontal wood-frame looms were no problem; they were constructed on the spot.

Haim has only one eye. He lost the other when he was five years old, helping his jeweler father "pull" the silver thread used in filigree work. Yet he became an outstanding craftsman at an early age, and had been the private jeweler of the ruler of Bayhan before he and his family came to Israel.

I did not learn these details right away; they emerged during the twenty years that Haim, Moshe Ben David, and Shimon Haim have been among our top craftsmen at Maskit. Long ago they moved from Agur, and today all the Bayhanim live in Ness Ziona, near Rehovoth, in neat modern flats. Their children finish high school, serve in the army, enter universities. But where is Bayhan, and what is the background of these people?

Wadi Bayhan, near the southern tip of the Arabian peninsula, separates Yemen from what was formerly the Aden Protectorate and is now Southern Yemen—an area with no definite borders and with traditional tribal rivalries. Thirty years ago, under the

British Protectorate, the ruler of the Arabs of Bayhan was King Hussein Ben-Nader Arzaeli. Bayhan was a place of small clay houses, but there was an airstrip where a British plane could occasionally touch down, bringing military and medical personnel.

In this Arab community of about 100,000 lived a small group of Jews, about one hundred and thirty families, whose forefathers had come earlier from Yemen to serve the king as advisers and mathematicians. What has always fascinated me about the stories of Bayhan under King Hussein was the unique friendship between the few Jews and the Arab majority.

"We all cried at the airstrip that morning in 1949 when we were leaving Bayhan for Israel," Haim told me. About a hundred Jews and thousands of Arabs wept like children. "And the good Sherif Hussein, who had tried so hard to persuade us not to leave, told us: 'If you decide you do not like your new home and wish to return, do not worry, for I promise that all your houses will be returned to you in the same condition as you left them.' "

I do not know why this handful of Jews happened to be on such good terms with this particular tribal leader. Moshe Ben David has tried to explain it: "Sherif Hussein was our friend because he respected us. He knew that we were different from merchants, because we were working in our crafts of jewelry and weaving as artists and not just to make a living."

The Sherif, he said, was a superb political leader: "He made a point of studying English, and learned to use British military power as leverage with warring tribes." Friction between Jews and Arabs was part of tribal life in Yemen, "but the Imam of Yemen was very correct towards the Jews." In other words, when no outside forces stir up trouble, friendship is not only possible but a fact of history. In his book *Modern Yemen,* Manfred Wenner says: "Despite reports to the contrary, Imams were usually scrupulously fair to Jews and apparently genuinely sorry to see the majority of them leave for the new state of Israel. . . . The Imam Yahya, on hearing the desire of the Jews to establish a national home, invited a prominent Palestinian rabbi to come to Yemen and explain personally the arguments and proposals. . . . When Imam Ahmad realized that nearly all Jews would be leaving Yemen, they were told to teach their trades to Arabs. . . ."

Haim was, as I have said, the Sherif's private jeweler. "Whenever a special gift was needed to express thanks to an important friend or appease a British officer, the Sherif would come to me and order a sheath for a dagger or sword. My father, who trained me, objected to my working independently, for he thought I was too young and should still learn from my seniors." The first time I heard Haim tell this story I was charmed by the idea of the "generation gap" in Bayhan. "But I was sure I could be an artist, an artist and not merely a craftsman. And I think you know, Ruth, that until this day I always try to introduce something new into every ornament, to keep it looking traditional and yet fresh."

Until 1948 the Jews of Bayhan and the Arabs under Hussein lived in harmony. But that year news came of the Palestine riots and the War of Independence. Echoes of this warfare began in far-off Bayhan when organized groups of Arabs began to attack Jews with sticks, stones, and ancient guns.

"We asked the Sherif to take measures. He assembled the whole community in our main square and spoke these words: 'In this country we do not hate. The British Consul and I have decided as follows. Whover kills will be killed himself. Whoever is interested in the fighting in Palestine, let him go there and fight. That is another country. Here, peace and quiet shall prevail.' And the Sherif enforced his policy, even towards close advisers and powerful friends, and towards his son, the Emir, who had come to hate the Jews."

Meanwhile, scholars of the Jewish community had calculated, according to mysterious hidden references in the Bible, that the time of the Messiah's arrival was close, and with it their return to the Holy Land. "With God's help, we will soon go to Palestine," said Rabbi Yitzhak Menashe, who taught prayers in the synagogue in the main square.

Help came in the form of an unusual British doctor who worked in the area and had a special liking for the Bayhanim Jews. "Dr. Walker was the only one, besides our own healers, whom we allowed to treat us," Shimon's wife told me; he once even took her to Aden when she needed special treatment. That belief in primitive superstition can run parallel with trust in modern medicine may seem strange, but it is understandable. It always depends on the personality of the man who brings new ways, as I was to see with Albert Schweitzer in Africa. I met Dr. Walker when he came to Israel, for he worked at the Scottish Mission Hospital in Tiberias. His arrival was cause for a celebration with his Bayhanim friends, most of whom keep a photograph of him in a place of honor in their homes. This is why I believe their health conditions may have been better in their native land than in the tent village where I first met them.

It was Dr. Walker who brought the Jews of Bayhan the news that in neighboring Yemen, transit camps were being organized from which Jews were going to Israel.

"We asked Dr. Walker to take letters from us to Yemen explaining that we, too, wanted to go to Israel," Haim told me. "We didn't want the Sherif to learn of our intention until we knew we could really go. We knew the Sherif loved us, and we didn't want to hurt his feelings. But we finally did have to tell the Sherif. We invited him and his bodyguard and all the tribe's notables to a meeting in one of our homes, decorating it as for a holiday with fine white tablecloths and steaming hot coffee served in the most beautiful cups.

"We told the Sherif about our ancient dream, and about the sudden real possibility through the Yemen transit camp, for Shimon had investigated and knew all the details. Then we saw that Sherif Hussein loved us even more than we had thought, for sorrow fell upon his face. He offered us money to stay and any help we might want and begged us to change our minds. But we were obstinate. Finally he made us this offer.

" 'You do not even know the country for which you have longed,' said the Sherif. 'Maybe you will be disappointed and will wish to return. Why not send two men there, on my account, and see for yourselves before taking all your people?' When I think of the conditions that actually did await the Bayhanim when they arrived, the Sherif's concern seems to have a special poignancy.

"But we told the Sherif, 'No, we do not need spies.' One of our elders quoted what happened when Moses sent spies into the land ['And they brought up an evil report of the land . . .']. We said we had only one wish, airplanes to take us from Bayhan to the camp in Yemen. The Sherif himself flew to Yemen to consult with the Israel immigration authorities there and arranged for planes to come for us. They came a week later, and that was when we said good-bye to our Arab friends, who embraced us at the airstrip."

All the Jews left that day except two—an old man and his son who simply could not believe they would go to Israel. The entire operation seemed too biblical to them, too fantastic to be really happening on a morning in the year 1949. "The Arabs were pleased that at least two Jews were staying, and helped the old man, Joseph Etrab, to acquire a large shop and promised to look after him and his son. But later we learned that Joseph fell into a depression after we had gone and died soon after. His son, the only Jew left in Bayhan, became an orphan.

"Sherif Hussein adopted the boy and raised him as his own son. He read him a passage from the Koran: 'It is said that in every royal house there is a stranger. You shall be the stranger in my house, and you shall live like a king.' "

According to Moslem custom, which is most tolerant in this respect though not always scrupulously observed, orphans of other religions are permitted when they reach the age of twenty to decide for themselves what their faith will be. The Bayhanim Jews worried about the boy after they arrived in Israel and tried to have him brought to their new home, at that time hardly flowing with milk and honey, but this was not possible. When he reached twenty, the last Jew of Bayhan told his adoptive father that he chose Islam.

Another account of the gap the Jews of Bayhan left behind is reported in a book by St. John Philby, the English Arabist—and father of the spy—who lived among Arabs and was converted to Islam. Philby was a friend of Sherif Hussein's and at the close of one of his regular visits, he asked, "Have you not forgotten something, my friend?"

"What have I forgotten?" asked Sherif Hussein.

"The scabbard," answered Philby. "Whenever I came before, you always presented me with a silver scabbard for a dagger. This time you did not."

"The Jews have left," explained Hussein. "They were the only ones who knew how to draw that fine silver thread, and now that they have gone to Israel there is no one left to do it."

Moshe Ben David and Haim can work today in any style of jewelry; the windows of the world have opened for them, and they can produce a piece that is cleanly modern or ornately Victorian. "But the original tradition that I learned as a child," says Moshe, "is part of me and will never leave. The style may change, but not the underlying technique."

For the Arab customers in Bayhan the Jews made rings, bracelets, earrings, necklaces. Today Moshe supervises such forms as the North African "Hamsa," the stylized hand symbol that protects against the "evil eye." And one of Haim's rings is made of intertwined parts, a pair of clasped hands and a heart, in a European style.

"When my students ask me what style to work in, I say, 'Whatever makes you happy.' " Moshe teaches jewelry-making evenings in his home in Ness Ziona, and his students include members of the diplomatic corps.

The Bayhanim love their work, which probably explains the affection the Arabs felt for them. It is also why I have been part of them, and they of me, for twenty-three years. "When you first told us about the idea of being able to go on with our work," Moshe Ben David reminded me recently, "that was the most important thing in our lives. We didn't care about wages, we didn't want to pick oranges. We wanted to do the thing we loved." A simple metal mold with about twenty little slits of varying designs, into which the silver wire is beaten, was brought from Bayhan by Moshe Ben David's uncle: "He didn't think he would ever do this work again, but he couldn't bring himself to part with his tool."

The Bayhanim met Eleanor Roosevelt on one of her visits to Israel when I took her to see their homes in Ness Ziona. Snow-white diapers were hanging from lines on the balconies, little flower gardens bloomed by each house, and a big placard at the entrance to the Bayhanim quarter read SHALOM, MRS. ROOSEVELT! I had nothing to do with this; Mrs. Roosevelt was deeply loved by everyone in Israel. As our car pulled up she said to me, "The people living here must be very clean and tidy!"

I noticed blond and black-haired children clustered together to greet us, and as we entered the home of Shimon and his wife, H'sena, our hosts, I was surprised to see that European women were there with H'sena, who is terribly shy. Over the sofa, of course, was Dr. Walker's photograph, and tables with white tablecloths were covered with Yemenite food delicacies.

Among the Yemenite dishes was a beautiful Sacher torte, the chocolate-covered Viennese layer cake. What was this doing here, Mrs. Roosevelt asked H'sena. She was flustered by her distinguished guest, but she explained, "When the people of Ness Ziona heard that the famous Mrs. Roosevelt would be visiting us, everybody wanted to help us Bayhanim prepare for the reception. Each neighbor did her best and donated something. Our neighbors are new immigrants from Austria, and they brought us this cake in honor of the event."

Mrs. Roosevelt was moved by this explanation and began to chat, in German, with the Austrian neighbor. "How are you getting on?" she asked. "You are from Europe and she is from Bayhan. You are so different, so far apart."

The Austrian immigrant's blue eyes rested on her dark-skinned neighbor, and after a moment she replied, "If I had to choose a lifelong neighbor for my family, I am quite sure I would choose this woman, and would not exchange her for anyone else in the world."

10 · Transition

When Moshe's assignment in Jerusalem ended in 1951 he was sent to England for a five-month officers' course at Devizes. Udi and Assi stayed at Kibbutz Maoz with friends of mine; Yael continued at school in Jerusalem and lived with my parents; Simha ran the big house, and I went with Moshe.

This English experience was completely different from our first, because Moshe could speak English and was learning things that fascinated him. Our living arrangements this time were fine, too. Reumah and Ezer had married and Ezer was attending an English officers' course for pilots at Andover. Their first child was born in England, as Reumah was. I had a room in Reumah's flat and our husbands came home weekends. I took courses in weaving, basketry, and ceramics; I wanted to know the actual techniques of the work I had started, and to be able to judge and supervise professionally in case I should be able to continue with it.

One of Ezer's colleagues in the pilots' course was an Egyptian officer, Afifi, who later became Deputy Chief of the Egyptian air force. He was called home when the British left Egypt and Ezer gave a little farewell party for him. I heard the two men joking that they hoped they would not use their training against each other. (Afifi was purged from his command after the Six-Day War.)

The gala ball at the end of the course was canceled by the

death of King George VI. As a little girl I had watched his wedding from a London curbstone in April 1925. Nobody had imagined then that he would be king, for the abdication of his older brother, Edward VIII, was still in the future.

After the course Moshe had another eye operation in Paris. For years he hoped to be able to live without his patch, and went through a series of operations that were attempts to give him an artificial eye. But the nature of his particular injury made this impossible.

After the operation, as Moshe was preparing to fly home, our friend Teddy Kollek arrived on his way to a Washington post as embassy minister. He and I discussed the project I had left in Israel, Eshet Hayl, and the three years' work with the settlements. I had hoped it would continue after my departure, but that did not work out. Still, having turned over the accounts in good order, I knew there were rugs left in stock to be sold and Teddy suggested that if I could get to America, he would put me in touch with new markets.

"If you agree to give a talk for the United Jewish Appeal, I'll be able to get you a ticket to America," he said. Though I had never in my life made a public speech, I agreed.

Moshe flew back to Israel and I flew to America, where I immediately got stagefright. "Don't worry," my dear friend Herzl wrote me, "I'll send you some tranquilizers." I never received them in America but they finally arrived in Israel months later, crushed to powder. It was probably my good luck that I did not have them to rely on. I learned I could stand on my own two feet without pills.

My speech was to be in Chicago. When I arrived I found that a comedian was to share the platform with me, and that my speech had already been written out.

"I'm sorry, but I can't possibly give this," I said when I read the speech. "It's not me and it's not the way I think or feel." The organizers were worried about this unknown and inexperienced young woman, and I can understand why they did not trust me, for I did the same thing I do now before any speech: withdraw into myself. I am sulky and refuse to open up; nobody could possibly expect anything to come from me.

But as soon as I do stand up I lose myself in my subject. That is what happened in Chicago, and has happened hundreds of times since. I was back in the tents of the Bayhanim, with the beauty and the filth; I was back with the plague of rats; with the jewelers of Hadhramaut, the weavers of Porat, and in all the villages I had come to know.

That is the only reason my speeches have some impact. I relive the experiences I describe. But even that first time, something made me unhappy about this kind of speaking, and after I came out of my trance I knew what it was. On the one hand, I hated speaking in order to draw tears—and raise money. On the other hand, I knew that by making Jewish audiences feel these emotions, they became part of us. I said, after that first time, that I would never speak publicly again, because I could not bear being a salesman at that level. But I have.

So my first speech seemed successful, and to my surprise I was asked to deliver more. Travel became hectic, with barely time for the merchandising contacts that were the reason for the trip.

There was a problem: four tons of wool remnants had been donated in England for handicraft work. Poor Moshe was very good about helping to arrange clearance through customs. His letters to me while I was in America were all about those four tons of wool; he went to a great deal of trouble.

Moshe's military career was advancing. His next assignment was to head the Northern Command and, after a little juggling of households, we returned once more to Nahalal. It was fantastically good to be back on the farm. We had a man to run it, since of course Moshe could not, and I was busy weaving. I had bought a lovely old Queen Anne loom in London and made upholstery, bedspreads, all sorts of things. Yael went to high school in Haifa, staying with my aunt and uncle and coming home for weekends; the boys were at school in Nahalal.

Perhaps this time, I thought, it might last. But it did not. When Moshe was appointed to General Headquarters in 1953 we had to leave the north and moved temporarily to a flat in Ramat Gan, which we all hated. It was the only time we did not live in a house. The boys went wild. They were trouble enough at Nahalal, but at least they had chores to do and trees to climb. In this Tel Aviv suburb there were no real trees; Udi and Assi used to climb up the drainpipe to our third-floor flat because they were always losing the door key. At Nahalal there was no such thing as a lock.

The flat, which the army assigned to us, had no separate room for Yael. She did not want to share one with the boys, so we took a room for her downstairs. She was delighted to be on her own, but it turned out to be far too much freedom for a young girl— and a girl whom, I realized, I did not know at all. Her involvement with an older man was one of the first blows to the foundation of our family. Yael's behavior was a profound shock to me. I was physically ill and spent three days at the home of Reumah and Ezer, who tried to help by talking to her; I was unable to, and her father was at the United Nations in New York. I am very good at shouting at other people, but I avoid bringing an issue into the open when it comes to people I love.

Until she was thirteen, Yael seemed a perfectly normal girl, very bright and entertaining, giving no cause for alarm. She was certainly very attached to her glamorous father, and she noticed early that he had contempt for certain laws of behavior; she saw that as his daughter she was in a position of power. She had always been precocious, trying to outdo her friends, who were usually older, not only in school but with boys—and men—as well. Yael was unlike me. She never played with dolls as a child, and, like my mother, she never cried. Yael and her grandmother Rahel always got on beautifully.

From this time on I simply did not know how to handle Yael, and her father was too busy to be concerned. It is a difficult age for many daughters and their mothers, but in Yael's case she grew up too quickly, and she seemed to have contempt for most people. She dazzled them with ease, but I had the feeling this did not bring her any real happiness.

In 1953 we bought a house in Zahala—again with a loan from my parents—and the day we moved, in December, happened to be the day Moshe was appointed Chief of Staff. I was washing the floors in the new house with Simha when the telephone rang. It was Ora Makleff, the wife of Moshe's predecessor, calling to congratulate me.

"Oh, but you should see the state the house is still in," I said, thinking she meant our new home. But she was referring to Moshe's appointment, which he had not mentioned to me, not considering this an important piece of news.

The next day we were told we could choose an "official residence." "What's wrong with this one?" I said. You could make a bit of money renting your own home and living in the official one, but, as in Jerusalem, I was against this; and again, I did not want to have to chase after the boys to keep them from ruining public property.

At the same time, I was approached by the Ministry of Labor about the possibility of going on with the handicrafts project. It had been discontinued by the Jewish Agency but similar work was going on within the Women's Labor Division of the Ministry, headed by Golda Meir.

"I'll look into it," I said; it depended on whether Simha agreed to stay and take care of the children. After a short time in Zahala I was again beginning to feel as I had when we moved to Jerusalem, a reluctant lady of leisure. And then, just as in Jerusalem, Simha joined our family and I knew the children and the house would be in the best of hands. She stayed with us until just before the Six-Day War.

People sometimes think of me as a mother who left her young children in order to work outside the home. Perhaps I have given this impression because I work intensely and become involved with many people. But the fact is that until Yael was nine years old I practically never left the house, and did not even dream of taking a holiday from the farm. Building my life around my family was what I wanted; and it was what I did until circumstances changed our way of life. Yael was certainly never left alone at Nahalal. I did not work outside the home—or join the Haganah—in the years before Yael was born, because all that I wanted was to be with Moshe.

My work, especially its human aspects, is a major part of my life now, and I am glad I went to work when I did. At first there was friction between me and the women running the projects; they were older, and I had different ideas, such as the need for research and the importance of good design. I had a good, tough board of directors—they kept us on our toes but gave us full support. I was given half of a secretary and a warehouse in the offices of the Ministry of Labor in Tel Aviv, which was Maskit's headquarters for seventeen years. In 1963, we moved into our present quarters in the El Al building.

The name "Maskit" comes from Proverbs (25:11): "A word fitly spoken is like apples of gold in pictures of silver." The English Bible translates the Hebrew plural of "maskit" as "pictures," but there are other meanings as well: image, figure, thought, imagination, ornament.

We worked very hard, lost money, made money, and had a great deal of fun. Our first fashions were stitched in the Tel Aviv atelier of Fini Leitersdorf, and many of her original workers still produce our fashions.

Finding the craftsmen I knew in places like Porat and Avdon was easy, though as soon as their crops became profitable these immigrants gave up crafts. With the Bayhanim, who have continued at Maskit, it was different. They had left Agur and all I knew was that they were somewhere in the orchards of Ness Ziona, for today's housing developments were not yet built. The families lived far apart in old watchmen's huts, and I spent days driving the jeep through rows of orange trees collecting my jewelers and weavers, who were not interested in oranges and only too happy to start working again, this time for Maskit.

Our first craft exhibition and fashion show was held in 1954 at the Dizengoff Museum in Tel Aviv, and it was a huge success. Our sales were about six thousand dollars within three weeks, a fantastic amount for the time. Whole classes of schoolchildren came to watch our craftsmen at work, the museum's attendance records were broken, and all of us worked from morning till night with a wonderful feeling of achievement.

Sheik Suleiman, of a Bedouin tribe camped near Beersheba, was one of our guests, and he and his Bedouin inspecting our merchandise in their flowing robes and daggers made quite a sight.

"I want to get a trousseau for my next wife, a German girl" was Sheik Suleiman's explanation for his visit. He was already something of a tourist attraction, with his thirty-nine wives and the inevitable jokes about the fact that he did not know which of his tribesmen were his sons. His fortieth wife was to be European and he had placed notices in newspapers abroad inviting interested candidates to reply. A young German woman wrote that she would like to marry a Sheik of Araby; she never arrived, but meanwhile the Sheik came to us for the necessary embroidered sandals and blouses for his intended.

"And this is for you," he said, putting in my arms a tiny desert gazelle. It was a lovely thing, but its little hoofs were sharp as knives and in a short time my arms were bleeding and my skirt was slashed. The solution was to pass it on to Udi, who was at a farm boarding school, and that day I drove north with the little animal. Udi and his friends built a large enclosure, where it had a happy life.

At work, I felt myself at the center of something important, and once more I made friends with a whole series of people whose problems I tried to help solve. Evenings, in my own house, it was different: I felt very much in the shadow of Moshe.

Planning the interior of our home, which I worked on over the years step by step, piece by piece, was tremendously important to me; but it was a background for Moshe, and I felt part of that background. I liked being a hostess in the casual style we had set at Jerusalem, but that again was a contribution I felt I could make for Moshe. At home in those days I rarely expressed my own view. The American trip showed me that I was capable of doing so; but every evening I came home to Zahala and the belief that this was not really true. It was years before I became convinced that the personality I projected away from home was not some sort of strange illusion.

The Zahala house, where we lived for nearly twenty years, was the last of the homes in which I spent countless nights waiting for the sound that meant Moshe had come home. When I was in some distant place at night, all my thoughts concentrated on home, at Zahala, with Moshe.

The sound of his homecoming changed over the years. In Nahalal, which was the opposite of Zahala in so many ways, both spiritually and materially, the sound was the clatter of the horse and cart that brought Moshe home from the fields, or the crunch on gravel of the car that brought him home from Haganah duty. Then there was the smoother sound of a better car pulling up at our Jerusalem home. At Zahala, finally, came all the mixture of brakes and bangs and footsteps of two cars and the bodyguards, and the sentry at the gate, signifying that that particular night of waiting alone in the dark had come to an end.

At Zahala our collection of eye patches expanded, for it was while we lived there that Moshe's fame grew to world-wide proportions. The seriousness, actual pain, and enduring effects of Moshe's injury cannot, I think, be imagined by most people. More than one psychiatrist has suggested that the injury had much to do with his behavior, since mutilation can make a man wish to prove himself in excessive ways; I have also heard that women may be attracted by the symbols of injury.

I cannot judge such theories, but it is clear to me that the patch played its part in Moshe's political and personal charisma. At the same time, because I was so close to him, I know the physical pain it caused; it is hard to express rationally, but many, many times I actually felt his pain with him. Again, there was never anything I could do, for, after discussions with specialists in Israel and abroad, the conclusion was that medical science could do nothing for Moshe's particular case.

At Zahala I took care of the patches that began pouring in from admirers all over the world—patches of varying types and construction that people thought might help Moshe. One, quite incredibly, was eighteen-karat gold adorned with a Star of David. Moshe was indifferent to each new sample arriving in the mail, but later he would remember one and decide it might be right. And then it too would be discarded.

All I could do was try to help find the best possible patch. This meant a great deal of running around, especially when I was abroad. Shortly after the Six-Day War, a package arrived from New York with yet another patch, very beautifully made, this time with an admiring letter from someone named Grace Forsythe. I sent a letter of thanks, as I always did. Moshe was not interested at the time; two years later he came upon it in one of the drawers where I kept patches, and decided it was comfortable. He asked our military mission in America to locate Grace Forsythe, but they could not. I was going to America on a speaking tour and, knowing that Moshe liked the patch and was wearing it, decided to try to find her.

She was not in the telephone book, and a note I sent came back marked "Not at this address." Assuming she had bought the patch at one of New York's many optical supply stores, I began making the rounds of them between speaking engagements; I had made a sketch of the design, and described it carefully at shop after shop.

"No, we have nothing like that. We carry only the standard type" was the response everywhere, for people who usually buy eye patches have nothing like Moshe's injury.

Finally I decided to do what I always disliked—explain that this was for the famous one-eyed general. Now I was given more attention, and at one shop a store in Los Angeles was suggested. I telephoned to Los Angeles, but no, what they had were fancy patches for women, made of plastic, some even with feathers.

At one of these encounters a woman standing next to me happened to hear the conversation and said, "There's just one place that might have such a thing, the oldest pharmacy in New York, the one at the Hotel Barclay." The Hotel Barclay was where I was staying. I rushed back there, produced my sketch, and explained that it had been sent to my husband by a woman called Grace Forsythe.

"Yes, that's right," said the salesman. "Grace Forsythe was a milliner who, on the side, used to make custom designs for patches for us. But she died a year ago." Miss Forsythe had worked with another milliner, Mary Supan, he explained. I went to see her.

"Grace was all alone when she died," Miss Supan told me. "Her body was not found for eight days. She would have been so happy to know that, in her way, she helped your husband. For you must not think he has only Jewish admirers." She agreed to make four more patches for Moshe, though she could not find the "bodies" Grace Forsythe had used, explaining that making this kind of patch was "like making a hat."

A very different reaction came from a group of our soldiers who wrote to my office several years ago. "Some of us have decided to ask you to tell us the truth," it read. "Is your husband's patch just a publicity stunt? We are asking because we have noticed that in newspaper pictures he is sometimes wearing it on his left eye, and sometimes on the right."

This cynicism hurt me. I realize that young people have every reason to distrust "public relations," but if they know enough to be so suspicious, they should also know that the negatives from which newspaper pictures are printed are sometimes reversed. I was also shocked for another reason. Obviously our schools do not teach the history of our country during the past forty years, and our children know nothing about such events as the Twenty-three and Moshe's episode in Syria. I wrote to the soldiers that Moshe was wounded in an action in which he fought with great bravery.

There is a connection, I think, between Moshe's eye patch and his interest in archeology. At first, there was pain and the need for adjustment; then came years of complications. Reading is now a great strain, so Moshe is denied the pleasure and relaxation he once had. His doctors have agreed that archeological digging is one thing he can do, and have encouraged it. I know that injuries to his spine make digging incredibly painful; yet he does it because he cares for it so deeply.

But it worried me when Moshe began selling his name, and it made me most uncomfortable to see references to objects "from the private collection of Moshe Dayan." Another reaction of mine—one growing out of my ignorance of the field—is purely aesthetic, for Moshe has never cared for discoveries that I consider beautiful. Ancient glass, for instance, holds no interest for him, and I see no beauty in some of the things that absorb him.

. . . . .

Our home in Zahala was crammed with gifts from all over the world, from the great and from the unknown; and because of our position some of my housekeeping worries were made easier than those of a normal housewife. But for the same reason it could also be more complicated. For instance, if I called the gas company to send a man to refill our tank, he would come immediately because it was the Dayan house. But then a second man might come half an hour later, again just because it was the Dayan house. We would have to pay twice, and things could get complicated.

Gamine, the lion cub from a French château, was one of our more charming gifts. She came into our lives four years ago, when Yael and I were in Paris at a dinner party. I was on my way to see Assi in Nice, where he was filming with Melina Mercouri. Yael, sitting next to a young French viscount, asked me in proper jet-set style, "Mummy, don't you want a lion?"

"Yes, why not?" I said. It turned out that the viscount had converted his marvelous château into a wild-game reserve and has as many as sixty lions, among other beasts. The place was wonderful, conditions delightful, and the food fantastic, so the animals' birth rate was much higher than in the wild.

"Is it for you, madame, or for your husband?" I was asked when I came for the cub. "Because if it is for you, you must take a male. For your husband, a female." I was fascinated to learn that such animals develop attachments for humans of the opposite sex and selection must be based on this fact. I had thought of giving the lion to Udi, but he turned out not to be interested; so I took a lovely little three-month-old lioness called Gamine. The rule about the opposite sex turned out to be true. I have a woman friend in Pittsburgh who keeps both a lion and a leopard —both males—in her flat; there is nothing to it, she assures me.

To get Gamine to Israel I telephoned El Al and asked what the regulations were for lions. "It all depends on the captain," I was told. The captain of my flight happened to be an American-born Israeli pilot who loved the idea of having a lion on board. The menu for the trip was condensed milk and vitamins, and Gamine was no trouble at all. Once, when I returned to my seat to check Gamine in her box, I found to my horror that the box was empty. "Oh, she's in the cockpit playing with the captain," the stewardess told me. At Lydda airport I did not tell the reception manager that the box with the air holes had a lion inside, and he put his fingers through the holes to carry it. Later, when he learned the truth, he became frantically nervous to think that his fingers might have been chewed off.

Back home I did not say a word about Gamine, but opened her box in the living room.

"Give her to the zoo tomorrow morning," said Moshe. I put

her in Assi's empty room for the night, and she didn't cry or make the slightest mess. Hours later I heard Moshe get up, go to Assi's room, and bring the little cub back with him. It was uncanny, but she knew she belonged to Moshe, and from then on she was his, sleeping on his feet at night and on the floor by his bed during the day. She used to wake up in the middle of the night, pad up to Moshe's pillow, carefully lick his entire face, and snuggle down again at his feet until daytime.

Moshe loved to romp on the floor with her, and she was beautifully behaved while he sat at his desk gluing pottery together. This is more than I can say of a Siamese cat we once had who became bored when Moshe didn't pay attention to her and used to take swipes at pieces of his ancient ceramics.

I drove to Nahalal with Gamine to show her to Udi and the children. Everybody loved her, and nobody was even faintly disturbed at the idea of a lioness. At the gas station in Nazareth the Arab children adored her, and when I picked up a soldier hitchhiker, he spent the ride playing with Gamine. The trip back reminded me of my ride with Sheik Sulciman's gazelle years earlier, because Gamine nibbled my hair as I drove.

We could not keep her more than six weeks. The veterinarian insisted that no matter how sweet their disposition, lion cubs do not know their own strength. The day would come, during play, when damage would be done; Moshe was already black and blue from those romps on the floor. So we gave Gamine to the men of the Army Central Command, and today she is their mascot at headquarters. To my regret they changed her name to Ruthie, which is certainly less pretty than Gamine, but at least she now has a mate. Moshe missed her and would go say hello on visits. Gamine, grown into a real lioness, recognized him immediately and licked him with joy.

So I came home to Zahala with a lioness; but then I was always returning with strange assortments of gifts. Once there were two hamsters for the boys, who adored animals; I had three turtles, too, one for each of the children, but hamsters were all the thing that year in New York. The El Al flight was a long one in the early days, and during the endless night across the ocean I suddenly heard an American voice scream, "Rats!" I quickly checked my flight bag, in which I had put Udi and Assi's hamsters, and found to my horror that they had chewed a hole in the bag and escaped. It was hard to convince the upset tourist that El Al was really not the one airline with rats aboard. I felt my usual emotions of fright and guilt, as I have in a lifetime of situations of this sort, and even a friend of mine on that flight, who had a glass of water near his seat for his headache pills, was angry with me when one of the hamsters was finally located balancing on the glass having a drink.

Once I returned home laden wth handicrafts acquired on a Far

Eastern trip for the World Crafts Council, plus two enormous straw hats for Yael and Assi's wife that I had bought in Bangkok. They were as big as lampshades, which is a nice use for them. I carried one in each hand during this complicated trip and that is how I arrived, unannounced, in Saigon, where hotel rooms were not to be had and practically no Israeli ever went—except Moshe, who had been assigned by several newspapers to write about the war.

Our interlude in Vietnam was an extraordinary example of my efforts to join Moshe. On the plane fom Cambodia—with a new "Grace Kelly" hairdo from one of Phnompenh's numerous hairdressers where you order your style from movie-magazine photographs—I met an Australian professor who had once been on a kibbutz. His very kind friends at the Australian embassy in Saigon drove all through the city with me—and my Bangkok hats and other handicrafts—to find me a hotel room. We traveled in an open jeep. The embassy men explained it was safest to travel with the windows open in case a bomb was tossed in, because that way it was easier to toss the bomb out again.

That did not bother me; I was too disturbed by seeing first-hand what war can do to a city as beautiful as Saigon must once have been. There were streams of refugees everywhere and sounds of bombing in the distance. And the soldiers. At one of the hotels we tried, I talked with a handsome and very young American pilot.

"M'am," he said to me, "don't be afraid of these people. They're very kind and friendly." He told me he had been out on sixteen sorties, and I thought to myself, What is a nice boy like this, who should be home studying, doing so far from everyone he knows, and killing people who have no quarrel with him?

We finally did find a hotel that had a place for me—one in a room with eight beds. The Vietnamese were kind and friendly, and did everything they could to help. There was no electricity —it had been bombed out—but the telephone was working, and a call was put through to the American embassy with a message telling Moshe, if he should turn up, where I was.

Late in the evening he called. Moshe was rarely in Saigon, for he spent all his time in the jungle with the troops; but this particular weekend he had come because of a luncheon meeting with General Westmoreland.

"What in the world are you doing in Vietnam?" Moshe asked over the telephone.

"I came to see you," I said, overjoyed at hearing his voice. "Aren't you a little happy I'm here?"

"A little," said Moshe.

That night, curiously enough, we had a wonderful time. We went to a Chinese restaurant, and we danced, something we hadn't done in a long while.

The Vietnamese women are so beautiful that it is impossible to be jealous of them. But the paradox of the conditions was terrible: people were sleeping in the streets among heaps of garbage and rivers flowing from burst water pipes, while the night clubs were full and music blared from the hotels. Darkness could not hide the tragedy of Vietnam.

Yet that night, for the first time in years, Moshe opened up to me about his work and described the jungle fighting and his thoughts on it. I was full of admiration for the way he was doing his job with the troops in the horrible, swampy jungle conditions. I was afraid Moshe misinterpreted my feelings, and that he believed I thought he was doing all this to make an impression. And yet for a little while that night, the understanding between us was as it had been years ago.

The next morning Moshe went back into the jungle. I spent two more days in Saigon, talking to bar girls and trying to understand their way of life; most of them were fascinatingly attractive, many were attending university. One day I was taken to the races. The grounds were jampacked and littered with betting papers; it was a horrible event in the middle of a war.

Fishing rods and bows and arrows were what I bore home to Zahala from another trip. I bought them in America for Udi and Assi when Moshe and I were there, where we were informed that he was to be given the Legion of Honor award in Paris on the way home. It was stifling hot in New York and I boarded the plane in simple sandals and a cotton dress—a very nice one, but it cost six dollars—and carrying my two sets of fishing rods and bows and arrows. In Paris it was pouring rain at the airport, where the diplomatic corps and distinguished military figures, accompanied by their conservatively dressed wives, had turned out to meet us. I sloshed through the puddles quite happily in my sandals, but the bows and arrows were whisked away with expressions of chagrin.

In spite of the Nahalal influence, it was in Zahala that the children really grew up and from there that all three went into the army. Each of them handled the heritage of the "Dayan problem" in a different way. Nobody knew how to deal with it; not the children and not their officers in the army, and certainly not I. I do not think Moshe ever considered it his worry, but more than one high-ranking army man said to me, "Our officers don't know how to take the Dayan children. Some are too tough on them, some too easy."

Assi hated the army, could not adjust, and was miserable throughout his service. He spent time in the army prison for desertion during training, after he could not meet the goal he set himself by volunteering for the paratroop commandos. I visited him often in prison, trying to help his inner turmoil, for the two of us have always been close, just as Udi and I have been. I understood the boys more easily than I did Yael.

Udi's army unit was one of the most secret and dangerous, requiring great independence and resourcefulness. He, too, was often confined to barracks for minor infringements of discipline during his military service. Simha, of course, considered Moshe and me terrible parents to let our sons suffer in jail, when, as she thought, we could easily get them out.

Assi stayed a private and Udi a sergeant; only Yael became an officer. Yael always managed to get permission to do what she wanted without getting into trouble, and handled well the problem of being the outstanding girl in her unit's basic training. She knew that if she were selected as the best recruit there would be difficulties, since her father was Chief of Staff. In the end the girls themselves insisted Yael receive the award, because it was so obvious that she deserved it.

Udi is a good sportsman, adventurous to the point of recklessness, always climbing the highest branch and always falling off, a trait his young son inherits. He was never interested in school, but then, he had been moved to three different schools by the time we settled in Zahala. From there we sent him to an agricultural boarding school whose social outlook was close to my own. Udi refused to have Moshe bring him to school the first day. He did not want the "Dayan name" attached to him. Of course everyone knew he was Udi Dayan, but he explained this away by saying, "Moshe Dayan is my uncle." This attempt lasted about a week.

After high school and before his army service, Udi went to South America as a deckboy on an Israeli cargo ship, just the kind of adventure Moshe had wanted but was turned down for twenty years earlier. The sailors decided they would give "the general's son" a hard time, but Udi took everything so cheerfully that they gave up.

Assi is in theory a political leftist and Udi definitely is not, but Udi is the one who has personal friendships with Arab families. And Udi, who always seems casual and lighthearted, was the one who wrote me a moving letter as soon as he knew I was divorcing Moshe. In it he examined which traits he believes he has inherited from his mother and which from his father: from me, "a good heart and good hands, and the capacity to care when I see a child who has been hurt." And from Moshe, "a sense of humor, which helps to get the car out of the mud." Udi, too, has begun to write, and some charming short pieces of his have been published.

Assi is a strange mixture, in many ways like me, for he can go into a deep depression and then switch to elation. His imagination, like mine, works hard. In elementary school, on a questionnaire the children had to fill in about their home and parents, Assi wrote, "My father is a plumber, and my mother is a dressmaker from Rumania." At the end of the form he added, "I'm answering this way because I don't want to be a guinea pig."

The school psychologist was interested, and called me in for a consultation. "He suffers from the 'Dayan Complex,' " said the psychologist, and added that Assi's future was problematical. Ever since he was a little boy Assi's sense of humor has been outrageous; yet during his school days one of Schopenhauer's gloomier quotations was tacked to the wall of his room, and he was already writing stories that were far too morbid for me. But I did not take the psychologist too seriously; I knew the children had their problems but I thought they would survive them, as they have.

Yet as late at 1960—when Assi was fifteen, Udi nineteen, and Yael twenty-two—I was still enormously concerned. In a letter to my friend Herzl, in whom I confided so many of my family problems, I wrote, "I can't understand the boys at all. They are so handsome, so egotistical, so unconcerned about others. I suppose I am to blame, because I adore them and can't say no to them." That was the year of Assi's flamboyant adventure in Cyprus, from where he and a friend planned to sail to Turkey and on to Africa. He bought his ticket to Cyprus by selling some of the things we had in the Zahala house; there was such a large assortment that we didn't miss anything until after he and his friend had left. Assi spent some time in a Cyprus jail and was then banished from the island, with a government edict that he must never again set foot on Cyprus. The story ended happily eight years later when Assi married, and the Cyprus government sent a message lifting the lifelong ban as a wedding gift. With this came an ancient pistol of Moshe's that Assi had taken.

Yael is without doubt her father's daughter, and that is what she always wanted to be. In her fictionalized autobiography *New Face in the Mirror,* published when she was nineteen, the narrator's relationship with her father is the serious one; her mother is a minor, neglected thing. I do not know whether this character is a figure of fiction, or the way Yael saw me, or the way she wanted her mother to be. To my regret, Yael never came to me for anything much beyond services or things she needed. The spontaneous gestures of warmth always came from the boys.

The names of our children come from the Bible. There Ehud was a "strong warrior" and is described as being left-handed. Assaf was "a leader of David's choir" and a composer. (Of our two boys, Assi is the left-handed one.) Yael was a fearless woman who killed an enemy with a tent-peg.

For their different achievements in their own right, I am proud of all three of my children. They are all standing on their own feet, they have always been good friends, they are all using their talents, and each has accomplished things I always dreamed of but never did. They have all coped with the terrible heritage of charisma, and to me they are all wonderful.

Moshe's mother, Devora, died in August 1956, after a long illness, just too soon to see her son's triumph in the Sinai Campaign. Shmuel was admirable; he did not move from her side for three months, and at Nahalal each morning he would carry Devora outside so she could lie by the bed of violets under the cypress trees. I was the first to arrive at the hospital after Devora died; and I was with Shmuel when he died in 1969. When Aviva died, a year earlier, Moshe was planting a poinsettia tree in our Zahala garden just as the phone rang with the news; from then on I thought of it as Aviva's tree. The morning of our divorce, after the storm of the night before, I saw that Aviva's tree had broken.

11 · The Orange Blouse

The name "Shimron" cropped up out of the blue one day in
1954 during a meeting at the Ministry of Labor. "We've heard
that one of the new immigrants there, a man from Baghdad, is
an outstanding weaver," someone said to me. "Why don't you
go have a talk with him? If he's really good, maybe you can
cook up some sort of weaving project."

The next day I drove the jeep north to the familiar crossroads
of the Nazareth highway. Sixteen years had changed Shimron.
The huts were still there; but in place of young people trying to
form a commune were discouraged immigrants from Arab countries. The one thing that had flourished over the years was the
King George V Forest, now a thick green strip along the ridge.

I found the hut with no difficulty: it was the one Moshe and I
had lived in. Inside, it was totally changed—the atmosphere, the
people, the problems. In the small, dark room I made the
acquaintance of George Kashi, his wife, Emma, and their son,
Albert. George seemed to me at the time rather elderly; he must
have been about fifty-five, while I was not yet forty. His wife
seemed a pleasant woman in spite of badly crippled legs. Working at a small table in the corner was their only son, a good-
looking boy of about twenty-two. There was a little daughter as
well, and another young man of Albert's age.

Mr. Kashi did not look healthy, and I noticed a half-empty
bottle near his chair. I introduced myself, explained what I
wanted, and asked him to tell me about himself.

"Ah, in Iraq we were well off," he began. I noticed that his eyes were bleary. The contrast between this scene and my Shimron was powerful, and I remembered the wonderful, still nights as I listened to Mr. Kashi's story. "I had a large weaving factory, and we did a big export business to England. Harris tweeds." Harris tweeds from Baghdad to the British Isles? Yes, that is how it was.

The family was well connected, he continued, with friends in high government places. I learned later this was all true. Mrs. Kashi's brother, who lived in Egypt, was said to be the dentist of King Farouk. In Iraq the family had been prosperous; in Shimron they were in a hut, and not as I had once been, out of choice. They had been in Israel just over two years.

"Here is Albert, my son," George Kashi went on. "A wonderful boy. He wants to go into the air force, and, you see, he's busy studying mathematics, which he needs to be accepted. But he's already done his military service, in the tank corps. If you're serious about this weaving factory, I must ask you to convince Albert to give up his air force idea. He's already trained in the weaving business, and knows all the technology." The other young man, he said, was a nephew and the couple had adopted him. He too knew the weaving industry, and his name was also Albert.

We began to discuss ways of employing new immigrants in a hand-weaving establishment. The site would be Migdal Haemek, a new town being set up nearby. Instinct told me that George's skill and experience were lucky finds. Our budget was limited and things were being put together on a shoestring, but a shoestring can do wonders. So it was more or less settled, there in the Shimron hut I knew so well.

I turned to Albert and said, "You must help your father. Don't talk to me about the air force for at least a year. Let's get this started." Albert, his father said, was a fine administrator and had such beautiful handwriting. I was pleased that in a sense I had returned Albert to his father for at least a year. It was an easy way of playing God.

The family moved from Shimron to a flat in the new town; looms were built, fabrics were designed and woven.

"You're right," Albert said some months later, "I can't leave my father and go into the air force."

In October 1956, George Kashi fell seriously ill and I arranged for his admittance to Tel Hashomer Hospital. But that October there was a cloud in the air that blanketed everything else: impending war. Nobody knew where or when the cloud would burst, though there was theorizing about a possible strike in the north, on the Syrian border. I was busy with Labor Ministry projects. About the war, I knew as much as I heard on the radio.

My sister, Reumah, knew more. She and the children lived on a military base with her air force husband, and towards the middle of October all families were evacuated from these bases.

One Friday evening in October I was home, alone with Simha. Moshe, who was almost always home on Friday evenings, had announced earlier that he would be away that night. Udi was at boarding school, Assi was with friends. Yael was in Europe. Suddenly there was a ring at the door, and there stood Albert Kashi.

"Ruth," he said, "I've been called up. I came to tell you there's work on the looms for four days. If you visit my father at the hospital, don't tell him about this, because then he won't go through with the operation, and that might kill him. But if I'm not back within four days you'll have to tell him, because he'll have to decide what new work to put on the looms."

Albert took two small swatches of cloth from his pocket. "Look, these are samples of two new designs. I think they're going to be fine." One was a beautiful brocade, the other was striped, and both used lurex, a bit of glitter new to hand-weaving and certainly new to the development town of Migdal Haemek.

"My father designed them," he said as he put the swatches in my hand. "And now I must go." The door closed, and I never saw Albert again.

The next day I went to visit George Kashi at the hospital. George knew all the gossip, of course, but not that Albert had been called up. On Sunday George's operation was canceled and he was sent home. Patients in all hospitals, except the most critically ill, were being sent home to make beds available for possible military casualties. Back at Migdal Haemek, George Kashi finally learned that his son had been called to active duty.

Moshe sent a cable to Yael telling her to come home immediately; with war about to break out, he did not want his daughter gallivanting around Europe. In the blackout, I drove to the airport to pick up Yael, who was not yet eighteen, and took her to the base to report for duty.

The Sinai Campaign lasted officially eight days, from October 29 to November 5. During this time Moshe telephoned me regularly to tell me where he would be—in Jerusalem, with Ben-Gurion, at headquarters. His enormous responsibility as Chief of Staff brought me closer to prayer than ever before, for this time there was the knowledge that soldiers were dying under Moshe's command, paying the price of Moshe's decisions. Evenings, I did not dream of leaving the house, even to sit with the neighbors, because he might phone. When news came of casualties, I had only my past experience in waiting to help me carry on with normal life, while Moshe bore the responsibility. I went to work, of course; Moshe turned up from time to time, sometimes at the office or at home for a bath.

The country was flooded with foreign correspondents. Yael, in uniform, managed to get leave from camp and sometimes met with them. I was practically unknown to reporters, even though the Dan Hotel, where most of them stayed, was across the street from our Maskit shop.

Suddenly, on November 5, the war was over. Mopping up continued, but the success was brilliant and complete. A day later I drove north to Migdal Haemek wtih my secretary, Esther. Like everyone else, the townspeople were excited; their boys had come back—all of them, that is, except Albert. Nevertheless, the Kashi home was festive.

"We've had a message from Albert through one of his friends who's just come back from Sinai," said Mrs. Kashi, beaming, when I arrived. "Albert's still with his unit down there, but he sent word that he's fine. And I'm so proud of him! He knew exactly what was going on. Everybody thought the trouble would be in the north, with Syria. Not my Albert! He told me, 'Mother, I'm going to see your brother in Cairo, and not only that, I'm going to bring him back to Israel to you!' "

Drawn to the place, I returned to Migdal Haemek and the Kashi home the following day. "We've had a message from Albert brought by another friend," said Mrs. Kashi this time.

After a few more days I began to find the situation peculiar. It was impossible that by now Albert could not have managed to come home briefly on leave; he was a devoted son. His cousin, "the other Albert," had been back now for a week. Even Mrs. Kashi was beginning to feel uneasy.

I decided that this was nonsense. It was ridiculous that everybody else had been released, and not Albert. I was going to find him and bring him back.

It was all so strange. That day Mrs. Kashi said, "Somebody from Albert's unit—most of them are now in Afula—came by this morning and said he'd be home in a few days." I drove to Afula with Esther, who was with me during this period and was a tower of strength. We located the unit and talked with every officer and soldier in sight. Nobody knew anything about Albert. Finally somebody said, "Yes, someone was here yesterday and said that he'd seen Albert at a village in the Negev." We drove south, located another portion of the unit, and repeated our questions. Again, nobody had an answer.

Now it was time for the last, inevitable inquiry: at the army chaplain's office in the records of the unidentified dead. There I learned that Sergeant Albert Kashi had died in his burning tank on the first day of the Sinai Campaign. But there was as yet no evidence of this, and so his family had not yet been officially informed. The only clue was a small sample of fabric, a tatter of a man's undershirt embroidered by hand with an intricate little stripe. That, and a small piece of a paper—a list of soldiers' names in a familiar and fine handwriting.

I drove back to the Kashi home. "Do you embroider Albert's undershirts?" I managed to ask his mother.

The woman gave me the one answer she thought might still save her son: "No."

I had Esther take Mrs. Kashi to the next room. Then I asked Albert's cousin, "Does your aunt embroider Albert's things?" Without a word he went to the clothes cabinet and opened a drawer. It was filled with neatly folded men's undergarments, all marked with an embroidered monogram A.

Each day of the following week, the traditional Jewish period of Shiva, during which the bereaved family gathers to mourn, I drove to Migdal Haemek to sit with the parents and friends. I felt a large share of guilt. If I had not interfered, if I had not done as the father had pleaded, then Albert would have gone into the air force and not have served in a tank unit for that fatal battle. I reflected on how people behave when they know some terrible truth: they pretend it does not exist so that perhaps, somehow, they will avoid the day of recognition. It took me a long time to understand how messages "from Albert" came to be delivered long after hostilities were over, when in fact he had been killed in the first day of fighting. The friends who brought them knew perfectly well that Albert was dead. They only wanted to give the family a little more borrowed time.

I gave George Kashi the two swatches that Albert had brought me on his last visit. He said, "We'll call the design 'Sinai.' And they'll be beautiful." He was drinking heavily again and never recovered from the loss of his son, though he lived another fifteen years. A plaque to Albert's memory was affixed to the entrance of the building where the looms stood, and which is still used today for special Maskit fabrics.

That is what I was doing during the Sinai war. Reporters abroad always ask where I am during our wars. At the front? Sleeping with a gun? The truth is of course far from that. During much of the Sinai Campaign I was in a development town with a family from Iraq who had lost their only son.

At the same time normal activity continued. Nearly every day, there were business meetings at Maskit—budget problems mostly, since we had practically no money. We were also planning one of our first fashion shows abroad. Our designer Fini Leitersdorf was to present it in London in mid-November. During the long jeep drives I thought about Maski's operating costs and how the new dresses for the London show should be priced. At the same time I reflected on the strangeness of human behavior, and the wish to postpone, at all costs, the shock of recognition.

One sunny November afternoon returning from my daily

visit to the Kashi home, I was driving towards the Maskit office when a woman crossing the street caught my eye. She was wearing a bright orange dress, and the color struck me as wonderfully gay and cheerful.

It was a marvelous day, in spite of the sorrow at the Kashi home. The victory under Moshe had been sweepingly brilliant and the whole country was alive with pride and joy. He was the hero for all Israel, and for me as well.

Even our own command had expected a higher casualty list. But Albert was one of only one hundred and ninety dead, and this was one of the Sinai Campaign's triumphs—the relatively small toll of lives paid for a total military decision. This in no way helped the individual tragedies of the families of the dead and wounded, but it might have been so much more terrible.

As I drove I noticed a blouse in a shop window. It was exactly the same bright orange as the dress I had seen a moment ago. I parked the jeep, walked into the shop, and bought the blouse. Unlike many women, I don't buy clothes as a way of expressing or coping with emotion. But this day was different, and everything seemed bright with potential. The blouse fit perfectly. I wore it out of the shop and went to the office. Everybody told me how nice it looked; they were not used to having me turn up wearing a brand-new purchase.

There was a message from Moshe's office that I was to be hostess to several French generals at our home that evening. In the afternoon I was expected at my cousin's house to celebrate the birth of a baby boy. Now it was time for a meeting at the Dan Hotel with representatives of the Finance Ministry about Maskit's budget.

As I hurried up the steps to the lobby, an Italian journalist came towards me. "You're Mrs. Dayan, aren't you?" he asked, stopping me just outside the entrance. "Please, I'd like to ask you a question."

"Yes, I am, but I'm terribly sorry, I know nothing about politics." That was my familiar reply. "There's nothing I can tell you, and anyway you must excuse me. I'm due here for an appointment."

The journalist persisted. "But this is a personal question, Mrs. Dayan. Actually, everybody in the lobby is talking about it. They're all waiting for the final word, and I decided to be the one to get it."

"All right, then, let's have it," I said cheerfully.

"Well, I'd like to be the first to know about your divorce," said the journalist.

"Perhaps you have me mixed up with somebody else?" I asked. No, there was no mistake. I asked him to repeat the question, and he did. It began to dawn on me that the conversation might be in earnest. "Look, I'd better go home and ask my husband about your question. Call me tomorrow, because, really, just now I haven't the slightest idea what you're talking about."

I turned and walked into the lobby. There, waiting for the Maskit appointment, was an official who was also an old friend. "We have a few minutes before the meeting," I said brightly. "Let's go to the bar and have a drink."

Something frightening had crept into this sunny day. Not really frightening, of course; nothing like this could ever happen to me—to others, possibly. But my basic reaction was the same as when the news came of Moshe's arrest: No, certainly not; the British would not do such a thing—how could they, when I was once a schoolgirl in London? Still, my reaction had already gone beyond the feelings one shares with every wife who watches her husband flirt with younger and prettier girls.

My friend and I sat at the bar, and I suppose it was a sophisticated scene—waiters, tinkling ice cubes, journalists' chatter in all sorts of languages, I in my new blouse. But sophisticated was not the word for me. My idea of love had been formed by *The Little Mermaid.* The reporter's question—a fair one, as I quickly learned—had to do with a way of life I could barely imagine. Yet every "informed" Israeli already knew that Moshe was leading a life of his own, and since it was such common knowledge, it was taken for granted that I knew too. The lobby of the Dan Hotel wanted an answer, but until the Italian journalist asked it, I was not even aware of the question. Naturally, I knew that Moshe was unusually attractive to women, and I had often been jealous of them. But there was a vast difference between that and what I was to learn now. During all the years in which Moshe's exploits with women provided newspaper copy all over the world, I think I took them more seriously than he did, for I am sure that today Moshe can barely remember the names of some of his "romances."

In the bar with my friend I had the presence of mind to talk in a carefree way. I mentioned the reporter's question in such a way that my friend would think I knew everything—except for a detail or two, such as a name that happened to escape me.

"You mean you don't know about her?" he asked in amazement.

It was time for our meeting, and Maskit's loan was approved. In my orange blouse, I went to my cousin's party and chatted with my parents and friends. Then I rushed home and changed into evening dress, to be hostess to high-ranking French officers. Finally, at the close of a day that had begun so long ago with the parents of Albert Kashi, there was time for a talk with Moshe.

He was first surprised by my ignorance, and then annoyed by it. I cried without a trace of self-control. In my eyes, no matter how many tears they shed, Moshe was a leader unique and indispensable to Israel; and my love affair with my husband was part of my love affair with my country. I was proud of him just as everybody else was, and although in my mind I separated family life from public life, emotionally they were interwoven.

The next morning I went to work. I thought how lovely it would be to have a nervous breakdown, lock myself in a room, close the shutters, and remain within myself. But the nearest I got to closing the shutters was wearing dark glasses for the next four months. Outwardly nothing had happened, and I was the wife of the conquering hero, met with joy whenever I arrived at some hopelessly muddy village. I think it was this—the realization that my double role gave so much to others—that helped me to carry on. The general's wife in her dark glasses all through that rainy season meant something to others, though not to herself. To new arrivals from Egypt, Iran, Morocco, Tunisia, my visits were a spectacular event.

Even to them, at times I was Mrs. Dayan and at times I was not. One day my jeep was out of order, no car was available, and I had to deliver two suitcases of wool to women who were knitting sweaters for us. I took the suitcases, boarded a bus, and got off at the stop nearest their village. Plodding through the mud with the suitcases, wearing heavy boots and an unfashionable coat, I stopped a villager to ask directions.

"Over that way," he said pointing. "But please don't go there right now. They're expecting a visit from Mrs. Moshe Dayan." Little did the villager know that he had made such an appropriate error. I really felt I had a split identity.

Determined to find out everything possible about "what everybody knew," I talked about the situation with many people. This is a thoroughly destructive thing to do, and there are women who handle themselves much more wisely. I was far from wise, but I have never been able to be anything but open with people. And now that it was quite clear that I knew about Moshe, all sorts of men I had known for years began flirting with me, including—to my astonishment—happily married ones. I suppose this is the usual pattern; but in my innocence, I found it dismaying.

Moshe simply thought I had gone mad. He tried to patch things up. We were barely on speaking terms, so not long after the Dan Hotel revelation Moshe put eleven-year-old Assi on the telephone to me, to say that his father thought it might be a good idea if the four of us—Yael was still in the army—took a holiday in Italy. We sailed that winter. The trip was not a success, hardly the second honeymoon it could have been, if only everything had been different.

It was supposed to be a private visit, but the Italian press learned that the glamorous general and his two bambinos were touring the country. The bambinos, very excited about their first trip abroad, visited the statues of Rome and dutifully listed the names in a notebook. This soon became boring, and Assi and Udi demanded to be taken to the amusement park. The wife of the Israeli military attaché volunteered to take them. What the boys liked was the rifle range, and they began to win the prizes, dolls and embroidered pillows, one after another. They had gone shooting with Moshe since childhood and knew all about rifles. "Will you please get those bambinos out of here," the manager of the shooting range pleaded, and Udi and Assi walked off with their loot.

I seemed always to be calling the police about the boys. They got lost in Rome and casually made their way back to the hotel by taxi while I notified the authorities of their disappearance. They vanished again at the race track and again I called the police; they had found the races boring and had gone off to the stables in the hope of being able to ride the horses.

Capri was beautiful. On the funicular, Udi as usual thought of a trick. He was in a chair behind me and pretended that his shoe had fallen off so that I would think he was going to fall off too. Actually he held the shoe behind his back and ended up grinning. The sea voyage was delightful; but travel does not change your emotional baggage, and we came home to things as they had been.

On a moonlit night in Jerusalem soon after our return, Tzippi's life again crossed mine. Esther and I had taken the jeep to Jerusalem, where I had been invited to speak about Maskit. There was also to be an informal reunion of girls from the Nahalal school. Driving through the empty streets I suddenly saw a women with long black hair standing alone on the sidewalk, holding a baby.

"Tzippi!" I shouted, slamming on the brakes. "What in the world are you doing here?"

"I'm waiting for the baby's father," Tzippi explained. "He's a doctor, but just now he's gone off with some friends." We talked for a few moments, and then a man walked towards us. Tzippi introduced him. He was a flashy young man who told us, "I haven't quite got my M.D. degree yet, so meanwhile I'm working in a record shop. But whenever there is an important operation at the Hadassah Hospital, they telephone me and I go over to help."

We drove to the shack where they lived—in a deserted slum. The baby lay in a tin washbasin and cried. On one of the wall beams, which served as a shelf, were a few baby clothes, all folded and neatly stacked just as I had taught Tzippi to do with Assi's things in Nahalal. It hurt me to see this one remnant left in the squalor. "I'll come tomorrow," I said and left.

At the record store where the young man worked I made the surprising discovery that the owner accepted the medical story.

"Yes," he said, "every so often there is a phone call from the Hadassah Hospital, and then he takes some time off."

I tried to convince Tzippi to get away from her man—she showed me marks on her back where she had been beaten—but it was no use. A baby born earlier, she told me, she had sold; this one, named after Moshe, she insisted on keeping. "Come back to Nahalal," I said. "Aviva will be glad to have you at the farm." No; she loved this man.

I talked to Zelda, who was working at the Ministry of Social Welfare and understood difficult family cases. "Don't take her into your home, or Aviva's," she warned me. "It's too late now to play God."

In Tzippi's eyes I was nearly all-powerful. In my own, I was crushed, unable to know what had gone wrong, where I had made mistakes. The more the situation engulfed me, the less capable I was of mastering it. It was so much easier to deal with other people's problems.

By 1957 Moshe was about to retire as Chief of Staff, in line with the army's policy of rotation. I had so many fears as I passed my twenty-first wedding anniversary and approached my fortieth birthday, and one of them concerned Moshe's future. His life as a fighting man had fascinated and suited him; what was going to happen now? How would he bridge this gap?

Once before, when political considerations had crossed my life with Moshe, I had gone to David Ben-Gurion for help—that day after the Acre trial, with Yael crawling on the floor. And in the autumn of 1957, I again went to see him, this time at his home.

Ben-Gurion was in the kitchen washing dishes. I did not know exactly what I had come for, but I wanted some sort of help. To Ben-Gurion, standing at the sink, I said, "Moshe is facing a gap now that he's finishing as Chief of Staff, and that can be terrible for him. How do you see his future?"

"You shouldn't worry about Moshe," said Ben-Gurion. "He won't get lost. A break of some kind at this point is probably going to be good for him. He's thinking of studying at the university."

"There's talk of that, but I think it's a lot of nonsense. After everything he's done, I know Moshe can't sit quietly in a classroom and read textbooks." (I turned out to be right about this, I am afraid, a habit of mine that has always annoyed Moshe.)

Ben-Gurion was aware of the rumors surrounding Moshe, but gossip and small talk meant nothing to him. His concerns were on another level entirely: his viewpoint was prophetic. Still, Ben-Gurion knew that Moshe, whose qualities he had early recognized, was considered a most attractive man.

This time—it was to be different a few years later when I once again went to Ben-Gurion—no word of this passed between us. Now, at least, I showed some self-restraint and talked only about Moshe's career. Ben-Gurion commented on our conversation to an associate, who later passed his remark on to me. "I admire this woman not for what she said, but for what she didn't say." It is one compliment I have never forgotten.

In 1963 a young woman published a thinly disguised autobiographical novel about a girl soldier and a famous one-armed fighting general. It caused less of a ripple in Israeli society than might have been expected. Duly reported in the local press and eagerly read by teen-agers, it is today barely remembered by well-informed adults. This demonstrates the pragmatism of the Israeli public. After all, this was some years before the wave of permissiveness which has since swept the world, and in another country there would have been a great outcry.

The story behind the book goes all the way back to Nahalal, and ahead to Ben-Gurion at Claridge's Hotel in London. For the young woman who wrote the book had married and borne a child to a schoolmate of Moshe's, an officer who was devoted to Moshe. The trouble was that by the time he met this young woman, he was already married and a father. Romantic and highly principled, he had left his family and divorced his first wife.

When his second wife left him for Moshe, he wrote a new letter to Ben-Gurion, pouring out his pain and disillusionment and referring to the biblical story of David and Bathsheba. In a detailed reply, the Prime Minister wrote that he understood the anguish felt by the officer; but he explained that the ways of historical figures are often different from those of ordinary citizens. "Their private and their public lives run parallel, but they never meet," wrote Ben-Gurion. He gave the example of Lord Nelson (also wounded in one eye), whose affair with Lady Hamilton did not detract from his heroic stature, "even in puritanical Victorian England." And Ben-Gurion took up the reference to David, whose private life is well covered in the Bible: "Whatever David did in his lifetime, remember that today we sing, 'David lives today, and is alive.' "

A copy of Ben-Gurion's letter came to me before the young woman's book was published, at about the time the Ben-Gurions and I happened to be abroad, in London, during the same week. I went to pay a call on them at Claridge's, in whose unaccustomed luxury they were staying. It is a good guess that the Scotland Yard detectives and the richly decorated suite escaped Ben-Gurion's notice, just as many human weaknesses failed to interest him.

Once again I did not know just what I wanted to ask, but I said, "Please don't go writing long letters to people." For by expressing his own philosophical viewpoint, Ben-Gurion was in effect giving his stamp of approval to a man he considered above the law.

Ben-Gurion was aware of, if disinterested in, the friction in our family life, through Paula, who had lively interest in what was going on and occasionally slipped something to him.

From her room in the suite, Paula called to the next room, where we were sitting, "Are you still having trouble with your daughter?" It was the famous, direct, Paula Ben-Gurion approach. Everyone knew that Yael lived a free, adventurous life; she had already written about it in her first novel. I began to cry, as I often did whenever anyone criticized my daughter. Ben-Gurion dismissed the interruption. He was not concerned with young girls but with Moshe.

"You must get used to the idea," he said, turning to the central problem and quoting himself, "that in the case of great men, the private and public lives will often run parallel but will never meet."

It was not difficult for Ben-Gurion to make this rational point. Anyone not emotionally involved could see it in such terms; perhaps even Moshe did. But my world had collapsed. Each day was a form of dying, and even more so the nights. I seemed to be drifting toward some terrible disaster, and all I could do was wait—wait endlessly. I felt as though I were being punished for loving. Searching for help and advice, I knew there was no such thing. And as I lived more and more in the public eye, I continued to feel this way.

But the years have finally accomplished what I once never dreamed could be done—put the shattered pieces together again in a new pattern of survival. Today I can still relive the anguish of that time, but I am no longer the same helpless woman. Today, when I recall Ben-Gurion's letter and his references to David and Bathsheba, I am also capable of noting that a curious biblical footnote is in order.

For Joab, the "captain of the host" after whom our street in Zahala is named, was entangled in an unhappy exchange of letters with King David during an early war—with the Ammonites—when Uriah the Hittite, Bathsheba's first husband, was sent to his death: "And it came to pass in the morning, that David wrote a letter to Joab, and sent it by the hand of Uriah. . . . Then David said unto the messenger, Thus shalt thou say unto Joab, Let not this thing displease thee, for the sword devoureth one as well as another. . . . But the thing that David had done displeased the Lord" (Second Samuel, 11:14–26).

Less than sixteen years after the day at the Dan Hotel, I did decide to divorce Moshe. The newspapers, both in Israel and abroad, had a wonderful time speculating on the reasons and on our separate futures. I read some of these stories with amusement and with the realization that it is best not to believe much of what you read in the papers on personal matters.

The correspondence between Ben-Gurion and the disillusioned husband was published, right after our divorce, in an Israeli weekly. Printed with this exchange was a letter I myself had written to the man at the time of his letter to Ben-Gurion, in the autumn of 1959, in which I tried to console him. I described Moshe's behavior in harsh terms. I wrote that while I, too, had earlier been betrayed by my husband, I had come to understand that this was simply his character in personal affairs.

When I gave an interview to this weekly—the only one I granted to any journalist—some people could not understand why I did such a thing, others understood the reason well. I knew that this material, and worse, had long been in the hands of the editor; and I knew it would not be published so long as Moshe and I remained married. What I wanted was to show that I, who had just left our home, would never be the source of an attack on Moshe; on the contrary, I had long been unhappy, but that was my personal problem. I had, in a way, made Ben-Gurion's "parallel lines" a reality in my own life. From now on Moshe would be for me only a national leader. The other part was finished.

In this interview I said, "For a long time now I have lived with the deep conviction that Moshe has left the realm of private life and become a kind of public property that belongs to the entire nation—and, in a way that is rather well known, to all the women of the world. In the good sense, and in the bad. No matter how he behaves, he will be forgiven. I think I truly know him better than anyone else does, and I certainly would not include him among the saints. But I believe in him."

"Is Moshe today the same man he was when you married him thirty-seven years ago?" That was one of the direct and provocative questions I was asked in the interview. "Certainly not," I answered. And this fact accounts, I think, for the long road people travel between marriage and divorce. Sometimes people just do not know each other when they marry, but I knew Moshe and he knew me, as we were then. We have both changed, though in him the change has been extreme, and in me, I think, much less so.

I loved Moshe for his dedication and his simplicity. He is not to blame that his historical role has elevated him to dizzying heights since then, and this fact has so changed him. My mother has said it: "When Ruth married him, Moshe did not have 'charisma.' "

The Moshe I once knew shines out from those letters he wrote me from prison in Acre; those thin, faded sheets, pasted into an album, are among the most precious things I own.

As his legend grew, women who had never so much as set eyes on him wrote Moshe love letters. Sometimes, incredible as it sounds, they even appealed to me for help. Not long before our divorce I received a phone call from a hysterical girl who demanded to know why my husband hung up on her. I told her that I really had no idea why he would do such a thing and suggested she call him at his office, for by this time I had developed a sense of humor about what once seemed a never-ending tragedy. The girl insisted on seeing me immediately because she was on the verge of a nervous breakdown. "That husband of yours is deceiving me with another woman," she screamed.

I wanted to laugh, but I said sympathetically, "These things do happen." I suggested that she take a sedative and lie down. What a child she is, I thought as I put down the phone. And this girl, whose voice sounded to me ordinary and immature, had had a well-publicized affair with Moshe. Perhaps it would all have been easier for me if only my husband had picked women who were beautiful, charming, and desirable.

For many years I tried to protect Moshe from himself as much as I could; and I saw to it that the "legend" always had his favorite cookies and cornflakes and milk. For myself, except for one fleeting romantic episode, I avoided emotional entanglements. I dislike the role of puritan and would prefer to have behaved differently—not for revenge, but to restore my self-confidence. Affairs with married men are not for me; I would never hurt another woman in the way I have been hurt. Moshe would often telephone, from home, to his longest-lasting romance, and I heard these conversations because he was never concerned about such details as lowering his voice. This woman, too, would complain that he was "deceiving" her with yet other women. He used to tell her not to believe such stories; and I heard all these exchanges.

I learned to live with this—though it was not really living. Far more important, as the years went by, I also learned that there were more and more things that I was capable of doing on my own. This was why I finally made the decision I did: because the price of living with a legend can be too great.

Sixteen years after the Dan Hotel episode, I was also no longer so naïve. Moshe's attitude toward women is not so different from the general rule; what is different is the power of his appeal, and the fact that he himself believes what Ben-Gurion described: that his public genius and his personal inclinations are entirely separate. He is also convinced—and circumstances support him in this—that his importance to the nation somehow excuses him from ordinary human standards. Yet I have never regretted our life together, and if I were asked to live it all over again, I would not choose otherwise.

When I finally fell asleep in the nights after the Sinai period, my dreams were horrible, full of scenes of drowning and being unable to cry for help. Two nights after our divorce, I had a dream of a very different quality; again it was strange and eerie, but this time the strangeness concerned not death but historical permanence.

I dreamed that I was with Udi, and we had to go to the house in Zahala for something, though in my dream I knew I no longer lived there. We saw that all of Moshe's antiquities had grown larger and larger so that now they were towers and steeples and even minarets extending from our house, and it looked like a mysterious city rooted in the past and rising into the future.

"Look, Udi!" I said, "It is *Ir Moshe*"—the City of Moshe, for in Hebrew we say *"Ir David"* for Jerusalem, the City of David.

12 · Charisma in the Jungle

It was considered quite mad, my idea of going to Africa to spend some time with Dr. Albert Schweitzer at his hospital in the jungle. Some of my friends suspected that I might even be thinking of remaining in Lambaréné, on the banks of the Ogowe River in Gabon, but I stayed only for three weeks. In 1960, I was feeling restless and dissatisfied, and when my friend Clara Urquhart invited me to go along with her on her annual visit to the famous doctor, I accepted.

Clara, who lives in London and is one of my closest friends, had by then been intimately associated with Schweitzer for about twenty years, traveling to Lambaréné each year to deal with the great man's accumulation of correspondence and translating his manuscripts from German to English. She and her brother were among the Lambaréné Hospital's main financial supports, and when Schweitzer died he left many of his manuscripts to Clara, who plans to donate them to Tel Aviv University. Clara was one of the very few human beings to whom Schweitzer felt close.

Clara, who is a saint, was widowed at nineteen and left independently wealthy; her own life has been starkly simple and all her resources go to help others. Her London home is a center for those in need of aid, particularly talented black Africans. She "knows everybody." Adlai Stevenson's visit to Schweitzer, for instance, was arranged by Clara, and she was instrumental in the negotiations to award the Nobel Peace Prize of 1960 to Chief

Luthuli, the South African Zulu leader, for his fight for a multiracial society. She is the co-author of a biography of Enzo Sereni, the Italian pacifist who came to Israel to help build the land in friendship with the Arabs, fought with the R.A.F., and was killed in Dachau in 1944. A kibbutz in Israel is named after him. What attracted Clara to Sereni's heroic personality was his hatred of hate.

Clara's involvement with Schweitzer had more to do with his philosophy than with his medicine. Her concern has always been people. After World War II, she went to Poland to help with the rehabilitation of women who had been victims of Nazi medical experiments. She has traveled widely but is not interested in sightseeing, only in people, as I saw when we visited the mud huts of Brazzaville.

Before we left she gave me some rather alarming pointers about Schweitzer; for instance, one must always wear white because he believed it to be the most appropriate and simple color for work in the jungle, and one must never disturb him, practically to the extent of not speaking to him until he speaks. In preparation for the trip I bought straw hats for Clara and me, which I thought were quite nice, but when we arrived Schweitzer refused to let Clara wear hers. He considered the style silly, and insisted that she wear the regulation white jungle helmet. What I chose to wear did not bother him, but he said that he would not let Clara walk around "looking like a fool."

We had three days' wait in Brazzaville, capital of the Congo, for the plane that would take us on to Lambaréné. All arrangements were made by the airline, so we stayed in a luxurious Air France hotel in the middle of the jungle, which is itself an interesting experience. But what I found most remarkable was the behavior of the native staff. The moment word got around that Mrs. Urquhart had arrived at the hotel, all the waiters and other employees clustered around her with enormous smiles. The next day I saw why. Our stay in Brazzaville consisted of visiting on foot in the native quarter every mud hut that every hotel worker called home, with Clara bringing gifts for the entire family and asking about all the relatives.

The last evening Clara felt tired—she is frail and thin and the efforts she demands of herself would tire a much more robust person—so she stayed in her room and I went to the dining room alone. On the menu that evening was French pâté and, very unwisely, I ordered some. Normally I have a cast-iron stomach but it is foolish to eat things like pâté in the jungle, where refrigeration is a problem. I was violently sick all night and when I shakily told Clara about it the next morning, she was of course worried. Here we were going to a jungle hospital to be of assistance; it would not be the thing to arrive ill. I made a quick recovery, however, and we caught the plane to Libreville, the capital of Gabon.

From there we traveled by canoe to the hospital, which is on an island near the village of Lambaréné, and the moment we stepped into that canoe, paddled by four natives in exact rhythm, everything changed. Schweitzer insisted on the canoe rather than a motorboat because he refused to disturb the surrounding wildlife. His philosophy of "reverence for life" and his belief that only through simplicity in living can this be achieved preceded the current ecological concern by fifty years.

It was beautiful being in the canoe. The paddlers would sweep away the overhanging branches that dipped into the water, and from time to time there would be a shout, "Look out!" And then we would see that a cobra had been looped around one of the branches.

A small landing pier came into view and standing there, dressed all in white, was the doctor. An enormous figure with a thatch of white hair, he waited between his two chief nurses, Ali and Matilda. As we stepped out of the canoe Schweitzer embraced Clara so that she practically disappeared from sight, and greeted me politely. I spoke German with the doctor throughout the visit. The only other language he spoke was French.

The first thing that gripped me at Lambaréné Hospital was a strange and overpowering smell, a mixture of the odors of human bodies, medicines, and something elusive. It took time to get used to it and much longer to get rid of it. Months afterwards all the clothes I had worn in the jungle still had the lingering odor, even after many washings. I did not understand what it was until the next day, when I saw the wards.

In my primitive room in the nurses' quarters I found a beautiful tin of delicious French biscuits on the rough wooden table next to the simple bed. That was a good introduction to the paradoxes of Lambaréné, for tons of marvelous foods and the most modern medicines were continually sent by admirers throughout the world to the saintly doctor living his simple life in the jungle. The food was eaten, although much had to be thrown away since any tin or jar spoiled almost immediately after it was opened.

Schweitzer did not believe in such frills as running water. Clara's brother wanted to donate money for a modern water supply but it was refused. The latrine was another example of Lambaréné's paradoxes. It was nothing but a big hole in the ground surrounded by newspapers and by boxes of fine facial tissues sent by admirers. Towards the end he did agree to permit a small generator to provide electric light in the up-to-date operating theater, but only there. Everywhere else, old-fashioned oil lamps were used.

And of course his philosophy of reverence for life meant that no disinfectant or anti-insect sprays were allowed. Finding a black widow spider in your room was not uncommon. Schweitzer was against swatting a mosquito just because it bit you, though wire netting was in use. In most of the books and articles written about this man, there is the recurring story of what happened when you walked along a jungle trail with Schweitzer and crossed the path of a colony of ants. *"Achtung!"* he would call out, and then everyone had to take great care not to step on the ants. I was present when this happened, and it is quite true. Perhaps all the publicity given to Schweitzer—after thirty-five years of unsung activity—made some of this seem phony. This bothered me, to say nothing of the matter of his charisma, a quality familiar to me. Yet the fact remains that this man actually lived his philosophy in the jungle for more than fifty years, under conditions that are hard to imagine. He arrived in Africa in 1913 with a brand-new medical degree, already known as a scholar on Bach and the Bible. He had earned a degree in philosophy, with a dissertation on Kant in 1899, and one each in theology and music. From then on he lived among what he called "the poorest of the poor," with practically all of his affection reserved for animals.

Towards animals, his attitude was fascinating. His pet jackdaw always perched on his shoulder, occasionally nipping at the doctor's ear. Once when Schweitzer left the hospital for a week, the jackdaw waited mournfully at the pier the entire time and refused to eat; the staff tried force-feeding, unsuccessfully. Finally, when Schweitzer's canoe appeared, the jackdaw took his last bit of strength, flapped up to his friend's shoulder, and was happy again. Schweitzer always carried grain in his pocket for the scrawny chickens we passed, and his big dog followed him everywhere. But since it was not permitted to remove the ticks that infested the dog, his sore and bitten ears were permanently bandaged.

Nor was Schweitzer a vegetarian, a fact that has confused some people; crocodile appeared on the menu. He did eat meat, although rarely. The point seemed to be that you must not kill for pleasure.

Every evening in Lambaréné was just about the same. First, one of the lepers brought a pitcher of water and a basin to each room. This man was a patient whose disease had been arrested; he lived in the leper colony nearby, which Schweitzer had founded and which of course I visited. The initial shock of seeing someone with limbs or part of his face eaten away was very great. But I got over it.

Then a bell rang and the doctors and nurses, all changed into clean white smocks, met in the dining room, which was lit by flickering oil lamps. After everyone had gathered, the old man would make his entrance, flanked by Ali and Matilda. We took our seats at a long wooden table beautifully set with German china and old-fashioned cutlery brought long ago from Alsace to the jungle. There were even little wooden holders for knives and forks. In a way, it looked like a formal dinner at the King David Hotel in Jerusalem, except for the day's antimalaria pill placed in the dessert spoons.

Dr. Schweitzer always presided at the center of the long table, and on the floor next to him sat the big dog with the bandaged ears. Opposite him were places for guests—sometimes as many as twenty—who happened to be visiting. After Dr. Schweitzer said grace, everyone sat down. The first evening I made a *faux pas* because, sitting diagonally opposite me, was a doctor who had lived in Israel, and I committed the error of talking across Dr. Schweitzer to him, and in Hebrew at that.

The food was good: fine cheese—as usual, gifts from abroad, but no ice to keep them on—and, at Dr. Schweitzer's place, little dishes arranged with things he particularly liked, such as radishes. I worked in the kitchen for a few days and one of the things I contributed were a few new ways of cooking eggplant, though the staff had excellent recipes of their own.

After the meal Dr. Schweitzer would rise and read a portion of the Bible in German. On my first night it was Luke, and after reading he gave his own commentary, explaining everything in the Bible in perfectly "normal" terms. For Schweitzer there were no incredible miracles. He saw biblical happenings as realistic events within the context of their time.

Every evening, he would sit down at a piano that stood in the dining room—one of the many with rotting wood and broken strings, the condition of most equipment after a short time in the jungle—and everyone would join in hymn singing. Sometimes it would be joyous, sometimes serious; but always the impact of that old man with his shock of white hair, sweating away under the oil lamps and bringing music out of a broken-down piano, was an experience that would not leave you. Apart from this there was no religion at Lambaréné. It was one of the few places in the jungle where a native could receive medical treatment without missionary flavor.

Schweitzer would then walk back to the table and take from his pocket some ancient yellow newspaper clipping. I do not know how these had survived, for they were from Alsatian papers of perhaps seventy years ago.

"Today I'm going to tell two stories," Schweitzer might say. "One about animals, one about people. First, naturally, about the animals." The story he told the first evening, taken from one of those old newspapers, was about a cat and a dog, great friends, who belonged to a farmer. When the cat had kittens, the farmer tied them into a sack and threw it into the river. The next morning the farmer found the sack with the kittens safe and dry on his doorstep; the dog had swum into the river to rescue them.

Afterwards we would break into little groups for coffee, and later Schweitzer and Clara would go to work on his papers. I would spend the evening with the nurses and doctors in their rooms, and there was fun and gossip—always the case where there are more women than men, and here the pretty young nurses outnumbered the doctors—and endless stories about animals, since everybody had his special pet. My friendship with the doctors and nurses was perhaps not appreciated by Schweitzer, or even Clara, since the two of them were very much above gossip.

One young Swiss doctor had a baby monkey that he always kept in his pocket, even during rounds in the wards. For cleanliness, he kept it tidily diapered, and used to come to the baby ward, where I also worked for a few days, to change the diapers. There was a Swiss nurse whose pet was a wildcat, a beautiful animal with a marvelously bushy tail. She took it home with her when she went on leave, and that wildcat traveled through Switzerland and even visited the Alps. When she returned she brought it back to the jungle with her. Another nurse had a fantastic tiny "rat" monkey with a long thin tail, the whole thing measuring only five inches. There was just one radio, because Schweitzer was not in favor of such gadgets, and that was our only source of news. There was no telephone.

Every evening at what seemed promptly ten o'clock there was a tropical rainstorm. Torrents of water poured through the trees, breadfruit dropped from the branches with great thuds, and "flying dogs," a kind of huge bat, went screeching through the night. Around midnight, as I walked to my hut, I would pass Schweitzer's window and see the old gentleman sitting alone at his piano, playing Bach. I know that musicians have criticized him, but I don't believe anybody could have played with more strength and love, or brought more beautiful sounds from that decaying instrument. Again the charges of phoniness and the myths created by public relations came to my mind. I thought about Shmuel, Moshe's father, but he was entirely different. Shmuel really believed he was saving the world with his particular philosophy, even though he was so often away from the soil. But Schweitzer lived his beliefs for half a century.

At five every morning everybody awoke to the sounds of chickens and goats, and I was reminded of life at a kibbutz. But at Lambaréné there was the added sound of coughing throughout the night, for my room was next to the tuberculosis ward.

One morning, I came upon the old doctor nailing some planks together—he did all sorts of simple carpentry himself. Another time I watched him supervising a group of natives weaving a simple rush mat. The maddening part of this, to me, was that the natives worked at such a slow rate that in a whole day they would manage to complete a strip of about five inches; a normal worker anywhere else might have finished ten times as much. This would have driven me crazy, but Schweitzer understood his people. I saw his principle clearly: you cannot create an instant revolution in the jungle. With his sense of humor he would quote the Bible—"In the sweat of thy brow shalt thou eat bread" —and then say, "Well, they sweat and sweat, and that's that."

Their slowness may have been due to the terrible climate. There was never bright sunlight, nothing but a hazy heat and great humidity. After a few days I found it an effort to climb the little hill to the leper colony; yet Schweitzer was doing endless physical labor in his eighty-fifth year.

When I first visited the wards I identified the all-pervasive odor. At Lambaréné Hospital the patient's family comes along and cooks for him. The menu is cassava, plantain, and banana, supplemented by a very smelly fish meal that Schweitzer had introduced to the patients' diet to provide protein; it was this peculiar combination that hung in the air. These wards came to my mind some years later when, after the Six-Day War, the Tel Hashomer Hospital "adopted" the El Arish Hospital in the Gaza Strip and I made frequent visits there. At El Arish the Arab patients' families often occupied the bed, while the patients lay more comfortably on the floor beneath. At Lambaréné you might find a goat under the bed as well. Schweitzer's view was that the patients must feel happy. That was the main thing, much more important than all the gleaming tile and modern conveniences that only alienated people from a totally different culture.

The natives flocked to his primitive place while a modern hospital in the village of Lambaréné that the French built before they left stood practically empty. Once, somewhat to Dr. Schweitzer's annoyance, for he disapproved of sightseeing, I left the jungle and spent the day in Lambaréné at the new hospital with the Swiss couple who ran it.

There was some opposition to the rigidity of Schweitzer's medical beliefs among certain members of his own hospital; one doctor left long before his two-year contract was up, and there were complaints among the natives too, but for different reasons. The witch doctor, for instance, with his painted face and horrible scream, hated Schweitzer. I often saw him standing just outside the hospital compound when a desperate case had left his care and gone to the white doctor as a last resort; he hoped Schweitzer would fail.

One night a pygmy arrived from a distant tribe; his people had heard about Schweitzer and wanted his help. There is something uncanny about seeing a grown human who stands just about waist high to the average man, naked except for a loincloth, and unable to make himself understood. Finally someone was found who knew a few words of his language. This little man was carrying a basket of roots with which to pay the doctor. That was the extent of his civilization. But the distance was too great for Schweitzer, so nothing came of this poor pygmy's efforts.

The degree of dedication that Schweitzer inspired in nearly all the doctors and nurses who volunteered to work with him was impressive. There were of course tensions and jealousies among the staff, just as there are in any small community, including kibbutzim and moshavim, but the devotion to Schweitzer and his cause among these young people was incredible. They came from Europe and America, and were paid only transportation and a holiday at the end of their two-year contract, plus money for stamps, practically the only major expense. Sometimes a medical specialist joined the group, motivated not by idealism but by the chance to study tropical diseases. When I was there, a Japanese doctor was in charge of the leper village. Neither he nor his wife could hold a conversation in anything but Japanese. She worked in the kitchen; it was hard to discuss eggplant recipes with her.

I became especially friendly with an American woman, Marie-Louise, who had arrived earlier as a journalist and decided to stay on for a year. She came from a rich family and was used to luxuries, yet something about the place held her. I think Marie-Louise saw Lambaréné in much the way I did: it gave you a fantastic perspective on yourself and on the world.

The baby ward was a good place to observe the dedication inspired by Schweitzer and his reverence for life. I watched the whole staff work tirelessly to save the life of a day-old infant. It was a baby nobody really wanted, but the care and devotion were fit for a queen's child. Actually, the mother was a native woman infected with bilharziasis who would no doubt have been better off without her new baby.

Among the children in the baby ward were twins. Native custom demanded that they be buried alive; the belief was that twins shared only one soul split between them, and so must not be allowed to survive. Until Schweitzer came, whenever a mother died in childbirth her baby was buried alive with her.

Marie-Louise sent me a letter from Lambaréné not long after I left describing a little orphan boy just under a year old, Christoph, to whom she had become attached; she herself was due to leave Lambaréné and return to her own children. "As you know," she wrote, "Dr. Schweitzer was against my taking Christoph to the States, so I've been looking for suitable parents for him and finally gave him to the chief of the tribe to which he belongs, the Akele. . . . I will continue to provide Christoph with food and clothing, and hope to arrange scholarships when he is ready. It was painful to leave him at the village, where he lives in a grass hut. . . . I've since taken the canoe early in the

morning twice to visit him—without permission from Dr.
Schweitzer, who would not like the idea—and found him naked
on a dirt floor, crying. . . . He is such a bright little boy, so
full of love for everyone. . . ."

I asked what motivated some of the volunteers and was told:
"Well, you should see the small, dull villages some of them come
from." At Lambaréné they found a challange and a great personality that held everything together. Even Marie-Louise, who
came from a background that many might envy, returned to Dr.
Schweitzer and stayed until a jungle ailment made her leave.

That was why we two were together so much at Lambaréné,
for I came from a rich—in experience—life as well. I considered
remaining; and perhaps if I had come from America, as she did,
and knew that my home might be described by the term "futil-
ity of riches," I would have stayed longer. But in Africa I
thought about the challenge of my own country. I did not have
to go to the jungle to look for one. My friends from school have
that dedication, have built their lives around it and are at kibbutzim today. In my own life it all turned out differently, although that was what made me go to Nahalal as a young girl.

I even had moments of nostalgia for the Shimron days, though
the physical surroundings were so different. Here again was not
only the dedication, but the gossip of a small community. Also,
Dr. Schweitzer's hospital was the only place in the world where
I was not "Mrs. Dayan" and was treated like everybody else,
which I liked very much. I dislike being whirled about as a
celebrity, much as I know such performances may be necessary.
And I loathe financial competition, which was nonexistent at
Lambaréné just as it was at Shimron and Nahalal in the old
days. So I felt unusually comfortable in the general atmosphere
of humility. Everybody felt this: you were just yourself and did
what you could. And if you were a nurse, you were that much
more useful than if you were merely a celebrity. Most of the
Lambaréné staff knew little about Moshe, and what they knew
they did not wholeheartedly approve of. Four years after the
Sinai Campaign his reputation was that of a conquering hero,
and these people had pacifist inclinations.

On Christmas Eve the residents of the lepers' village put on a
Nativity play which was beautiful to see. We had walked up the
jungle track to this village before, so by this time I knew what
to expect. The people are terrible to look at, but in a way they
are happier than others at the hospital because this is their
permanent home. They live with their children and their chickens; some of the children have had the disease and some are
perfectly healthy. These people are the remnants of a once in-
curable plague. Two boys from the leper village have finished

high school and one young man, whose arms and legs have been eaten away, is a marvelous sculptor in wood. The stumps of his arms are very sensitive and can grip anything. He gave me a little carved crocodile and a canoe, which I still have.

The Nativity play told the Bible story through songs; the costumes were sheets and sugar sacks. The mother of Jesus, a black woman in a white sheet, held a tiny black baby in her arms throughout the performance; when he started to cry she simply uncovered her breast and fed him.

Towards the end of our stay Clara became exhausted by the conditions of Lambaréné and I helped with her secretarial work. The doctor was receiving about five hundred letters a week from the outside world and the rule was that all had to be answered, but there was such a backlog that the staff was about two years behind on correspondence. Another problem was that paper clips and pins rusted, so one had to sew each letter to the copy of its reply. When I went through the stack of unanswered mail, I saw letters from doctors and nurses, and people who believed Schweitzer could heal them; one from a ninety-one-year-old woman had been written two years earlier.

Facing the hopeless task, I was tempted to dump them all into the river. I restrained myself; and out of the blue I came upon five letters from children at a kibbutz in Israel who had heard Schweitzer's animal stories and decided to write to him.

Near the end of our visit Dr. Schweitzer invited me to his room after the evening meal. His attitude towards guests was, I thought, paradoxical, like so much else at Lambaréné. Clara had assured me that visitors tired him, but I noticed that he always clipped on a little black bow tie to meet important arrivals. But this is how it so often is with charismatic personalities. If the celebrity did not function in this way he might not command the attention he does.

A divided opinion about Schweitzer often rose in my mind— the conviction that he was a saint, against the conviction that he was making his own myth. But when I saw the feelings he aroused in those near him, as well as people the world over, it was clear to me that he had an undeniable, mysterious power. It was not his fault that he became the center of a cult.

There is great similarity, I am sure, in the behavior of charismatic personalities, whether they are political or military leaders, or people who are saving some part of the world. At Lambaréné I thought a good deal about Moshe. When a personality becomes widely celebrated, there are both positive and negative effects on normal human relationships. I probably spent most of my married life looking for the right balance in this. If you are emotionally involved in the charisma, as I was at some level every waking moment and often in my dreams as well, this can be a heavy load. Charismatic personalities tend to live with-in themselves, and sometimes this becomes their burden. I think, for instance, that they cannot maintain normal friendship but draw strength instead from sources the rest of us do not have. We who live around them must learn to adjust. And whether the charisma has evolved unaided—which probably never happens, because there is always some feedback—or whether it has been blown up by today's media is really not important. The fact is that this power exists. Schweitzer and Moshe were totally different in their aims and methods, but they shared a rare strength. The other man of this caliber, whom I have known most of my life, is David Ben-Gurion.

It was strange to walk through those jungle rainstorms at midnight thinking about Moshe, and our home in Zahala so full of tributes to him. That I was the one who lived side by side for so many years with such a man is ironic, because I have always loved simplicity and closeness. Thinking about Schweitzer, whose simplicity was complex and whose tenderness was reserved for animals, gave me a perspective about Moshe that was obscured by daily contact.

When I entered Schweitzer's room the evening of my invitation, he was sitting at his desk under an oil lamp, holding an old-fashioned pen and wearing a mitten on his right hand, for he suffered from writer's cramp—in his lifetime he wrote about two hundred thousand letters, all by hand. Two baby antelopes were asleep on the floor; the jackdaw sat on his shoulder and pecked at his ear throughout our conversation.

He had made most of the furniture in the room, except for the old bed he brought from Europe when he first arrived, and a big, old-fashioned cupboard. On this was written in Germanic script, "Schweitzer-Breslau." Breslau was the maiden name of the doctor's wife, who was of Jewish descent. She had been a nurse and had died years earlier, crippled by arthritis. Their only child, a daughter, was married to an organ maker. She took over the Lambaréné establishment when Schweitzer died in 1965.

Schweitzer told me something of his life story. He had arrived in the jungle as a young doctor and missionary and had seen, on an island in a river, a mother hippopotamus with her baby. He watched the mother feeding it, caring for it, worrying about it. "That huge animal with its comparatively tiny brain was capable of reverence for life," said Schweitzer, "and that sight led me to my belief that people must observe this, above all."

But what about the criticism so often made, I asked, that he showed more concern for animals than for human beings? Schweitzer replied, "True. Because humans can take care of themselves."

I have never seen a lion lie down with a lamb, but I did see a pelican standing on the back of a goat at Lambaréné; pelicans and goats and all the other animals followed Schweitzer about the place, nobody else, though he was certainly not the only one who fed them. I heard many of the animal stories that have become legends at Lambaréné—about the gorilla, for instance, that Schweitzer raised from infancy and that was eventually sent to the Paris zoo. When he visited the beast there later, it became frantically excited and, according to the zookeepers, cried real tears. And of course I saw the famous sign along the trail by the hospital: SPEED LIMIT 10 KILOMETERS, with a picture of a mother duck leading her babies across the road. Schweitzer had finally permitted jeeps, but they were not allowed to go above this speed.

His main concern was such man-made devices as the atom bomb; he kept up to date on scientific measurements of fallout and other effects, and knew exactly what the seismographs throughout the world recorded. He was worried that all the fish were going to die through some unnatural catastrophe. For these developments he followed the news; for politics he showed no particular concern. The war against nature, he believed, was far more crucial than the war of man against man.

"I would like to send the General and your children some cards," he said after we had talked. He asked their names; Moshe's, of course, he knew, but he asked about the spelling of Yael and Ehud and then laboriously wrote them out in his small fine script. I saw that the old gentleman was straining himself writing all these greetings, and so I stopped him at Udi. Then Schweitzer said, "But what about the little one? Don't you love him?" He knew about Assi and insisted on knowing exactly how his name was spelled. The next morning Matilda brought in a letter opener carved in the shape of a crocodile. "This is for the little one," she said. The doctor had been worried that perhaps I did not love Assi enough.

Clara had become really ill and the difficult conditions and climate made Lambaréné unsuitable for her. The Swiss doctor in the village examined her and prescribed medicine. When Schweitzer found out about this he asked why she had not come to him directly, for he adored Clara and took a dislike to me because I was trying to get her away from Lambaréné. But it became clear to him that she would have to leave, and on the first available day we took the canoe back to the village, the plane to Brazzaville, where Clara soon recovered at the hotel, and back in stages to civilization.

Schweitzer was interested in Israel and informed about the country. He corresponded with three Israeli intellectuals—Martin

Buber, Ernst Simon, and Hugo Bermann; when I left he gave
me letters for them, and one for Ben-Gurion as well. In 1962,
for the ninetieth anniversary of the Sharei Zedek Hospital in
Jerusalem, I wrote to Lambaréné inviting him to attend the
ceremonies as the guest of honor. His reason for being unable
to accept had, I thought, something of the spirit of David Ben-
Gurion: time was running short, and he still had so many things
to do. In January 1965, he was hale and hearty for his own
ninetieth birthday party at Lambaréné, but later that year he
died.

The reply to my invitation came to me in a letter written in
German by the doctor's assistant, Ali, in her fine small handwriting so like his own, on two thin pages joined by a little loop
of thread. I was pleased to find that I was well remembered as
"a quiet, dear modest guest who understood the doctor's great
pressure of work." She wrote of Dr. Schweitzer's deep regret that
he could not come to our hospital, "which, like his own, serves
the poorest of the poor," and that it would have fulfilled "a very
old desire of his to come to see the country whose history he
knows so well."

After my return we put on a Maskit fashion show in the
garden of what was the most luxurious house in Jerusalem. Everybody was talking about it; we were not yet used to such things.
Everything went off well, except that by mistake somebody
turned on the sprinkler system and showered the audience.

There is a wall at the back of this garden, and on the other
side of the wall is a leper hospital. In the midst of our beautiful
fashion show, we suddenly saw a row of bandaged faces peeping
over the wall. One of our mannequins was so appalled she nearly
lost her footing. Without knowing anything about it, I used to
be vaguely frightened of this hospital whenever I passed by in
the days when we lived in Jerusalem. The contrast between
leprosy and luxury is terrible; when the reality of a plague in-
trudes, it is the luxury that fades away and you are left with
the stronger reality. There are more than ten million cases of
leprosy in the world, with five hundred thousand new cases
detected in the past five years. There are lepers in Europe and
America; in Israel there are about three hundred known cases.

Looking at the well-dressed women in the garden, I thought
Schweitzer had a point when he made everybody wear the same
uniform. The purpose of our show was to display beautiful
dresses, though it was for the benefit of a working-women's welfare association, and of course the basic purpose of Maskit was
employment and to help people find their way in life. Leprosy
was brought to Israel by new immigrants, especially from India
and the Arab countries, who were the principal beneficiaries
of Maskit employment. The wall in that Jerusalem garden di-

vided two worlds, but I was glad that our jewels and embroidery had an aim beyond self-gratification. I should have gone to the hospital to learn something about the lepers of Israel, but after the show I had to drive the dresses back to Tel Aviv.

Nearly ten years later, I visited a leper home for Arab patients in the Judaean hills. Through a roundabout chain of events, I found myself there with my mother. We were on our way to a luncheon with the Armenian bishop in Jerusalem at which Yael was the guest of honor.

My trip with mother came about after I had been told that an interesting and unusual Arab woman, Jerusalem-born but living abroad for the past twenty-four years, was about to visit her home to see her elderly mother. This woman, whom I shall call Theresa, was known for her strong nationalist views and opposition to Israel and Zionism. I knew, though, that she wished to meet with Israeli leaders and her list included my name.

Theresa's family had been rich and influential in Jerusalem. Her father had been a physician, and when I heard his name in the autumn of 1971, a childhood memory came back to me: a big brass plate, always highly polished, with the doctor's name in Arabic and English on the door of the house next to the building where my father worked in Jerusalem, nearly fifty years ago.

Theresa's mother, ill and infirm, was living at some sort of institution near Jerusalem; I will call her Mrs. D. On the morning of our luncheon with the Armenian bishop, a few days before Theresa's arrival, my mother and I found a rare two hours to spend together and decided to find Mrs. D. I wanted to learn a little more about the family before meeting this Arab nationalist.

My mother is always ready for exploration and adventure, and after I had located the institution—the Moravian Lipra Home near Ramallah—telephoned the head nurse, and found out how to get there, Mother and I took her little car and set out. Yael had come to Jerusalem earlier, and we were to meet at the King David Hotel and go together to the Armenian church.

We had a wonderful drive through the Arab villages. No more than three or four minutes' outside the city and you are in tranquil countryside, with magnificent old trees and peaceful villages. I know that new urban centers must be built; yet there is no question that the old villages are more beautiful. My mother is always pleased with the chance to speak Arabic and we had a lot of opportunity for that—we managed to lose our way and had to stop often to ask directions.

One Arab policeman began chatting with us. Mother spoke to him in Arabic and he answered in English, for my benefit, on the assumption that I didn't understand Arabic. Mother assumed so, too, and this annoyed me; for although I speak the language haltingly, I understand practially every word.

"Wouldn't you ladies like to have coffee?" the policeman asked us after a few minutes. He did not, of course, have any idea that my name was the magic one of Dayan. This was a pure example of the Arab hospitality that is a famous tradition.

We said regretfully that we had no time for coffee but would certainly come again. We made our way through two more villages and finally arrived at the home. It is set in a beautiful garden on top of a hill from which Tel Aviv can be seen in the distance.

The head nurse greeted us kindly—my name, during this conversation, was not yet connected with the Minister of Defense—and sent word for Theresa's mother to be brought to meet us. Suddenly we realized where we were. Mother said it had been clear to her as soon as she heard the name—Moravian Lipra Home, since "lipra" means "leper." We were at a leper hospital established years earlier by Theresa's father; his widow, in her late eighties, was spending her last years here.

It was getting late and we certainly were not going to be on time for our appointment with Yael. I thought perhaps we ought to leave before meeting Mrs. D., but Mother said, "No, now that we're here, a few minutes more won't matter. We'll telephone from somewhere and tell Yael to go ahead, and we'll meet her at the Armenian church."

Just then an attendant came in sight helping two elderly women towards us. Both had white hair and blue eyes; it turned out that they were German by birth. Mrs. D. had married an Arab intellectual more than sixty years earlier, not a tremendous rarity in those days, and her sister had come to stay with her. I spoke German with them. It was also the language of the staff; this hospital was supported by funds from the province of Moravia in what was formerly Germany and later Czechoslovakia.

Mrs. D. was practically blind and very deaf, while her sister, though in her early eighties, understood us quite well. We were introduced; my mother's name was no problem, but mine took a bit of shouting and I felt slightly embarrassed.

"It must sound like a terrible name to you," I said.

"Oh, no," said Mrs. D.'s sister. "It is a very great name."

On the drive back, we again passed through the sleepy villages with their goats and chickens, which will soon give way to a more modern form of life. Our car stalled several times, and I was glad I was with Mother instead of almost any other woman; the two of us were driving past Arab homes, and a visitor might have been frightened. But Mother isn't afraid of anything, and I'm not afraid of situations like this. It was peaceful and safe.

We found ourselves in another lengthy conversation with an Arab when we stopped at a village post office to call Yael. I noticed that the signs were written in Hebrew and English only, not in Arabic, and that the telephone book was in Hebrew only.

"This isn't right," I said to the postmaster, as usual getting into a chat with a stranger. "Your signs should be in Arabic, and you should make a fuss about it to the Israeli authorities."

"Wouldn't you ladies like a cup of coffee?" he asked, inviting Mother to come in from the car. There was no one else in the place and the three of us began to talk. We introduced ourselves, which in no way changed the tone of the conversation. It developed that this man had been a postman under the Mandate, on the delivery route that brought mail to Nahalal; and his wife turned out to be the cousin of one of the Arabs who used to help Mother at her playground in Jerusalem.

"How strange it is," said our new friend. "You two ladies, whom I've never met before this moment, turn out to know friends and relatives of mine!" He made us promise that we would never again pass through his village without stopping to see him. "And if I'm not here, the house across the road is where I live."

This is an example of my philosophy that the human being is what is important; there must be rapport between individuals, not on an abstract level as it was with Schweitzer, but in actual behavior.

I returned again to the leper hospital with Clara during one of her visits to Israel. Conditions for the eighteen residents were excellent. Each had his own room and most, I noticed, were decorated with photographs of Nasser. But the patients seemed lonely; perhaps in a way the lepers in Schweitzer's village were happier, for they were living a normal life with their families. The more developed a society, the more isolated are its outcasts.

13 · The Six-Day War

Lydda airport was practically deserted on the evening of the first Sunday in June 1967. I drove out to say good-bye to an Arab family from Nazareth I had known for years. Mary, the mother, was born in Bethlehem, married a man from Nazareth, and was one of Maskit's best embroidery workers there. Nim'r, her husband, made good money as a construction worker for kibbutzim. But during the recession of 1966 and early 1967 nobody was building, and Nim'r left for Canada to start a new life—as many Israeli Jews were also doing at that time. Now Mary and four of her children were to follow. The youngest, a boy of four, was very attached to me and cried at the airport. He said he didn't want to leave "without Ruth Dayan."

During the Sinai Campaign I had been involved with the Kashi family. Under completely different circumstances, the connection continued with Mary's family. The same thread was to lead, after this short war, to Bethlehem, where I met Mary's mother. There were countless such coincidences during this strange period.

That evening Mary carried a big string bag filled with garlic and vine leaves. Nim'r had written that garlic was expensive in Canada, and vine leaves were not to be had at all. The little boy clung to me as Mary thanked me for the arrangement I had made to help get her to Canada. I had also asked

Clara, in London, to help the family during their stopover there.

Mary's relatives from Nazareth came to see her off, but they sat at the other end of the lounge and would not come near me. Their car had been stopped several times on the way by security police and they looked at me with dislike. They had been listening to Cairo Radio for days and were convinced an Arab victory was near. None of us had the slightest idea the war would start the next day.

"Aren't you bringing your husband any arak?" I asked Mary. Nim'r was fond of his arak, but Mary was so busy with the garlic and vine leaves she had overlooked this essential. I bought five bottles, the number allowed, counting one for each of the children, and then the time came for Mary, in tears, to board the plane. The only other passengers on that flight were two priests.

Moshe had been appointed Defense Minister three days earlier, on Thursday, June 1, ending a period of general depression that had been hanging over the country from the time the tension began in the middle of May, when the Egyptians closed the Straits of Tiran. This evaluation of the impact of Moshe's appointment is not my personal feeling; it is a matter of record, and I saw it everywhere about me at the time.

In those weeks before he joined the government, nobody knew what was going to happen, and practically everyone was convinced that only Moshe could provide the necessary leadership. He was a member of the Knesset and a representative of the Rafi Party, a small group with Ben-Gurion at the head that had broken away from the ruling Mapai Party. When the Straits were closed and the reserves began to be called up, Moshe decided to go on his own to the Negev to observe the situation. He asked for, and received, permission from Prime Minister Eshkol to do this. He was not interested in any headquarters appointment but wanted to be with a combat unit. For about three weeks he was in the desert, coming home occasionally for a bath.

I went to work every day at Maskit, where about twenty mothers of soldiers were employed. I think they would have lost their minds if they had not had their work. They already imagined us overrun by Egyptian tanks, and conversations in the empty store ran along such lines.

At Maskit we had no customers, but plenty of accumulated merchandise. On May 28 one headline in the *Jerusalem Post* read, "Tourist Exodus Proceeds Smoothly," while another said, "Journalists from Abroad Arrive in Strength." Long lines of tourists gathered at the El Al building, where several airline offices are located; and we tried to get them to do last-minute shopping with us. American Ambassador Walworth Barbour, who of course did not leave, was one of our few customers in that period.

Yael was abroad in May in connection with a book she had just finished, and returned as soon as things became serious. I picked her up at the airport, just as I had in 1956, and drove her to the Army Spokesman's unit, to which she was assigned as a lieutenant. After one day she decided she wanted to be nearer the front and arranged to be reassigned to the Beersheba office. I took her to the Negev and drove home alone in the evening, a lonely and eerie experience along the blacked-out highway.

Assi was in the antiaircraft reserve and he was called up. But when the war did start, antiaircraft units had no potential targets after the first day, and Assi spent the war playing chess with elderly reservists at an installation in the north. He is our pacifist son, but he was outraged at this fate.

Poor Udi, who is a frogman in the reserves, was not called up at all. He was by now practically the only able-bodied male left in Nahalal, which was bad enough; but to make things worse, all the village wives were asking him to help with their farm chores. He telephoned me every day to complain. It was his theory that he had not been called up "because he was Moshe Dayan's son." Finally, during the action on the Syrian front, he and a friend who was also a frogman traveled north on their own, found a Syrian jeep, and went looking for action, an enterprise for which they were later court-martialed.

The streets were empty of young men, and most of the middle aged were gone too. We had several at Maskit who had not received orders and they were in a terrible state, going to their units and insisting that they be allowed to join. The mood of our country during those weeks has often been described—the delivery vans and buses gone from their familiar routes and conscripted for troop transport, schoolchildren digging trenches and delivering mail. It is sad that only the threat of war seems to create such unity of purpose and willingness to sacrifice.

Many housewives shopped for staples such as sugar and oil in a mood of panic, but I have always disliked shopping and bought nothing beyond our normal requirements. I went to the hairdresser as usual and overheard what other women were saying. One admitted that she was so frightened she was spending her days in the cellar. But another said she had just taken her children on a picnic.

The *Jerusalem Post* of May 29 ran an assortment of headlines that help recall the feeling of those days: "Nasser Warns of Total War"; "What to Do if the Siren Sounds." There was editorial comment on the "lack of national leadership and the need for additions to the cabinet," and "political negotiations to bring Moshe Dayan into the cabinet as 'minister without portfolio.' "

That day, too, Yael had a story in all the newspapers, which described how three Egyptian officers and two soldiers had mistakenly wandered into our lines and been taken prisoner by an astonished Israeli patrol. As Yael had written, our soldiers were bewildered by the ignorance of the Egyptian officers in making this blunder, and also by the enormous difference in quality between the uniforms and equipment of the officers and those of the men. In our army, both wear the same boots and receive the same battle rations.

The newspapers also printed a picture of Winston S. Churchill, who had arrived as a war correspondent, donating blood to our blood bank. The story quoted part of a report he sent from the Negev: "During the past week General Moshe Dayan has been visiting units in the field, and his progressive changing from civilian to military dress is perhaps significant. He has great popularity among the soldiers. . . ."

A few nights earlier our telephone had rung at midnight, and when I answered a voice said, "Winston Churchill speaking."

"It's for you," I said to Moshe, "but he says he's Winston Churchill."

On the telephone, the explanation came. "I'm Randolph's son, and Father said I might call you." I invited him to lunch, and everyone who met him was charmed by this modest, pleasant young man. He and his father later wrote an excellent book on the war. Just a few days before it started, poor Winston was told that there was not likely to be any excitement, so he left the country, as did several other foreign journalists. They returned with difficulty after the fighting suddenly began.

On Thursday, June 1, in addition to a little item headed "Knesset Discusses Air Pollution," the newspapers carried a story about "woman power" at a most effective moment. This described a demonstration of women in Tel Aviv who believed that Moshe should be appointed Minister of Defense. They carried signs reading WOMEN AND MOTHERS FOR NATIONAL UNITY and WE DEMAND THAT MOSHE DAYAN BE GIVEN THE DEFENSE PORTFOLIO. That same day the decision was made, and news of Moshe's appointment was broadcast at midnight.

The moment this happened, the scene changed completely. Everybody greeted everybody else as though we had already won the war. If a nation's morale and this thing called "charisma" are among the decisive elements in a battle, then we had indeed already won it. Military men of course see things differently, but for me the impact of Moshe's appointment was electrifying.

The difference in the women, alone on the home front, was unbelievable. At Maskit our staff of mothers felt that Moshe personally had saved their sons—and I felt the same thing. As usual I picked up pedestrians on the streets of Tel Aviv, for there were no buses and very few private cars. On the day after Moshe's appointment I had two women in my car, both strangers. One said to no one in particular, "Now that Moishele is Minister of Defense, I've had my first good night's sleep in weeks." The other said proudly, "Yes, yes, I've known him since he was a baby." I asked who she was, and she turned out to have been a kindergarten teacher in the village where Moshe was born.

And it was not just the women. I went to the Government Press Office, where Moshe held a press conference with foreign journalists on Saturday, June 3. There I saw hardened newspapermen, not Israelis but visitors from abroad, excitedly drinking toasts to the new situation. I saw the same reaction among officers who, for one reason or another, had not always enjoyed serving under Moshe. When I tried to telephone Yael at Beersheba, it took some time before a girl soldier finally answered the telephone and said, "I'm sorry, I can't find anybody; they're all celebrating."

Although Moshe was already hard at work at headquarters, he was not yet officially sworn in. This was scheduled for the following Monday in Jerusalem, at the Knesset. As it turned out, he was not sworn in even then, after the war had started.

Sunday evening, the fourth of June, he came home late, long after I had returned from the airport. "I understand you're going to be sworn in tomorrow," I said. "I'm going to be in Jerusalem myself, because I have a meeting at the Ministry of Labor, so I'll be there to watch."

Moshe has always considered ceremonies a waste of time and did not understand why I wanted to be there. But wives generally are present—usually automatically, except in my case—and this ceremony coincided with my job. Moshe left early the next morning and was at his office by seven. I drove off early too, and as I was passing Ramleh, a little after eight, I heard on the radio that the war had begun. Past Ramleh I slowed down at an intersection and noticed several people crying by the roadside. It struck me that this might already be the tragedy of an early casualty. But when I stopped to pick them up, I found it was a natural calamity: the father of the family had died that morning in a nearby hospital and I drove them there.

I arrived in Jerusalem in plenty of time for my meeting with one of our directors, an old friend and a kibbutz member. (He was killed less than three years later, on February 21, 1970, in the Swissair explosion caused by Arab terrorists. Forty-seven passengers were killed, including thirteen Israelis.)

Jerusalem was quiet and I had breakfast with my parents. I wondered if Moshe would be sworn in after all, now that the war had begun. Mother told me that everybody had been congratulating them for the past four days on Moshe's appointment. Both my parents have always been tremendously proud of Moshe. They too make the separation between his public and private lives. Reumah, they said, had called early to say that all was going well. My sister, a pilot's wife, has always known what was happening within the air force, and this is because the air force wives hear air force talk continually, and have an unusual degree of closeness with their husbands. This is something that is not found in other military branches.

At about eleven I left for my meeting. I needed gasoline, and drove to my usual gas station, just across the road from the King David Hotel and a few hundred feet from the former Jordanian border. And that is where I spent the next four hours, though being next to gas tanks while shells are falling is not an ideal situation.

The attendant had just unscrewed the gas cap when the shelling started. There was nothing to do but go into the little office, which was separated from the row of tanks by a large glass window. There were eight of us at the station, seven men and myself, and we all sat on the floor and wondered who was shooting at whom. A policeman came by and shouted at us to go down to the shelter, but there was none. I did manage to turn on the radio in my car, standing just opposite our window, and we heard the broadcasts, which at that moment were not informative. We noticed that everyone who tried to cross the road separating us from the King David Hotel was sniped at from the Old City wall.

I started making calls from the station phone. I was the only one of our little group who did, and I had some interesting conversations. First I called my parents, who were on their way down to the shelter; all citizens of Jerusalem were ordered to do so. The next person I called was Reumah, who was at home in Tel Aviv. My sister was wonderful all that morning, calling us at the gas station every half hour. In one of our talks she said that there was nothing to worry about, since we had already finished the Egyptian air force. Reumah even managed to check the position of our station with respect to the Jordanian artillery units and reported that "the trajectory is such that you won't get a direct hit."

I also telephoned Moshe's office in Tel Aviv. I certainly did not want to trouble him at that moment, but I spoke to his secretary and left the number of my temporary war headquarters. He called back in a little while and asked, "What in the world are you doing in a petrol station in Jerusalem?"

"I told you last night I would be here today," I said. "How was I to know the war would be starting?" He was to be sworn in as scheduled at five that afternoon, and I told him I would be there, an insistence on my part that he still found hard to understand.

Teddy Kollek, the Mayor of Jerusalem, was another person I telephoned. Teddy spent the morning cruising about the city in his Plymouth, visiting children in the shelters and generally inspecting life in this crisis. He was terribly proud of the behavior of the people, and of the fact that the city was functioning—water, electricty, necessary services. Teddy is a most unmilitary character, but when his car was struck by a bullet, he felt very proud. He was going to the Knesset for the ceremony and said he would pick me up at five at the King David.

By then—it was about three—I had had enough of sitting on the floor near the gasoline tanks and decided to cross the road. This turned out to be easy, and I joined the people downstairs in the hotel's elegant Regence Bar, which was being used as a shelter. They were mostly foreign journalists, plus a group of village children who had been in a bus when the shelling started. There were also people who worked in offices in the neighborhood, among them several women I had known since childhood and who had shared with me the shelling of Jerusalem in the 1948 war. I telephoned my friends at the gasoline station, for you can quickly develop a closeness to strangers under such circumstances, and convinced them to join us. Perhaps it is a little curious, when you think of it, that not one of those seven men had thought to leave earlier.

At the Regence Bar we had several radios and listened to both Kol Israel and the Arab stations. Our own radio made me feel proud, for it was reassuring and calm. There were many songs, including of course "Jerusalem of Gold," written by Naomi Shemer just a few weeks earlier; what we heard then was the original version about the city with the wall through its heart. Later, Naomi revised it to refer to the reunited city.

At the same time the Arab stations were blaring out hysterical messages. I translated some of the slogans for the foreign newsmen. One of the words that kept recurring was "Itbachum" ("Slaughter them"). I almost felt like apologizing to the journalists for our enemies, and said that I could not understand how civilized people could permit such a performance. While we were listening to the Arab stations the maître d'hôtel, Reuven Gat, begged us to turn off the horrible noise. Two days later, his nineteen-year-old son Avraham was killed in the battle for the Old City trying to rescue wounded friends.

Among the correspondents was Flora Lewis, who later wrote a fine report of those hours in *The New Yorker* magazine. Flora had come through Mandelbaum Gate from Jordan earlier that morning, a very cool thing to do, and when Teddy Kollek arrived promptly at five to take me to the Knesset, she came along. In Teddy's car, with its bullet hole, we took a little tour of

Jerusalem on the way. It was strange to see the city absolutely quiet except for the sound of artillery. There was no one in the streets, no traffic, no soldiers, for they were all at the border. When we arrived at the Knesset, everyone was waiting for Moshe and there was an air of fantastic excitement. In the Knesset shelter we found ourselves with the country's leaders, Ben-Gurion and Golda Meir, Abba Eban, and Menachem Begin, so long in the opposition. When Moshe arrived, everyone began to clap. It was a remarkable atmosphere; political antagonists who for years had barely spoken to each other practically fell into each other's arms. By this time word was spreading of the air force victory that morning, news I had learned from Reumah hours before.

The one person who had not yet arrived was Prime Minister Levi Eshkol, whose presence was, of course, required for the ceremony. Moshe, as always in such a situation, was restless and impatient to get back to headquarters. Finally he decided that he would go, and skip the ceremony. So leaving the others behind, we got into his car with his driver and aide and began the journey to Tel Aviv. Another driver recovered my car from the gas station, after finishing the interrupted job of filling the tank, and followed behind us.

That afternoon Moshe had come to Jerusalem by the main road, under fire. To return we took another, safer route. Part of the time there seemed to be no road at all, and we drove without lights. Coming towards us most of the way was a long line of tanks, reinforcements making their way to Jerusalem. The tanks looked huger than usual in the darkness, without lights; the soldiers were singing.

This was one of the times I really was at the center of operations, for Moshe was in radio contact all the while with the Chief of Staff, General Rabin. As we drove, we heard constant reports of new advances, and with each change Moshe issued further orders. It was a dramatic drive into the darkness along an unknown road, with the silhouettes of the tanks and the singing, and Moshe making decisions.

From headquarters, I drove my car through the blackout to Zahala, arriving just half an hour after a missile had flown over our home. Aimed at this army suburb, it landed instead in a nearby community. There were no casualties, except for one of our neighbors, who died of a heart attack in his trench shelter. That afternoon a single Iraqi plane—a Russian Tupolev —had appeared over Natanya and bombed a civilian neighborhood. There were twenty-one wounded and one fatality, a mother of four children. Her name was Violette Dayan.

Later, some kind neighbors, concerned about the fact that I was alone, invited me to spend the night in their trench shelter. I thanked them but declined, since sleeping in a trench is un-

trench is uncomfortable. I slept in bed with a transistor radio at my ear, waking up every hour to hear the news. The headlines next morning, Tuesday, June 6, summarized what had happened: three hundred seventy-four enemy planes were destroyed; nineteen Israeli planes were lost; there was a breakthrough in Gaza. The following morning we read that the Old City of Jerusalem was encircled and that two hundred Egyptian tanks had been smashed. That was the day King Hussein said in his famous speech, "Kill the infidels wherever you find them, with your arms, hands, nails, and teeth if necessary." We also heard about the deaths of friends.

My job was to keep Maskit and our house running. Yael returned one night for a bath, bringing with her Colonel Dov Sion, of General Sharon's division. I had never met Dov in my life. Yael was to marry him in about six weeks, but she did not mention a word about it that evening.

One night, after much banging at our door, Udi appeared with three friends who had somehow gotten down to Sharm-el-Sheikh; a day or so later he made his excursion to Syria. My brother-in-law, Ezer Weizmann, telephoned to say that Uzi, Moshe's nephew and a paratrooper, was safe and sound. Ezer had just come back from an inspection tour at Sharm, and the first person he saw was Uzi Dayan. In family matters Ezer is always most considerate. Mimi always listens to casualty lists and I telephoned her at five in the morning to tell her that her son was safe.

My telephone was a kind of communications center for wives and mothers, among them Moshe's sister, Aviva, whose son Yonatan was fighting on the Golan Heights. Yonatan wrote a number of poems about the war and dedicated them to the friends around him who were killed; but he will not let these poems be published. A friend and neighbor, an officer in the reserves who lived on our street in Zahala, was killed on the Golan Heights. But the greatest number of our dead and badly wounded were young boys.

As I arrived home one evening during the first days of the war, I saw a cluster of people at the house four doors from us. I knew that Oren must have been killed. He was a handsome and outstanding young officer, and I had known him since he was a boy. I used to pick him up in my car when I met him coming home from school. In high school he had headed a youth program, which brought together young people from different backgrounds. I went into Oren's house. His father was not dry-eyed but his English-born mother was in complete and terrible self-control. Oren's best friends from Zahala and from his unit were telling his parents about the action. In the years since, Oren's parents have continued his work with youth and have built a clubhouse in a nearby slum district. The money came from an inheritance

Oren would have received on his twenty-first birthday. This is how it is with us; instead of the children continuing their parents' work, parents must often continue the work of their fallen children. When I left the house that day, I kissed Oren's mother and she said to me, "Tell Moshe not to give in on anything, so that Oren will not have died for nothing."

The next day a cousin of mine who lives at a kibbutz told me that her husband was seriously wounded; later I heard that the husband of Aviva's daughter was wounded by a bullet through the throat. Only the combat doctors' skill saved his life. Through all our wars there is first the upsurge of joy at the victory, and then the terrible depression as we count the dead. Our feeling for the value of human life is different from that of the Arabs. For us each boy is an entire world, and with his death a world is lost. This is not just because we are a small country. It is because of the huge investment in love and preparation for living that we give each young man. The loss of these irreplaceable worlds is felt not only by the bereaved family, but by all Israel.

While the fighting raged on I met and talked with paratroopers, boys brought up to revere life and never to kill unless there is no alternative. I saw their shock at suddenly confronting Arab military mentality, especially in Sinai, where they came upon thousands of simple Egyptians deserted by their officers and left to die. Our soldiers learned that Egyptian soldiers may be sent to fight without identification tags, since no importance is attached to their fate. One of the many tragic effects of the war is that our boys became hardened. Israeli soldiers were killed while giving water to thirsty prisoners who asked for a drink— prisoners who had not yet been searched for concealed weapons. Such incidents have had their effect.

One of the greatest victories of the Six-Day War lay in the relatively small loss of life for us—fewer than eight hundred killed during the actual fighting. A village like Nahalal lost many more of its best young men during the War of Independence. In the one hundred hours of the Sinai Campaign, just one boy from Nahalal was killed; in the last war and the no-war-no-peace years that followed, Nahalal lost five of its youth, including the pilot son of a cousin of Moshe's. These are now the third-generation children of Nahalal, and we are still here to bury them.

The number of military funerals Moshe has attended cannot help changing a man, and I know he is no longer the impetuous fighter of 1948: the price we pay in human life weighs heavily in his military decisions. And it is not only the funerals. There is the long waiting for results of even unimportant, day-by-day operations, the waiting for news of actions that only he knows about.

Nobody who has not done so can understand the impact of attending military funerals year after year. To visit widows and parents afterwards can be even more terrible. There have been times when Moshe has been to four such homes in one evening. I have been to many myself and have learned strange things. For instance, it is almost more painful in homes where the families have disciplined themselves to self-restraint. In homes where cultural tradition encourages tears and emotional release, it is somehow easier; everything comes out. So there is a special tragedy in visits to pilots' widows; they do not lose control, and it is harder when there is no sobbing.

The funerals have gone on through the cease-fire period. When an ammunition truck exploded in Eilat in January 1970, at a cost of nineteen dead and forty-two wounded, Moshe was still recovering from his nonmilitary injury incurred during an archeological dig, when he was nearly buried alive. That evening he was to deliver an address at the Hilton Hotel and we were dressed for dinner when word came that the wounded would soon arrive at two Tel Aviv hospitals.

We went straight to Tel Hashomer and saw the helicopters land. The minute anything happens Moshe is there; and his presence at the front and at the bedside is profoundly important.

Some of these wounded were charred lumps, no longer resembling human beings but still speaking. Others had been wounded in terrible ways by flying metal from the truck. When you see such a sight on such a scale, you know that nothing in the world is more important than preventing it. Nobody could sleep after that evening; I thought all night of the ghastly price we are forced to pay in our wars for survival.

For our dinner engagement that evening I was wearing a silver-embroidered dress—embroidered by Arabs in Bethlehem, as it happened—and found I could not go up with Moshe to the wards. Not because I could not face the horrors: I have done that. Not because my dress was embroidered by Arabs: that was nothing. But because of the glitter. I could not go among the dead and dying in a gay dress worn to attract the eye.

When Moshe had visited everyone and received the medical reports at Tel Hashomer we drove on to Beilinson Hospital. After he had been in the wards for some time, a nurse came down to the car and told us the following story. One of the doctors on duty there, who performed a difficult and successful operation on a boy wounded in the abdomen by a piece of metal, turned out to be an Arab doctor—an Israeli Arab, of course. When Moshe learned of this, he asked the doctor, who happened to be light-haired, if this situation wasn't hard for him.

"No, and sometimes it's even amusing," said the young man. "Anyway, at this hospital it's the Iraqi Jewish doctors who are mistaken for Arabs." And that is the way false assumptions about human beings are made in the Middle East.

Long ago I learned that in hospitals, comedy and tragedy are constant companions. Joking helps the staff keep going. On that night of horror, the Arab doctor told many anecdotes about what can happen to an Arab doctor in an Israeli hospital.

"A woman who needed an operation," he told Moshe, "called me to her bedside and told me confidentially she very much wanted me to be the surgeon. She had heard that there was an Arab on the staff and she certainly didn't want him; she wanted me." Another story was about the patient who was a religious Jew from the Sephardic community. He was trying to get together a *minyan*, the required group of ten men for prayers. "He saw me coming through the ward," said the doctor, "and asked me please to join for prayers. I decided the simplest way out was to say that I was sorry but I was very busy. 'Oh, you Ashkenazim,' said the offended patient. 'It's just because I'm Sephardic that you don't want to pray with me.' "

After the cease-fire I traveled to Jerusalem as often as I could to visit the side we weren't allowed to see for nineteen years. For this, one still needed a special permit, though everybody in Israel seemed to find a way to get one. On June 29, "the day the wall came down," I was in Jerusalem for a meeting. The decision—largely Moshe's—to permit free movement for all Jews and Arabs in both sectors of Jerusalem is to me one of the most brilliant he has ever made; and I have heard the same opinion expressed by violently patriotic Palestinian nationals.

On that day many people were worried by the possibility of violence. I was not; I was thrilled. As if by magic, the entire western sector, the "New Jerusalem" built and inhabited by Jews, was filled with Arabs in *kheffiyas*, wandering about staring at the sights. At exactly the same time the eastern city and the Old City within the walls were filled with excited Jews, many seeing the beauty and mystery of Arab Jerusalem for the first time, others looking for spots they remembered from years before. It was as though Arabs and Jews had temporarily exchanged cities.

Everybody who was in Jerusalem that day has his own remembrance of how things were. At Damascus Gate, Arab peddlers sold eager Jews "friendship pencils," made in the People's Republic of China, while over in the western sector Arabs looked for bargains in Jewish shops. Three carloads of culture-minded residents of the Old City visited the Israel Museum and saw the Billy Rose Sculpture Garden.

A family of Jerusalemites I have known since childhood had a strange experience. They had lived for decades in an old Arab house on the western side of the city, and before the 1948 war an Arab nurse lived with them and cared for their children. After the city was divided the Arabs fled; they were told—and many believed it—that Jewish Jerusalem had become desolate and impoverished, and that in general all Israel was starving. So nineteen years later, the Arab nurse, then over eighty, packed into her kerchief sugar, olive oil, and a few eggs to take to her old employers. She knocked on the door of the familiar house and presented her gift; that day, in that house, everybody cried.

The lack of real information even on the part of educated Arabs seemed strange to us. A sophisticated Arab couple living in a Jerusalem suburb, whom I later came to know well, arrived for a look on the first day this was permitted without passes. They came by car and happened to arrive at Mea Shearim, the neighborhood of very religious Jews whose houses and streets are neither clean nor modern.

"Well, it's still the same old Jerusalem," they said to each other, deciding the city was not worth any further investigation. But this story has a good ending. The next day, old friends from Tel Aviv, with whom they had been classmates decades earlier, invited the Arab couple to Jewish Jerusalem and to Tel Aviv so they could show them what the country was now really like.

During this same period of the shock of recognition, I had an experience that sums up many things. At Maskit I received a formal note mailed from East Jerusalem and signed by two brothers who were tailors. "Would her honor come to visit us? We would be honored to serve her," they wrote. On my next trip to Jerusalem I found the tiny shop and the two brothers, both in their early twenties. I had with me a length of Maskit wool, and asked, without identifying myself, if they would make me a suit. They agreed politely; we set a price, one took my measurements, and we decided on the day of the first fitting. Then I produced the note and asked why they had sent it. One of the brothers looked at the other and shouted, "You see, you see, she did come!" They explained what had happened.

On the day of the bloody battle for the Old City, one of the soldiers who took part in the hand-to-hand fighting through the alleys was a young lecturer at Hebrew University. This tailor shop was in the path of the fighting, and the Israeli decided then and there that when peace came he would help the brothers rebuild their business. He returned to their shop a few days later and learned that they both came from Ramallah and of course had never seen an Israeli in their adult lives. They hated us without knowing us. The university lecturer recommended the tailors to all his wife's friends and the wives of his friends at the university; he gave them my name, too, because he was sure I would come. When I arrived for my next fitting, the brothers proudly showed me their appointment book, now filled with the names of the wives of professors and Hadassah Hospital doctors.

"Under the Jordanians, not even a police officer's wife would come to a simple shop like ours," one of the brothers told me.

The Israeli, who shortly before had been a soldier with a rifle, was a guest in their homes and they in his; and the two Arab tailors came with their families to see Tel Aviv and to visit Maskit as our guests.

I have told this story, which sounds sentimental and rather too good to be true, because it is true and because it illustrates a point about that period on which I feel strongly. For a short time after the war, both Arabs and Jews were in such a state of shock that there was an opportunity for peace. But nothing was done, attitudes hardened, and pressures from powers with no direct interest in our conflict began to bear down on both sides. That was a time when any exchange of views between Arab and Jew was exciting and revealing, and both sides suddenly saw that the enemy was not as had been imagined. Moshe and those who supported him in removing the border through the city were absolutely correct, and the results were incredible. In all the masses of excited jostling throngs, there was, in those first days, not a single instance of violence—or probably even a harsh word. Those days were among the wonders of the times, and they had an impelling spontaneity that can never occur again. I hope that the base they created can be built upon, and that a constructive arrangement will in time be achieved.

It was only three weeks since I had said good-bye to Mary and her family on a seemingly long-ago Sunday evening at the deserted airport. She had told me that her mother lived in Bethlehem and was a dressmaker, one of the best in the area. Two of Mary's brothers specialized in a rare old craft—cutting vases and platters on a lathe out of gray stone found only in one area of the Dead Sea, Nebi Mussa, "the Prophet Moses." The stone is immersed in pomegranate juice, which gives it an unusual blackish color. The two brothers were the only artisans left who used this technique, and when Mary used to visit her family for the Christmas holidays—family reunions were permitted by the Jordanians—she always brought me back a little gift made by one of her brothers. Such items were unobtainable on our side of the border.

I drove the short distance between Jerusalem and Bethlehem and found the address that Mary's daughter Rose, who had stayed behind in Nazareth, had given me.

As soon as I got out of the car, everybody seemed to know exactly who I was, for over the years Mary had told her family about me. The neighborhood children crowded around, shouting excitedly that "Mussa's wife" had come. I met Mary's mother, a well-dressed elderly lady, and took a photograph of the whole family to send to Mary; that evening I cabled her that everybody was fine.

Mary's mother was delighted with our visit and the following

week invited me to lunch with her in Jerusalem. She took me to
my favorite restaurant, the National, which I remembered well.
The food was still delicious. She helped us start an embroidery
project for Maskit; the women of Bethlehem were eager to find
a source of extra money. And her sons began to produce their
black stoneware for us.

She also gave me long lists of friends eager to be reunited with
relatives in other Arab countries and some of her women clients
met with me at her workshop to ask if I would present a
petition from the citizens of Bethlehem requesting that their
city be given the same status as Jerusalem. As Christians, they
did not wish to be part of the Moslem areas. I explained that
I was not the right person for a political request and referred
them to the area's military commander.

I continued to worry about Mary. Her husband did not find
work in Canada and fell ill. She could not adjust to conditions
there and returned to Nazareth about three years later, though
she had sold her house and most of her belongings to go abroad.
She was certainly not a victim of the war in any real sense, but
by a quirk of fate she had become a misfit. If her trip had been
planned for just a few hours later, she would not have been able
to leave the country. In just a week she could have been reunited
with her mother, and in the subsequent building boom, her
husband would again have been employed in his native land.

In addition to going to West Bank villages such as Bethlehem,
I began visits to Gaza, just as I had after the Sinai Campaign. I
returned to the same weavers I had worked with in 1956 and
again ordered rugs, this time in larger quantities. In the summer
of 1967 the city of Gaza was thronged with Israelis; Jewish
housewives from southern towns and settlements used to shop
regularly at the Gaza market for cheap vegetables and fish. Some
years after the war, Gaza became a place where terrorists destroyed
and killed—their victims rarely being Jews but nearly always
their fellow Arabs, and often Arab children. But as I write this,
the Strip is tranquil, and its population enjoys a prosperity it
never knew before. Throughout Israel today, you will see people
from Gaza selling their products along the road—pottery, cane
chairs, and rugs; and a whole convoy of Gaza taxis comes to
Jaffa every day with fresh fish. Gazans feel perfectly safe to
move freely within Israel. In spite of tensions, individual or
national, they know that no harm will come to them among us.
Arab terrorist organizations have failed to frighten the local
Arab population, as much the victim of terrorism as the Jewish
population of Israel.

I learned in Gaza that under Egyptian rule the people lived
with a permanent nightly curfew. Under our administration
curfews are imposed briefly only in order to track down terrorists.
I think we would be incapable of ordering a permanent curfew;

our aim has been to give Gaza citizens, for the first time, the chance to lead normal lives. For twenty years it was Arab national policy to maintain the refugees as a "show window" for their cause, with no regard for human suffering, something we could never do with our Jewish refugees from Arab and other lands. Now this show window has been shattered—not by terrorist bombs, but by our determination that these Arabs return to stable lives. It is to the credit of the Gazans that they themselves defy the terrorists by working and trading with us.

For various historical reasons, developments in Gaza were different from those of the West Bank, which through the years attracted tourists and maintained contact with the outside world. Gaza under the Egyptians was isolated; the Egyptians had contempt for the local population, who in turn had contempt for the Palestinian refugees who filled the camps in 1948, and were left there. The atmosphere of Gaza has never been pleasant, though physically many places such as El Arish, with its superb grove of palm trees along the seashore, are magnificent.

The name "Gaza," incidentally, is associated with the word "gauze," for the city was an ancient trading center known for its fine weaving. In recent years weaving has continued to be important, but the products now are coarse Bedouin cloth and rough rugs. At Maskit we were interested in all Gaza crafts—the rugs as well as Gaza embroidery, whose style is different from that of Bethlehem or Ramallah, and cane chairs. For the chairs we brought new designs based on traditional Philippine styles, and introduced a kind of chic to Gaza canework by suggesting that it be painted white, a touch of elegance I first admired in Acapulco. And we suggested mini-chairs for children's furniture.

In the midst of the excitement of seeing new places and discovering new handicraft possibilities, we were concerned about Maskit sales. In early July, we badly underestimated the flood of tourists who would soon come to Israel and it was decided that I would go to New York to put on a Maskit fashion show.

Naomi Barry of the *Paris Herald Tribune* was immensely helpful. She was in Israel then and began firing off letters to friends in the fashion business. She had met Mary in Nazareth and was excited about our embroidery possibilities. Pauline Trigère helped us plan the fashion show, and Eleanor Lambert of the American Fashion Institute handled publicity. My visit coincided with the annual meeting of women fashion journalists and editors, and I met with four hundred of them. Jerry Silverman, a fashion manufacturer who was my host for this trip, gave an enormous party in his penthouse, where I spoke with many of the fashion writers.

But it was perfectly clear that I was in America as the wife of General Moshe Dayan, and what was supposed to be a Maskit venture turned into a victory celebration for Israel. I felt again what I experienced in Israel at the beginning of the Six-Day War: Moshe's charisma and the impact of his personality as a hero. People who knew practically nothing about him, Gentiles as well as Jews, felt an immense trust in him; as for the women of America, there was a mass falling in love with Moshe. I was swept along, at the same time uncomfortable at being identified so incorrectly with all the glory.

I probably could have been on television twenty-four hours a day. But my seven-day schedule was crowded; there was no time for me to go to the television studios, so the crews came to my hotel. Radio interviews were conducted by telephone—an unusual experience. The questions I was asked were practically always political ones which I was in no position to answer, though I did give my opinions. I told stories about my meetings with Arabs, especially Arab women, and described the new atmosphere of the possibility of friendship.

The inevitable question came up, the one I find so silly: what was I doing during the war? Countless times I had to apologize for not carrying a rifle, and confess that the only tank I came near was a gasoline tank near the King David Hotel. We had Bethlehem embroidery in our collection and our fashions were enthusiastically received, but there was no question concerning the focus of this visit: it was the victory of the Israeli army.

I returned on July 15, giving myself the week to prepare for the double wedding to be held in our garden, for Assi and Yael. Assi and his fiancée had planned their wedding long in advance. Just a week before the event, Yael told us she and Dov would join them.

It was supposed to be a quiet wedding, in the words of so many parents, but in our case it was perhaps harder than usual to decide about whom "we just could not offend." We wound up with two thousand guests. In 1967 the stone wall behind our garden had not yet been built, so we used the field on the other side as well. It was really more of a community outing than a formal wedding. Our guests included the Armenian and Greek bishops; Druse and Arab sheiks, some from the West Bank; all of Nahalal; and hundreds of kibbutz friends. There were no little sandwiches or canapés; we had Greek *meze* and barbecue dishes, and a Greek orchestra. Television crews from all over the world covered the wedding. Some of them came in the early afternoon and made Moshe very nervous. He does not make much effort to be gracious on such occasions. There was really far too much fuss about the whole thing.

I am never particularly interested in wedding fashions, but, for the record, Yael wore a dress made for her at Maskit; my dress was made by Mary's mother. She heard that "the children were getting married" and insisted on being the one to make my dress, which was black silk with beautiful beading, a Bethlehem specialty. Black is not, I know, traditional at most weddings, but it is customary among Bethlehem Christians, and it did look elegant. And I liked the idea that an Arab woman, who six weeks earlier had been living under a government committed to our destruction, had made my dress.

During the war it was obvious that I could do nothing except what all civilians did—continue, as much as possible, normal activities; industries and services had to operate even though the men were gone.

Once the fighting stopped and the new situation permitted open contact with our former enemies, I realized that I did have a real job. It started with handicrafts, through my travels for Maskit, and led to friendships. War and peace, I know perfectly well, are made by military men and politicians. But all sorts of things are possible when people learn to understand each other and realize that such understanding is in their interest. Moshe is in a position of historical power, while I work with hand-woven rugs and jewelry; but our thinking is similar.

I can feel very close to individuals in a way that Moshe, whose character is so different from mine, does not. One path to this closeness has been handicrafts. For twenty-five years I have seen it happen between myself and strangers, and I experienced it again in Gaza and the West Bank after the war. As long as people work with their hands, they are thinking; when they operate machines and push buttons their behavior becomes something different. When you explain a needlework design or a jewelry setting you are talking to a human being. It is a simple-minded thing to say, perhaps, but when you see someone working with his hands, it is possible to take his hand.

In the Arab villages I found that the more "undeveloped" an area, the more rich and beautiful its crafts. In Arab villages long under Israeli rule, crafts have largely disappeared, because progress and prosperity bring work in factories, and industrial wages are higher than earnings from home crafts. Furthermore, in isolated villages the women's laboriously embroidered dresses are simply not for sale. This is still true among the Bedouin in Israel's Negev, where the work of creating beauty is not to be measured in money. These traditions are quickly fading, a process which began after the war with the economic activity.

Bethlehem, for instance, has long been the center of a mother-of-pearl industry. Many craftsmen are traditional carvers of the shell, which is imported from Australia and made into intricate boxes and religious items. The usual market is pilgrim tourists and, during recent years, Eastern Europe. With the new tourist boom in Israel, Bethlehem shops are busier than ever; and with assistance from the Israeli government, foreign markets have been opened on an unprecedented scale. I was delighted to watch this happen, though it was not always in Maskit's interest. By the time we suggested our ideas for mother-of-pearl—butter-knife handles, for instance—the manufacturers were too busy to bother with our relatively small orders.

Bethlehem skills were more developed than those of the Arabs we had worked with in Israeli villages. Little camels carved of olivewood that I saw in a factory impressed me; I learned that the men who made them came from families whose fathers and grandfathers had made the carvings for the massive wooden doors of churches throughout the Holy Land. Now this type of work is done by machine, with some loss in quality but of course greater output. Asked a week after the war's end whether he would produce little camels for Maskit, one of these men answered, "I'm really sorry, but I'm already in partnership with another Jewish firm." With an Israeli government loan he bought a piece of equipment—from a kibbutz, incidentally—which now produces thirty olivewood Madonnas an hour, instead of eight as formerly. Some of the shifts in tradition do not make me happy. Within two weeks after the war, for instance, Bethlehem workshops were turning out olivewood carvings of the Wailing Wall. These sell well, but I cannot bear to see them.

On my first trip to Gaza I watched an age-old method of pottery production and learned something about human realities, too. I drove to Gaza alone to look for a man in the Jebalya refugee camp near the city of Gaza. This man's brother has been a Maskit weaver for fifteen years, and the son of the Israeli Arab has since married a girl from Gaza and lives in the Israeli town of Lydda. This is the pattern of many Arabs whose families had been separated by the border.

The moment I saw the Jebalya camp I realized that, like practically everybody else, I had long held serious misconceptions about these camps. The Palestinian refugees had been, in my mind, something like the refugees I had seen in India. But, to my surprise, the children were well fed—shabbily dressed, certainly, but not undernourished. I also was impressed by the educational level in the Gaza Strip, for the UNRRA educational program operated many schools. (I am not discussing here the fact that pupils were being taught to hate Israel and that the mood was bitter: I was simply impressed that schools were functioning and that malnutrition was not a problem.)

I introduced myself at the Gaza Municipality, where I was sullenly received, and asked to see the pottery production. Quantities of Gaza pottery are sold along the road throughout the Strip, and I was curious to watch it being made. I was taken to what looked like an ordinary field, though several chimneys rose from the ground, and led down some steps to a vast underground area with arched ceilings and tunnels connecting a maze of chambers. It was an astonishing sight. Here sat the potters, each in a sort of little hole in the earth, running the wheels with their feet. Thousands of jars—water jars, cooking jars, butter churners, all of exactly the same ancient design—were lined up to dry before being fired in the ovens. Each potter produces about two hundred vessels a day, and practically all are perfect. Gaza pottery is either a dark smoky pewter color, which is the effect made by closing the chimneys, or a natural red, for which the chimney is left open during the firing. The ovens burn wood, and the smell is wonderful. This is the way it has been done for thousands of years.

But changes came quickly. I loved the absolutely simple, dig-nified look of the pottery. Yet a month later, along the road-side, hundreds of children were busily painting gaudy camels and date palms on the jars, dipping their brushes into tins of Israeli house paint. The beautiful unadorned jar had cost about ten agurot (under three cents) when I first visited. The improved version by now cost exactly ten times this price, and was selling nicely.

On a later trip to Gaza, I was walking past the Jebalya camp with a sergeant major in our military government who by now knew the local problems intimately. He speaks Arabic, was born in Ethiopia of Yemenite parents, and has been an army man for over thirty years, including service with the British army. We were being trailed by a group of curious children, and from be-hind a mud wall I heard the voices of other children, in what sounded like a regular chorus.

"What is behind the wall?" I asked the sergeant major, whose name is Ovadia in Hebrew, but whom the Arabs called Abdulla.

"Come along and I'll show you," he said.

We entered a two-room mud hut—a real hovel. In each room about fifty children were sitting on orange crates, facing a black-board. All were clean, wearing smocks, and healthy looking. It was a private kindergarten in the middle of the refugee camp. The parents paid a shilling a month (half an Israeli pound) and the children were learning to read and write by shouting out the lessons, which seems to be the Arabic method.

I liked the way the room was arranged—pictures on the wall, and a study plan for the week. The teacher greeted me indiffer-ently. We sat under a big map of Israel and Sinai, both painted black, that showed an Arab standing on the seashore with a rifle; the slogan, in Arabic, read "We Shall Return." I was given a cup of coffee. The woman's husband, I learned, had deserted her and their two children. She had lost one leg when she was ten years old during the fighting in Jaffa, where she was born.

"We'll fix up your kindergarten with desks and benches," I said. I had been asked to become vice-president of the Israel

Variety Club not long after the war, and I knew funds could be found for such a project. You can do a great deal with little money.

On my next trip I brought toys for the children and arranged for desks and benches in bright colors to be made by a carpenter in the camp. I also brought a carrousel for the children, but that carrousel was a terrible mistake and I should have known better, for hundreds of other children from the camp practically tore the kindergarten to pieces trying to get to it.

On the following visit the teacher, who had barely spoken to me the time before, suddenly addressed me in fluent Hebrew, which she had never forgotten from her Jaffa days. She read me a long letter from her husband, who wrote that he missed her and wanted to return (a point on which I felt dubious). She asked for help in getting supplies from the Israeli Ministry of Education, and over the years we have provided equipment for her kindergarten. The woman has kept in touch, and writes to me, but as a result many people in the camp now look upon her with mistrust, a feeling rarely absent in my contacts with Arabs. Those who do not know me are sure I must worm secrets out of those I talk to. I have often told Arab friends that until they overcome this basic mistrust of one another, they are not likely to become a unified nation.

I am encouraged by the changes here in Gaza: the weaver we worked with who operated twenty looms in 1956 today works with a thousand; the cane-chair designs we introduced have been copied by other Gaza establishments, which is not good for Maskit but is good for Gaza; the number of girls and women doing embroidery has declined because factory jobs, one of the surest signs of normal modern living, are for the first time open to Gaza women. The end products are not as beautiful, but the pay is much better.

The results show up in Maskit designs as well. We have had to enlarge the whole scale of embroidery because labor for delicate stitches is no longer available. The embroidery is now big, dashing, and effective in a different way. We have only two hundred women available for home crafts, compared with six hundred after the war. Perhaps, indeed, this kind of craft work is coming to an end.

About two years after the war I visited Yael at Tel Hashomer Hospital. She was in one of the wards for treatment. As soon as I arrived, an old Arab woman in a patient's smock fell at my feet and kissed me. (There are so many Arab patients at our hospitals now that a visitor who did not know better could easily think he was at an Arab establishment.) Yael explained that the old woman had been waiting for me since early morning, and that she was desperately anxious to see Moshe and kiss his feet too. She turned out to be the mother of the kindergarten teacher at Jabalya, a frail old woman fatally ill with cancer who had been brought from the refugee camp to have the best possible medical care. I doubt whether there is another country in the world where the daughter of the Defense Minister of the victorious nation would share a ward with a destitute old woman from the defeated nation.

14 · Daggers and Rings

Mary, my Arab friend from Nazareth whom I left at Lydda airport just before the Six-Day War and whose embroidery was perhaps the most beautiful in Nazareth, was one of the threads linking me to Père Gauthier. This unforgettable priest, who had been a professor of theology at the University of Dijon, lived and worked among the Arabs of Israel, and later in Jordan, in the conviction that by sharing his life with the poor he would be truly following in the footsteps of Jesus.

Radical in his thinking and critical of the church establishment, Père Gauthier and a handful of priests and nuns—fewer than twenty altogether, of whom about eight were working at various times in Israel and Jordan—were members of a group within the Franciscan Order called the "Companions of Jesus." The name was later changed to "Companions of Jesus—Carpenter" to emphasize the proletarian role of Joseph, the husband of Mary. By working as simple laborers instead of living off the fat of the land as so many highly organized groups come in time to do, they believed they would be practicing true Christianity. Two whom I came to know well were Sister Marie-Thérèse and Sister Bernadette.

What Père Gauthier believes today I cannot say. I have tried to find him because I want very much to talk to him face to face. If he reads these lines I hope he will come to me, because he knows how many beliefs and ideals—and arguments—we shared.

He has been expelled from his order, I am told, and now works with Arab terrorists. I would like to understand the long road this priest has traveled from the time he learned Hebrew by working and living at a kibbutz on the shores of Lake Galilee, fascinated by the communal way of life that exists in democratic form only in Israel.

During the 1950's Père Gauthier formed co-operatives of Arab workers in Nazareth. One was a housing project for Arabs living in slums; it is a fact, I am afraid, that most wealthy Arabs who run Israel's Arab towns do not worry about their own poor. Another was a needlework co-operative formed to employ women, and Mary was a leading figure in this organization. It was called "Tabitha," after the woman of Jaffa in the New Testament who was "full of good works" (especially making clothes for the poor) and was raised from the dead by Peter. Mary was also working for Maskit; we were beginning to hire Arab and Druse women as well as Jews. From Druse villages we bought basketwork, while Arab women in Nazareth embroidered tableclothes in a style similar to European embroidery and unlike the traditional Arab work done in villages controlled by Jordan; Christian Arab girls of Nazareth, like those of Bethlehem, were often educated in convent schools and instructed by nuns whose needlework style was European.

"We would like to work with you," Père Gauthier told me in my office at Maskit when we first met; after that we saw each other at Maskit and in Nazareth on various projects. One was a plan to produce hand-woven, hand-embroidered vestments for priests; Fini Leitersdorf met with a Belgian priest from Jerusalem who was the fashion expert for the order. I was delighted to learn that there was such a specialty in the church—priests who designed changes in vestments and modernized them with the changing times. Fini saw some beautiful simple flowing costumes with a leather cross stitched to the cassock. We were going to use the marvelous new fabrics just being woven by George Kashi: off-white with gold, the same fabric Albert brought to my home before he went to his death in the Negev.

But this interesting project was never developed, because Père Gauthier was not much of a businessman, though we collaborated profitably on a line of skirts made of embroidered sacking that were sold in France. Reproductions of icons were also made by his Arab workers, and we sold hundreds at Maskit.

In the stony hillsides around Nazareth are grottoes in which people lived during the time of Jesus, and in one of these Père Gauthier preached his sermons. Inside was a manger, for the early Jews of Galilee lived together with their animals, just as some of our new immigrants did, and as a few Arab and Druse villagers still do.

"Look at that inexcusable waste of money," Père Gauthier

said to me one spring morning. We were standing near the cave where he preached, looking down at the enormous Church of the Annunciation then being built at a cost of twenty million dollars. "How much good could be done with that money," he continued. On that we agreed. The opulent church with its Italian marble seems to me an aesthetic as well as a social error, because its style is so foreign to the stark, austere hills of Galilee. Père Gauthier lived his beliefs absolutely, spending what money he raised abroad on the poor, eating and living as they did. He and his companions always wore workers' clothes. Church vestments were only for church ceremonies; but their work with the people, they felt, was the most important ceremony of all.

On the simple altar near the manger inside his cave I noticed a beautifully embroidered red velvet altar cloth worked with gold. "Where did it come from?" I asked.

"It was a gift from Jews who came to Israel from Shanghai, and who brought it with them originally from Russia."

My gift to Père Gauthier that Christmas was an ancient pottery oil lamp, which Moshe gave me for this purpose from his collection. It fitted the manger-church perfectly, for this was the illumination used by the people who had lived in the place in Jesus' time.

Poverty in Israel, Père Gauthier soon realized, was a far less serious problem than in the refugee camps of Jordan, and he decided that he must work there as well. In the period just before the Six-Day War he was dividing his time between the two sides of the border, continuing the Nazareth projects but also organizing self-help programs in the refugee camps.

"The most I have gotten out of King Hussein so far are twelve houses," he told me on one of his return trips to our side, following several months in Jordan. It was harder to get things done there—by that time three hundred families were living in Père Gauthier's Nazareth housing project.

We also met during Pope Paul's visit to the Holy Land; Père Gauthier was active in the planning of this event. On one of his trips from Jordan, he brought me a pamphlet he had prepared, and wanted to have published in Arabic and Hebrew, on peace and mutual understanding between the two peoples.

I had had no word from Père Gauthier for some time before the Six-Day War, and certainly not afterwards. In 1970 our paths crossed again in Dublin, though we did not meet.

I was in Dublin for a World Craft Conference and was aware of a certain tension, as though I was being protected from something. On the last day I learned what it was: bitterly anti-Israel pamphlets were being distributed at the door, though great care was taken that I should not see them. I finally managed to get one. The title was "The War in Jerusalem," published by the Irish-Arab Society and written by my old friend Sister Marie-Thérèse of the Companions of Jesus.

The essay was written with deep sincerity, the writer obviously stirred by the horror of witnessing the deaths of children. It happened; it happens in any war, though incidents have been documented in which our soldiers lost their own lives because they acted to protect innocent women and children. But to anyone who knew the facts, the pamphlet was unconvincing. For instance, the scene of one Israeli "atrocity" described was the Ecce Homo Convent in the Via Dolorosa. By the time I read Sister Marie-Thérèse's pamphlet, I was well acquainted with the convent, whose nuns are dedicated to the promotion of understanding between Jews and Gentiles; they treat all Israelis as welcome guests because they know we share their aims. Immediately after the war, the scholarly and devout Mother Superior Aline formed close ties with many Israelis. Her death last year was mourned by hundreds of Jews who felt the loss of a great and understanding friend. I counted myself among her admirers, as Mother Superior Aline knew. She was a member of Brit Bnei Shem, an organization whose purpose is to promote understanding between Arabs and Jews. (In 1969 I accepted an invitation to become its chairman). Several nuns at the convent are also members. For the past five years the convent has been holding classes for the teaching of Hebrew to the Arab residents of Jerusalem, and of Arabic to Jewish Jerusalemites. Mother Superior Aline had attended both classes and could speak both languages, as can many nuns of this teaching order.

I am not happy about the name Brit Bnei Shem, which existed before I was asked to join; it has a somewhat racist flavor—it means, roughly, "Pact of the Sons of Shem." (Shem was the oldest son of Noah, and the word "semitic" comes from his name.) The organization was founded soon after the Six-Day War by nine Israelis, both Jews and Arabs.

It was partly because of my name that I was asked to head Brit Bnei Shem. But my personal involvement with Arabs was by then well known. I was spending more and more time with Arabs—through Maskit among craftsmen on the West Bank, among Nazareth families who have worked with us for years, with their newly reunited relatives from the West Bank, and among the new generation of Arab students studying at our universities. I visited Arab homes, attended their weddings, helped arrange hospital care in emergencies, listened to their views and complaints, raised money for scholarships, celebrated family reunions of those separated for twenty years, and met visitors from Arab lands.

I became the friend of a brilliant young man who served briefly as the mayor of an Israeli Arab village, but was unseated by the vested powers of his own people. This is something our young Arabs feel strongly: their plight is caused largely by the blindness to progress of their elders, and by the dead hand of certain aspects of Arab tradition.

I worried about problems of employment and housing for Israeli Arab students, areas in which the Brit is trying to help. Most of all I realized that it is one large step forward when an Arab and a Jew can sit down and talk together. This is not much, and it may be followed by two steps backward; but it is something that happened far too rarely during the first twenty years of our state.

In this, Moshe and I agree. His policy since the Six-Day War has been to create a climate in which the Arabs themselves will find the way to determine their own fate.

"The real problem and its solution," he said in a recent interview, "is not a matter of relations between states, of encounters between troops, but of the attitude towards the Israeli of the Arab people, the relationship between two groups of human beings. In a way we are very lucky that we have to live in close contact with many Arab peoples—on the West Bank, in Jerusalem. Otherwise, if we had the desert between us and them as we have between us and Egypt, there would be the problem of how we would meet Arab people and live with them. . . ." On the morning of our divorce, Moshe told me that he wished to continue to help me in the work I was doing with the Arabs.

Here I want to make something clear. I am not a "do-gooder." It is true that I try to help individuals, whether Arabs or Jews. But this is because I like to help people; perhaps it is a way of helping myself. When it comes to politics, I know perfectly well that problems cannot be solved through good deeds—and it is clear each of us must help himself. Only the Arabs can solve the Arab problem. Only the Arabs—I am speaking here of the Palestinians—can make their own state.

It is tragically clear that they have not yet been able to do this. Mistrust and suspicion are deeply rooted. Even within Arab families the unity of one family is usually split against another. This is the history of politics within Arab villages in Israel, and on a national level as well. I have been in the middle of the bitterest exchanges between Arab parents and their children, between brothers who do not trust brothers. We Jews have our own family troubles, but by and large we also feel a degree of responsibility for one another.

I say openly to the Arabs—and some days there may be as many as six or eight in my office, with as many problems: until you begin to put aside your internal quarrels, to have faith in one another and stop informing against your own people, you will never have the unity necessary to make peace with us. You have not achieved unity among yourselves even for making war against us, and making peace is much more complex.

An Arab came to me recently for help. He had been arrested by our authorities on suspicion of collaborating with the terrorists, was questioned by our people, and then released. He refused to inform on his own people, for which I admire him. But the result was that all his people were convinced that he had indeed betrayed them. He wanted me to clear his name—not with the Jewish authorities, but with the Arabs.

Every Israeli Jew knows that it is hard to be an Israeli Arab. I greatly respect those who, by their own honesty, have worked out the problem of maintaining their national pride and loyalty to the state in which they live simultaneously. Our first generation of Israeli Arab intellectuals is a fascinating phenomenon, for in 1948 practically all Arabs of means and education fled, leaving the poor and illiterate. It has taken a generation—the life of the state of Israel—to educate from the bottom up, elementary school, high school, and finally university. Only now is a new leadership beginning to emerge. The fault is again partly with the Arabs themselves: why did the leaders run away? Why did they not remain with their own people, of whom nearly four hundred thousand live within the pre-1967 borders of Israel?

"Where are your Arab intellectuals?" is a question I have been asked by Arabs from abroad visiting here for the first time in two decades. They themselves do not realize their own responsibility, or the fact that under Israeli rule education has a broad, democratic base. Unfortunately, many of our new university graduates tend to leave the country—for it is a complex challenge to be a loyal Israeli Arab intellectual.

"For you Jews, we are Arabs; for the Arabs across the border, we are Jews" is how it has been put to me by Arab friends. Until the Palestinians unite to form their own state, I do not see how the problem can be solved permanently. The policy Moshe follows, "normalization" of relations however slow the process, is a way of providing the atmosphere for a rational solution, whatever form it may take.

Not all of my encounters have this undercurrent of political tension. Recently, I was a guest at a wedding that I enjoyed more than most. It took place in the trackless wastes of the Negev, far from the main road, at the encampment of the Azbarga tribe. It was a double wedding; Jum'a, a young man of the Azbarga, and one of his brothers—there are ten children in the family—were both being married.

"Oh, I'm so happy you came!" said Jum'a when I drove to our meeting spot by the side of the main road. He had been waiting there for nearly an hour; without a guide to direct me to where the tribe's two hundred tents are encamped, I could never have found the place. Jum'a put his head inside the car and kissed me before getting in himself. He is twenty-four years old and a teacher at his tribe school, which has thirteen hundred pupils, including twenty-four girls.

We had become friends when Jum'a sent me a letter after reading an article about me in a local paper. "I am most interested in your work with the Brit Bnei Shem," he wrote, "but disappointed that you did not mention the life of the Bedouin in our country. I think people should know that in Israel an Arab boy born in a tent can still finish high school and become a teacher."

Jum'a writes very good Hebrew, something not every Jewish boy can do, in addition to classical Arabic, and he speaks English well. His dream is to become a film director; he has written a script about the Bedouin, complete with professional camera instructions, as well as many short stories. They all have color and imagination, and show a very lively eye.

"Please come to my wedding," Jum'a wrote me some time after visiting me at Maskit, in the big Tel Aviv office building. "And please invite everybody on the floor above you, and the floor below you," he added. Bedouin hospitality is still a living tradition.

Horses—with embroidered saddlebags—were tethered outside the wedding tent, camels stood haughtily not far off, and a baby goat wandered into the tent during the proceedings. No Bedouin women were present, but there were many Jewish women among the hundreds of guests. We all sat on the floor, on the rugs I knew so well, and ate roast lamb and rice with our fingers. It was served in big bowls, lined with sheets of flat Arab bread; these were passed among the guests by the young men of the tribe. Our army officers, who have close contact with the Bedouin, were there; two of the colonels, Jews of Yemenite descent, chatted with their hosts in Arabic.

It really was a mixed wedding party; the guests also included two families of recent immigrants from Russia who spoke only Yiddish and had just settled in Beersheba.

As gifts I brought Jum'a a picture album about Moshe, with his personal inscription and autograph, and a check donated by children of the Happy Valley School in Ojai, California, to whom I had spoken about the life of the Bedouin. Yael sent a bottle of French perfume and an Italian scarf. We met the bride and her mother later—the bride is not allowed to mix with the guests. Both were wearing long traditional black gowns embroidered with red, the kind of embroidery a few Bedouin women still make for such events, but never for sale. Their white headdresses could be drawn to cover the face. The bride's necklace was of gold coins.

"No, there is no friction among my wives," I overheard the

sheik say to a friend of mine. The sheik of Jum'a's tribe has three wives and ten children. "Much less, I suspect, than your customs involve." What the sheik was really worrying about was the weather; there was a drought that summer, and the Bedouin are dependent on desert crops to feed their animals. "What we need is rain," he said more than once.

After the feast I was taken to the tent of the women, who were swaying and singing to a Bedouin dance. I was drawn into the center; I still know how to snap my fingers in the proper noisy way, and the women embraced me. Some of the words they were singing sounded familiar, and Jum'a translated: "They are asking for rain, and they are saying, 'Mussa, Mussa, Mussa Dayan, bring us rain!'" That same day, incidentally, Moshe was in Jerusalem visiting Sheik Ja'abri of Hebron, who was ill in the hospital.

On rare occasions throughout my life I have met women who have become my friends in the deepest sense, whose way of thinking and feeling corresponds to mine, and to whom I can unburden myself knowing that my weaknesses will be understood. Relationships of this kind are entirely different from those between women and men, and are essential to me. One or two such friendships remain from girlhood, and while I do not see these old friends now as often as I would like, their importance remains unchanged.

Some of these women live in distant countries, but when we meet it is at though we had never been apart; I think most women will know exactly what I mean. I have noticed that men, by comparison, seem less capable of such friendships among themselves, friendships based on trust, understanding, and unselfishness.

Not long before Moshe and I agreed to divorce, I met a woman who quickly became this kind of friend. Our relationship is, first and foremost, based on understanding as people. But it is terribly complicated by the fact that she is an Arab patriot just as much as I am an Israeli, and the tension in our conflicting feelings is a powerful emotion between us. We both spent our youth in Jerusalem, and that is part of it, too. She is the "Theresa" whose mother I visited at the leper home near Jerusalem, and she has lived away from her homeland for more than twenty years.

"My husband has sworn never to set foot in Jerusalem so long as it is under Israeli rule," Theresa told me when we met; like her, he is an Arab nationalist and activist. "But he agreed that I should come to see my mother, and he also said he was curious to hear my report when I returned." One of Theresa's sons heads an Arab students' group at a European university.

Our first conversations were polite and restrained; we spoke over the telephone and then met at the King David Hotel. "Mrs. Dayan, I am so grateful to you for visiting my mother," she said. "But why? The very least I could do was visit your mother. And I enjoyed it." It was clear to me that she saw me purely as the wife of Moshe Dayan. It was only later, though it came in a sudden surge, that we spoke as two women with no reservations. Still, from the beginning I was struck by her intelligence, sophistication and compassion, and by the feeling that we had so much in common.

At the same time there was the chasm in our beliefs. Thoughts went through my mind: I don't want to argue with her or try to convince her. Most of all, I don't want to put her in an impossible position with her own people. How different our roles were; if I were seen with a classmate of the terrorist leader George Habash, as this woman had been at Cairo University, none of my people would therefore consider me a traitor.

We talked for three hours and began to touch on politics and I was hopelessly late for the wedding for which I had come to Jerusalem. She said, "I've come to this country as a representative of my group, to find out what's going on here." And I thought, You have been away from your own people too long.

The U.N. decision of 1948 came up in our talk, and I silently replied, We would never have been the side to start a war with threats of destruction, not in 1948 or 1956 or 1967. And so I went on mentally answering her, for I still did not wish to argue: If the refugees who have spent twenty years in camps had been Jews, we would not have let them stay in camps for the purpose of making propaganda for the world. All this came into the open later; now she still thought of me as Mrs. Moshe Dayan and was only beginning to realize that I did not for an instant think of her as "the enemy." The meeting was painful for both of us, and later meetings became more so. I did not think that my impact on her was as strong as hers on me, but I was wrong. For the first time I understood what it meant to be a Palestinian who had become a wanderer. She had to admit that all was not exactly as she had imagined. We spoke about ourselves as human beings; we tried to solve problems that were beyond us.

We had many meetings, and each time I found it an increasing pleasure—mixed with pain—to talk to her. She knew where I stood; I knew where she stood. I felt she had been indoctrinated; she thought the same was true of me. Yet she had an open mind. When she was ready to leave our country after her two-week visit she said, "I am in a state of shock. I have been exposed to the rays of your country." The very fact that she had fought and won the inner battle about coming to see things for herself proves a great deal about her.

One morning Theresa and I left early for a long day's trip to the Golan Heights. With Willy, Maskit's industrial designer—just back from a year in Singapore, where he had been invited to help build up the local arts-and-crafts industry—I was going to investigate developing handicrafts in the Druse villages of the Golan Heights, formerly Syrian territory. (These must be distinguished from the Druse villages in pre-1967 Israel, where about thirty-six thousand Druses live, practically all of whom have relatives among the ten thousand Druses in the Golan villages.) In the Golan Heights the Druses remained in their homes as the Israeli army made its swift advance, while the Arabs fled.

As we drove past factories and soldiers on the road, Theresa spoke of her father's wealth—all lost in the 1948 war, for his extensive property was in the western sector of Jerusalem—and her views on the Palestine problem.

"One of the places we used to go for our holidays was an experimental farm my father developed. The Jews were anxious to buy it, but my father on principle refused to sell land to the Jews." Without saying so, she indicated that some of his best friends were Jews, as were her first serious boy friend and many of her husband's girl friends before they married.

"Finally Father sold it to a Syrian, who offered a quarter of the money the Jews were ready to pay. A few days later, the Syrian turned around and sold it to the Jews."

"How are your people going to achieve unity?" I asked. "That is your whole problem."

"Yes," she said, "that is what must come. That is where we admire and envy you. My elder son, at the university, is an optimist. He reminds me of myself when I was twenty and marched in parades. And he's always lecturing me on environmental pollution. . . ."

I turned on the car radio to the B.B.C. so that my friend could hear a program in English. We had tuned in a discussion of the national aspirations and obstacles to unity of the Australians, so I switched it off and we took up the subject of our children. Her second boy, sixteen, was a slight problem: "He doesn't want to do anything, just loaf and listen to records."

"That reminds me of Assi," I said, and told the story of Assi's adventures at fifteen—running away from school to Tiberias and Cyprus.

"Yes," said Theresa, "our children must find their own way." She paused and looked across the rich green countryside through which we were driving. "It's beautiful here. I don't remember this road at all. You know, some of the most magnificent scenery in the world is in Lebanon. The wild lupin grow so tall a child could be lost in them."

Willy asked whether there were laws in Lebanon to protect the wildflowers and I replied, "My eldest grandchild gives me lectures on what may and may not be picked."

"No," said Theresa. "It seems a characteristic of the Arab not to want wildflowers in his home. The most miserable rose grown in his own garden means more to him than the most beautiful wildflowers. We do love our gardens, and we have such marvelous ones." Then she added, "Or, rather, we did."

A few miles farther, and the subject was no longer wildflowers: "If I lived here I would help to blow up every Israeli military installation built in the areas taken in the 1967 war—if only to give the Arabs hope, and to show the Israelis they are not there to stay." She spoke bitterly of our building program in Jerusalem and the changes made in the city's character. She knows us Jews well and kept returning to one point: "Because you are as you are, because you are committed to justice, you are the ones who must be generous, who must make the concessions."

She told us about two of her experiences in Jerusalem. "I was wearing a cross around my neck"—she is a Christian Arab and wears a cross in Israel, to keep from being taken for a Jew— "and on the street a boy of about twenty-one spat at me. I spat back and took him to the police station." A friend who later heard this story remarked that the boy's target had undoubtedly been not Islam but Christianity, under which the Jews have suffered far more.

"The other experience was just the opposite. I was in a shop in the Old City about to buy some fabric when the proprietor said, 'Now I must do my evening prayers,' and spreading out his rug on the floor, he began to pray. Then I noticed that a religious Jew was just entering the shop. I thought to myself, I can't bear it, another of these awful confrontations. The Jew waited until the Moslem had finished his prayers and was rolling up his rug. Then the Jew said, in broken Arabic, 'My brother in the faith of God, you cannot imagine how I appreciate your taking time out from the making of money to worship God.' And the two men embraced each other. . . .'"

We were winding through the hills of Galilee. "I don't agree with many things your husband has done," said Theresa. "But opening the bridges and permitting contact between Jews and Arabs was a stroke of genius."

At a certain curve, by prearrangement, we met two Druses— one a sheik, in traditional Druse dress, the other a young man in his twenties in shirt and slacks, the university-trained generation wanting to break with the past. Both were from Israeli Druse villages and were joining us in their car for the ascent to the Golan. Farther on, also by prearrangement, we met Mordechai Cohen, a Jew who had immigrated from Syria and has been with our Ministry of Commerce for fifteen years, trying to find ways to bring industry to Arab villages in Israel.

"We have a German investor putting up a knitting machine

in a village with no industry, and a French investor interested in starting a plastics firm," said Mr. Cohen eagerly to my friend, in Arabic.

The sheik looked pained, for he was anxious to talk about his people, the Druses. "Let him talk now," I said. "The rest of the day is for Druses."

For the next leg of the trip, Theresa moved to the other car, sitting between the sheik and Mr. Cohen. I said to Willy, "It's very likely that she wants to throw us into the sea. But she has an open mind, and she cares about people."

Our cars crossed the narrow bridge that before June 1967 had marked the border between Israel and Syria, and began the climb to the Golan Heights. Here the land has a wild look and the earth is black, but near the villages you can see orchards and children by the side of the road waving and selling baskets of fruit. Our destination was a village with a population of about two thousand, two miles from the Syrian cease-fire line. A delegation was waiting patiently for us outside the grandest house—mostly older men in black robes and baggy trousers, a style that long ago disappeared from our Druse villages.

There were also four men in uniform to welcome us. One was Colonel Shmulik, who heads the military government there. He is an old friend from a village not far from Nahalal; I have known him and his wife, a Jerusalem girl, for years. Shmulik's parents came from Russia but he has spoken Arabic from childhood, and commanded a Druse fighting unit in the war. The two enlisted men were both Druses from Israeli villages, and the young captain, wearing a mustache in the Druse style and with the fearless look of these hill people, turned out to be a Jew from Iraq.

Inside the big, many-windowed room, we were met with an air of celebration—tables covered with white embroidered linen and huge platters of fruit. In addition to the village notables, the place was thronged with women and girls, all in white headdresses. There were speeches to the effect that several of the girls had studied at a seminar in Tel Aviv and that they were eager to make handicrafts for Maskit. Theresa listened intently, whispering to some of the women sitting near her—about reunions with family members from Lebanon, employment for women, and the nearby medical clinic.

"I've never seen men and women join in a Druse celebration," I said to Shmulik.

"I'll tell you something," he answered. "In all my years with the Druses, I've never seen it either. I can explain it only as a mark of esteem for you."

Now another group of women filed into the room, most carrying babies, to shake hands with the guests, and then several girls brought samples of handicrafts—raffia handbags, knitted children's clothes, crocheted scarves, handmade lace. "We had an instructor from Nazareth who showed us the patterns," one girl announced proudly.

We must have made a pretty picture. Tough Shmulik, a big man in his colonel's uniform, inspecting a roll of white lace; my activist Palestinian friend admiring a frilly scarf; and I holding a handbag of pink raffia. Theresa and I have similar tastes and both of us disliked seeing plastic strands worked into the raffia. "I don't think much of the patterns," I said to her in English, "but the workmanship is fantastic. Look at this embroidery. At Maskit we've developed some fine patterns, and all we have to do is introduce them. What skills they have!"

Turning to the group and changing to Hebrew, which was translated into Arabic, I said "About payment—I know a shawl like this represents a month's work. But crochet work is going to be important in fashion again. I'll be back in ten days with wool for you, and with our crochet designer, and we'll discuss wages." In English, I said to Theresa, "It's all so different from when Maskit started. With full employment today, hardly anyone is interested in crocheting, not even the older women. . . ."

The next appointment was still farther north—the village of Majdal Shams, practically on the cease-fire line, on the slopes of Mount Hermon. Our meeting was at the military government headquarters, and the subject was daggers. On a low table were twenty-two of them, each about a foot long, with a curved blade in an embossed brass sheath and a handle decorated with geometric inlaid designs.

"Majdal Shams is famous for its daggers," explained the mustached captain, the Iraqi Jew who knows the Druse world so well. "Before the Six-Day War they were shipped from here to Damascus, where they were popular with the Russians. Now the craft is dying out. There are only six men in this village who make them, and they do it only as a hobby. Their main work is agriculture and they get good prices, so there's no real incentive except as a source of pride. Each dagger is a day's work. I'd estimate the people here could produce about thirty a month for you."

Mr. Cohen, the Syrian-born government executive, also knew about Majdal Shams daggers: "The main work, you see, is in the handle. The materials are goat horn, sheep horn, silver for the inlay, bone that looks like ivory, and the red and blue colors are plastic. The metal used to come from automobile springs but now they get it directly from a factory."

The young Druse who had come with us, born under Israeli rule and a university student, picked up one of the daggers. "But these things are meant to kill people with," he said, in a tone of great disapproval.

I asked, "What is your opinion, Willy? My idea was that we

might adapt the handle designs for other things, like desk sets or mirrors or dressing-table sets."

Theresa, who had been silent, could no longer contain that side of her that makes her an excellent executive: "You must be very careful, because I can tell you that the Damascus market is now flooded with cheap plastic imitations of these daggers. But there are customers and money for fine work, too, and that is what you should aim for." Now carried away with the marketing and design possibilities, she jumped from her chair and held two daggers at right angles against the bare wall: "I've seen picture frames made of this work too, and they can be absolutely beautiful!"

"But you can't make just the handle," said Mr. Cohen. "All the inlay is worked into the base of the blade, and without it everything will fall apart."

Willy sketched a diagram on a piece of paper to show how this could be solved—a handle with a short shaft. Somebody suggested that for the *femme fatale* who has everything else in her boudoir, a combination mirror with concealed dagger might be a useful gift.

We agreed on prices and deliveries and went on to our next appointment, lunch with the muktar of Majdal Shams. It was a feast with no women in sight. All dishes were served by men—grilled spiced meat called *"sinia,"* potatoes stuffed with meat, platters of grilled fish, rice with lamb and pine nuts, steaming string beans and tomatoes in sauce, hard-boiled eggs baked in a thin coating of meat, tomato and cucumber salad. Shmulik sat next to Theresa and they joked in Arabic. Willy was on a diet and ate only salad; I worried about that, because I love to see good food enjoyed.

But there were undercurrents of other problems. Our host, the muktar, had only recently become leader of the village after his cousin, a wealthy and educated sheik, was arrested for spying for the Syrians—a case widely reported in our newspapers. After lunch we moved to another room, to tables heaped with flawless peaches, grapes, melons, apples, and pears, and were served coffee. From here I was taken to another room for an unavoidable confrontation with the wife of the man jailed for spying. Surrounded by four beautiful blond children, she embraced me. Pretrial prison conditions were excellent, I learned. That term "pretrial conditions" always takes me back to the helpless days of Acre when my own husband was in prison. This woman's youngest child was about the age Yael was then.

"But couldn't you just let him stand trial, pass the sentence, and then quietly release him?" The weeping wife's request was translated for me. It was difficult to explain that I was powerless, that under Israeli law there is no such thing as intervention by the privileged. The Druses of the Golan Heights, accustomed to Syrian inequality under the law, do not yet understand this, and are sure a general's wife can do anything. I tried to explain that if the man actually spied he must take his punishment. Like the rest of the Israeli public, I did not know whether he was motivated by financial gain or by pressures on his brother, a high Syrian official.

Two other sobbing women came to me, embracing me through their tears. Colonel Shmulik explained the first case: "Her son is in prison and she asks your help in arranging his release."

"What has he done?"

"He killed his sister and was sentenced to five years."

The second woman's son had been sentenced to eight years for killing an elderly Circassian (a Moslem minority living in these hills). Here the details were complicated: he did not actually pull the trigger, but passed the weapon to someone else.

I said to Shmulik in Hebrew, "I'm relieved that their crimes were not against Israel. But why, actually, should we interfere when these people follow their own customs? In the case of the boy who killed his sister, isn't this a question of honor in the Druse tradition?"

The colonel explained. "We follow Syrian law here, and since our military presence is the only authority, we must apply it. Syrian law goes like this: If someone finds his sister in bed with a man and kills her on the spot, the assumption is that this is an unpremeditated act, and he will not be punished. But if, after finding her, he goes to his house to get his gun and returns to shoot her, he will be tried for premeditated murder.

"We take into consideration the fact that the Druses have kept their identity by strict observance of their own customs. Don't worry about it. He's not in prison for drinking a cup of coffee, but for killing somebody. Anyway," he added, "I was there for his defense. If it had been somebody else, he'd have gotten a longer term."

The captain said, "He's really a very nice young boy. He won't serve the full term."

Theresa had her confrontation over fruit and coffee with the Druse men in the other room, including one who had recently come from Lebanon under the family-reunion scheme. The Israeli Druse, long white robe flowing beneath white head-dress, set the tone. "Now that you've seen we're not barbarians and that we live under a real democracy, why don't you stay and live with us in Israel? The country needs Arab women of your intelligence. I'm sure you could learn Hebrew in just a few months, and then you could be elected to the Knesset. . . ."

One of the Druse soldiers, blue-eyed and blond, said, "You've just seen a colonel eating with us, joking with us, on equal terms with me and these ordinary villagers."

The irony of this scene was not lost on Theresa. "I know perfectly well that these are not the arrangements in Arab armies," she said with a smile, but she cannot have felt comfortable.

The sheik went on urging Theresa to return to her homeland. Fortunately, she is a sophisticated woman.

"I couldn't possibly make such a move without my husband's agreement," she said, successfully changing the subject.

Theresa was one of the first people outside my immediate family to know about my divorce. After I made the decision to leave Moshe I went to America for a speaking tour, stopping in Europe to see Theresa. Each of us was eager to see the other. We talked again about many problems—Arabs and Jews, husbands and wives, parents and children. I brought her a gold ring made by Haim, the one with clasped hands entwining a heart.

"Ruth," she said when she saw it, "now I must tell you something about rings. More than twenty years ago my husband was sentenced to death by the Haganah. He escaped. I swore then that I would never wear a ring until our rights were restored. But because this ring is from you, I will wear it around my neck, on a chain."

Rings also play a painful part in a Jewish divorce. The woman must remove her wedding ring and all other rings she may be wearing. She is allowed to put them on again (I did not), but their removal under the searching eyes of the presiding rabbis is required.

Nobody had warned me of this. On the morning of my divorce, a day of pouring rain and black skies, I arrived at the home of Rabbi Goren, Chief Rabbi of Tel Aviv, wearing seven rings. I had been sick in bed with influenza for a week and had a fever that morning, but the ceremony had to be that day. It was a fast day, so the Rabbinical Court was not holding its usual sessions at the Chief Rabbinate. A special court of three rabbis was convened in Rabbi Goren's home because this was the divorce of Moshe and Ruth Dayan, and the Chief Rabbi of Tel Aviv was formerly Chief Rabbi of the Israeli army and had known us both for years. Special arrangements like ours are called "*proteksia*," meaning that if you have important friends you can arrange all sorts of things to your convenience. Of course we are all firmly against this in principle, but I must admit I was happy the Dayan name gave us this "*proteksia*" because the ceremony is bad enough among old friends and in a private home. At the public building, one entrance is thronged with couples coming to be married and another with those seeking divorce; this is a mixture of blessings and curses, for shrieks go with some divorces—and perhaps this lack of restraint is healthy.

My collection of six rings included one of the few gifts

Moshe ever gave me—a copy of a Hellenistic ring in the form of two serpent heads and a ruby. I wore it on the third finger of my left hand instead of a wedding band; mine had long ago slipped down the drain while I was doing the laundry.

Moshe's serpent-head ring was very slim, so I wore a band on either side of it; with these I wore another ring of three interlaced gold bands. So altogether there were six rings on that finger; and on the little finger of my right hand I wore a ring made of a coin of the Emperor Trajan, a gift from Teddy Kollek.

"Take off all your rings!" came the sudden command. I panicked, because it was so unexpected and because I never remove my rings. As I struggled with them, I began to think how ridiculous the situation was, how degrading but at the same time funny, and this saved me from crying.

What if I can't get them off? I thought to myself, twisting the bands against my knuckles. Will that mean there will be no divorce? And what would have happened at such a ceremony two thousand years ago? Would they have cut off the woman's fingers?

Finally I did get them off, with Moshe and the rabbis watching in fascination. As I removed each ring I dropped it with a clink into my handbag; by this time I was smiling to myself, it was all so ridiculous. What kept running through my mind was the old nursery rhyme, "Rings on her fingers, bells on her toes."

While the conditions of the Jewish *Get*, or divorce, were once progressive and protective of women by comparison with divorce procedures in other cultures several hundreds or thousands of years ago, I do not find this true today. I had to read aloud from a card that I would never speak evil against Moshe, while he, as the man, was not asked to do anything of the kind regarding me. And it is the man who "casts out" the woman; she is the passive one. When the document has finally been written out—a long process, since it must be done by a scribe with a quill pen—the woman cups her hands and the man drops the document into them.

"But you must be careful not to touch each other at this moment," said the rabbi.

One of the questions asked was about our previous marital status. To Rabbi Goren's great surprise, Moshe answered that he had been married before—to Wilhelmina.

Because the day was so rainy, the ink on our *Get* would not dry. Mrs. Goren thought of a solution. She brought out her electric hot plate and we put the document, with its age-old terminology, on the hot plate and plugged it in. This worked very well. But if we are going to use modern appliances to dry out our divorce certificates, I thought, perhaps the ceremony itself ought to be modernized; there is little dignity in many of the customs we preserve.

After Moshe dropped the *Get* into my hands, I was told to tuck it under my left arm, walk to the door, then return and give it to the rabbi for safekeeping. The walk to the door covers a certain prescribed distance and is supposed to represent "acquisition," but what the left arm symbolizes I have no idea. After I had been "cast out," I was told I could not remarry within three months and three days, though Moshe was free to marry immediately; and I may not marry a "Cohen"—member of the priestly class.

During the ceremony I had with me the gray chiffon scarf embroidered with pink flowers that my Grandmother Pnina—who had been divorced twice from the same man—had given me for my wedding veil thirty-six years earlier. What I was wearing had as little importance for me this time as it had at my wedding; but this filmy memento did matter to me. I have grown up since that day at Nahalal, but I will always be sentimental, and will always look for the ceremony that is meaningful to me: the closing of the circle.

The reporters were waiting for us when it was over, and Udi and Assi came to take me to lunch. Their father and I drove off in separate cars, and our photographs appeared in the papers the next day, each of us seen through car windows streaked with rain.

Miki, my secretary, was by my side, as she had been since early morning, and through the week of my illness, and indeed whenever I needed her. I have been more than lucky in the devotion, far beyond the line of duty, that both my secretaries have given me—Miki for eight years, and before her for twelve years, Esther.

Miki's first decision that morning was typical of her concern. Without asking, she brought a hairdresser to Zahala to arrange my hair, because Miki would not let me make this public appearance looking as one does after a week of influenza, though I myself could not have cared less.

I did not cry till the next day, and for reasons that had nothing to do with the divorce. Miki telephoned early. She knew I was not yet well enough to go to work. I had just finished the move from the Zahala house, with the help of friends from Maskit.

"Anna's baby is dying," Miki said. "You must get to the hospital." I am grateful to Miki for knowing me perhaps better than I know myself. She realized that I felt weak and miserable; but she also understood that I would want to be with Anna and her baby.

Anna is an immigrant from Czechoslovakia who arrived with her husband just before the Six-Day War, penniless and friendless but with a great talent. She makes pictures in lace, which hang in museums abroad. There is only one other person in the world who does this. I took care of Anna when she arrived: we sold her work at Maskit; I saw that she got a flat, and I organized classes so that she could teach her technique to others. A year and a half ago, a child was born—a blue-eyed, flaxen-haired boy. Two weeks before my divorce the baby suddenly developed cancer and within a few days changed from a chubby infant, the picture of health, to a weak, fragile little thing gasping for breath.

"He would point to the door and say, 'Out . . . out,'" Anna had told me, for during those days of rain the child found it easier to breathe outdoors. So Anna walked for hours in the rain, pushing the stroller with her dying blond son.

At the hospital it was almost more than I could bear. Anna stroked his forehead, and his eyes moved from her to me. The doctors rarely entered the room except to give the tiny body a dose of morphine, for the case was hopeless. The baby could barely swallow. Anna tried to help him take a little water, moistening his lips and encouraging him in Czech, in Hebrew. He wanted terribly to live; that we both knew.

"Look at my child," said the mother. "We know he's going to die. But he has such a strong heart, such a strong will, and such a strong mind." I cried nearly all day in the hospital. My troubles seemed insconsequential at that bedside. The death of a baby is one of the real tragedies in the world. I wondered about all the things that would never be for him—to die for his country, perhaps.

That evening, my first away from the Zahala house, in a house by the Mediterranean, the storm clouds finally cleared and the sky turned pink. The only star in sight was Sirius. I felt selfish to be crying again, for this time I was crying for myself; it was Anna's tragedy that had permitted me to break down. I have cried so many tears, and in Zahala I felt imprisoned by them: I could not go into the garden for a good cry because the guard in his tower, by the wall at the back, would see me.

The baby died. Miki and I arrived late at the cemetery—the one place I knew I had to be. That day everything had gone wrong. The handful of mourners had gone, but the mother was still there by the small new grave. Miki had arranged a beautiful wreath of white anemones, our wildflowers, and yellow narcissuses; it completely covered the little mound. Anna knelt and stroked the fresh earth between the flowers. I watched her fingers, and they seemed like those of a harp player, or a weaver; her art is a little like both. She was far beyond tears, though Miki and I were sobbing. I thought of George Kashi's fingers, when he went back to his looms after Albert's death in the Sinai Campaign, and I knew that Anna, soon, would go back to her work.

. . . . .

The reactions of friends to news of the divorce were a complete surprise to me. Feeling guilty has long been such a habit that I felt I was to blame for this step. Suddenly letters and cables began piling up in my office; the telephone did not stop ringing and I heard nothing but expressions of affection and concern. My new home was filled with flowers and gifts; I had never thought giving presents a divorce custom. Some of the gestures were touching: a friend from Zahala told me she knew a sure cure for influenza—hot milk with Suchard chocolate and a little coffee—and made the long drive to my new home to leave a big tin of Suchard chocolate on my doorstep.

Some people did not know exactly how to act, since the newspapers had already married me off to a number of candidates. A woman who said I had once done something for her brought flowers to the office as a wedding gesture. My mysterious fiancés changed from day to day, but always included several millionaires. This upset me only because it is so far from the truth; anyone who knows me at all should understand that the last reason I would marry would be for money. The truth is just the opposite: the qualities that would make a man a kibbutznik —my old dream—attract me much more.

Warm good wishes came from people as far distant as Moshe's cousins in Nahalal, artists in Europe, a member of the Bahai sect who ten years ago ran our Maskit shop in Haifa, and Arab friends abroad.

Two letters arrived on the same day from Jum'a, the Bedouin boy whose wedding I had attended. In his first letter he inquired about my health—he had heard about the influenza—and announced that he was writing a book about Moshe, to be called "The One-eyed Leopard."

A little later he wrote,

> Geveret Ruth, this is my second letter to you in one day. The first I sent two hours ago. The reason is that as I was walking from the bus stop, and turned right on the sandy path along which you once came to us, I turned on my transistor radio and heard the 2:00 P.M. news.
>
> Suddenly I heard the report that Moshe and Ruth Dayan were divorced this morning. The news struck my heart like a heavy stone and I ran all the way home. I took the album which Moshe sent and looked at the beautiful pictures of the days of your happiness which once were. I told the whole Azbarga tribe and everyone was terribly upset and saddened by this rare event.
>
> Only today I wrote you about the book I was going to write of the life of Moshe Dayan, and how I was going to send the first copy to you—and now in the space of two hours everything has changed completely.
>
> Geveret Ruth, I am so sorry about this. And, forgive me, but what should I call you now? Ruth Dayan, or what? I wish you a life filled

with happiness and peace, with serenity and tranquility; I wish that you may live to 120 years.

If there should be a change in your address, please let me know so there can always be contact between us. And I have some advice for you. Don't brood about this too much, and don't worry; you have very nice—and very famous—children. . . .

Jum'a Suliman el-Azbarga

In my appointment book are some recent meetings:

With Maskit personnel to discuss plans for expanding our outlets in America.

With a friend's daughter who is having romantic complications and feels I am a person she can turn to.

With Rose, from Nazareth, who needs medical treatment at Tel Hashomer Hospital; and on another day with her mother Mary, and her grandmother from Bethlehem about employing women there to crochet for Maskit.

With Rabbi Darai of Jaffa about a group of Jews from Ethiopia, whose problems I saw when I visited their community in Africa; and about other projects at "Beit Ruth," the community center Rabbi Darai is building for all social groups in Jaffa.

With Jewish and Arab students at Haifa University.

With a new immigrant from France who makes handbags.

In Gaza with a unit of border police, mostly Druses, for the dedication of a clubhouse. Willy came with me, and we photographed Gaza's ancient weaving and pottery techniques for a book I am preparing on handicrafts. An hour and a half after I drove my car home from Gaza, a terrorist bomb was thrown on the same road at another car, killing an American nurse who worked at the Baptist hospital in Gaza and wounding the American director and his young daughter.

With a friend, an expert in these things, to plan the garden of my new home.